W9-AVK-245

Learn Winning Strategies from a Pro!

Boost your skills and your score as you learn:

- how to play the weaker combos from your rack in order to save the good ones
- all about hot spots and finding the highest scoring placement for each word
- your score—as you test yourself against the experts
- which play to use when you need a bingo and are short of time
- how to use your opponents' play to guide you, and more!

Let **The Official Scrabble® Puzzle Book** be your hands-on guide to playing your best in the game that keeps America thinking!

THE OFFICIAL SCRABBLE® PUZZLE BOOK

JOE EDLEY

BARNES & NOBLE BOOKS
NEW YORK

This edition produced exclusively for Barnes & Noble by Simon & Schuster

2005 Barnes & Noble Books

ISBN 0-7607-7093-X

Printed and bound in the United States of America

05 06 07 08 09 10 M 9 8 7 6 5 4 3 2 1

CONTENTS

ABOUT THIS BOOK *vii*

PART ONE

READING THE BOARD

1 Notations, Definitions, and a Short Word List *3*

2 Two-Letter Words *9*
Answers *30*

3 Placing Your Words on Hot Spots *32*
Answers *43*

4 Bonus Squares, One at a Time *44*
Answers *55*

5 Bonus Squares, Two at a Time *56*
Answers *67*

6 Bonus Squares, Choice of Five *68*
Answers *79*

7 The J, Q, X, and Z *80*
Answers *91*

8 The Highest-Scoring Play, No Hints! *92*
Answers *103*

PART TWO

BALANCING YOUR RACK

9 Three-Tile Plays *107*
Answers *118*

10 Four-Tile Plays *119*
Answers *130*

11 Five-Tile Plays *131*
Answers *152*

PART THREE

PLAYING ALL SEVEN TILES

12 Bingos: Beginnings and Endings, the Key to Success *157*
Answers *188*

PART FOUR

MAKING THE IDEAL PLAY

13 A Practical Guide for Choosing the Ideal Play *193*

14 Actual Game Positions: Your Move! *204*
Answers *255*

ABOUT THIS BOOK

There is a certain mental process that good SCRABBLE® game players undergo as they look for good plays. The puzzles in this book are designed not only for entertainment but to help the average player develop that process. It's possible for someone with an average vocabulary, enlarged only with the two hundred extra words listed on pages 7–8, to solve every one of the puzzles in this book.

Here is a suggestion for the aspiring expert: Start with a board and tiles in front of you. Recreate the diagrams and racks and rearrange your tiles while trying to find the solutions. For each diagram of five puzzles, take at most thirty minutes to solve them, and then look at the answers. Ask yourself what you could have thought that would have led you to the answers. This process of replaying in your mind how you can improve your thinking can have a profound influence on developing your crossword game skills. If you don't get useful results from this "questioning" process, then don't labor over it. Let the questions simply alert you that you'd like the answers at some future time, and then forget about them.

Of course, for those who aren't easily frustrated, you may enjoy the challenge of spending extra time to earn the very best score attainable. For those readers, I say good luck!

Part One is all about learning how to "read the board." "Reading the board," in part, is being able to find the open rows and columns where you'll be able to score the most points, and where you cannot.

Chapter 1 shows you how to read our notational system and learn some important and useful definitions. There's also a short word list of about two hundred words, including all ninety-seven two-letter words, that you'll want to learn in order to solve all the puzzles and increase your word-game skills.

Chapter 2 is all about learning the best way to utilize two-letter words. There are a hundred puzzles, and every two-letter word is showcased in order to familiarize the reader with them.

Chapter 3 is about using bonus squares, two-letter words, and making parallel plays. 50 puzzles.

Chapters 4–6 are designed to increase your ability to use bonus squares effectively. The complexity increases with each chapter. 150 puzzles.

Chapter 7 shows how to take advantage of the J, Q, X, and Z. 50 puzzles.

Chapter 8 will give you a tougher challenge. These puzzles combine all you've learned in the previous chapters. 50 puzzles.

Part Two is about playing the weaker combinations of letters from your rack in order to save the really good ones.

Chapter 9 gives practice playing off three tiles at a time. 50 puzzles.

Chapter 10 can help you learn how to play off four tiles at a time. 50 puzzles.

Chapter 11 is devoted to practicing finding five-tile plays. 100 puzzles.

Part Three is all about playing all seven tiles of your rack at once.

Chapter 12 shows how to find seven- and eight-letter plays. 150 puzzles.

Part Four is about the theory and practice of making the Ideal Play each turn.

Chapter 13 explains how to go about finding the Ideal Play.

Chapter 14 gives real game positions and analyzes them in order to give you a framework for how experts think. 50 puzzles.

PART ONE

Reading the Board

To ''read the board'' well is to be able to evaluate where, specifically, on the board either player may score well, and where s/he cannot.

The puzzles in these chapters will help you to expand your ''reading'' abilities. The quicker you read the board, the quicker you'll find better plays.

Knowledge of the two-letter words is inseparable from the ability to read the board. And so, that's where the puzzles begin. On page 7 you'll find all 97 acceptable two-letter words.

■ CHAPTER 1 ■

Notations, Definitions, and a Short Word List

Below is a representation of a SCRABBLE® Brand Crossword Game board. Following it are explanations for some of the symbols used in this book.

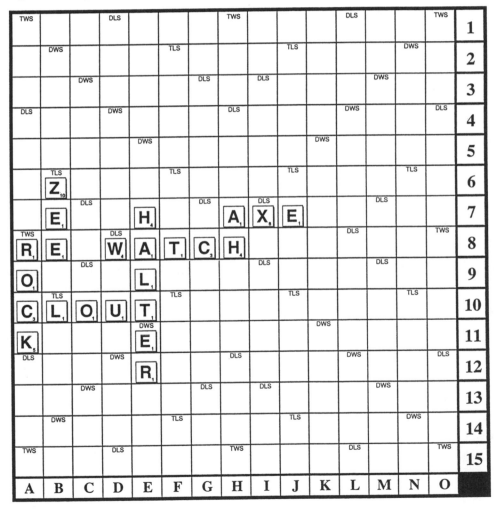

A	B	C	D	E	F	G	H	I	J	K	L	M	N	O	
TWS			DLS				TWS				DLS			TWS	1
	DWS				TLS				TLS				DWS		2
		DWS				DLS		DLS				DWS			3
DLS			DWS				DLS				DWS			DLS	4
				DWS						DWS					5
	TLS Z$_{10}$				TLS				TLS				TLS		6
	E$_{1}$	DLS		H$_{4}$		DLS	A$_{1}$	DLS X$_{8}$	E$_{1}$			DLS			7
TWS R$_{1}$	E$_{1}$		DLS W$_{4}$	A$_{1}$	T$_{1}$	C$_{3}$	H$_{4}$				DLS			TWS	8
O$_{1}$		DLS		L$_{1}$				DLS				DLS			9
C$_{3}$	TLS L$_{1}$	O$_{1}$	U$_{1}$	T$_{1}$	TLS				TLS				TLS		10
K$_{5}$				DWS E$_{1}$						DWS					11
DLS			DWS	R$_{1}$			DLS				DWS			DLS	12
		DWS				DLS		DLS				DWS			13
	DWS				TLS				TLS				DWS		14
TWS			DLS				TWS				DLS			TWS	15

DIAGRAM 1-1

TWS: TRIPLE WORD SCORE

When a TWS square is covered, the player covering it scores triple the value of the sum of the individual letters of the word covering the TWS. Example: Adding the letters R, O, and K in Diagram 1-1, forming ROCK, scored R (1) + O (1) + C (3) + K (5) = 10 × 3 = 30 points. Notice that ROCK was played after CLOUT but before ZEE.

DWS: DOUBLE WORD SCORE

When a DWS square is covered, the player covering it scores double the value of the sum of the individual letters of the word covering the DWS. Example: The play of HALTER in Diagram 1-1 scored H (4) + A (1) + L (1) + T (1) + E (1) + R (1) = 9 × 2 = 18 points.

TLS = TRIPLE LETTER SCORE

When a TLS square is covered, the value of the letter covering the TLS is tripled. Example: For the play of ZEE in Diagram 1-1, the Z alone was worth 3 × 10 = 30 points.

DLS: DOUBLE LETTER SCORE

When a DLS square is covered, the value of the letter covering the DLS is doubled. Example: For playing AXE in Diagram 1-1, the X alone was worth 8 × 2 = 16 points.

? = BLANK

The blank tile is worth zero points and is represented in the text as a question mark—"?" In the diagrams, the blank is represented by the shaded letter it represents. When the blank is used as a letter in print, the letter is underlined.

Recording Plays

Notice the numbers 1 through 15 printed down the right side of the board on Diagram 1-1, as well as the letters printed across the bottom. With their help we can describe any square of the board with only a letter and number. Thus, the center square is represented as either 8H or H8. When the number is listed first, the play is horizontal. That shows the word is played across a row. When the letter is listed first, the play is vertical. That shows that the word is played down a column.

EXAMPLE:

In Diagram 1-1 the opening play of WATCH is recorded as: WATCH 8D. The 8D represents the square which is in the eighth row and intersects the D column, and is the location of the first letter of the word. The second play, HALTER, is recorded as HALTER E7. The E7 represents the square which is in the E column and intersects the seventh row, and is the square on which the word begins.

Useful Definitions

Here are some definitions for words used repeatedly both in the answers in the back of this book and in the SCRABBLE game culture of clubs and tournaments. This is not a complete list. Only terms used in this book are included. For a further glossary see *Everything SCRABBLE®*, by Joe Edley and John D. Williams, Jr., a paperback Pocket Book publication, 1994.

Alphagram: The alphabetic arrangement of a group of letters. Example: BEGNU is the alphagram of the word BEGUN. Many players place the letters on their rack in alphagram order. All the racks in this book are so arranged.

Anagram: A word that is spelled with the exact same letters as another word. Example: KITCHEN is an anagram of THICKEN, and vice versa.

Balancing Your Rack: Making a play that leaves the letters on your rack that will most likely help you to score well next turn. This often means leaving a favorable ratio of vowels and consonants. Also known as Rack Balance.

Bingo: A play that uses all seven tiles. The player earns a bonus of an extra fifty points.

Bingo-Prone Tiles: A group of tiles that are likely to produce a bingo. Often used to describe a player's set of three to six tiles just before drawing his or her replacement tiles. Example: ERST, ALS, or AERST.

Blocking: The act of playing a word that stops the opponent from making a large score on a portion of the board. Also called "closing the board."

Extension Play: The extension of one word by adding two or more letters. Example: With QUEST on the board, adding CON to the front creates the extension CONQUEST. Also called Front Extension or Back Extension.

Hook Letter (or Hook): A letter that will spell a new word when it is played either at the front or end of a word already on the board. Example: With HARD on the board, the Y is a hook letter, since HARDY is acceptable. "Hook" is also used as a verb. Example: The letter C can "hook" onto HARD, since CHARD is acceptable. Also called Front Hook or Back Hook.

Hot Spots: These are either specific squares or areas on the board that have excellent bonus-scoring opportunities. Players will do well to look for these areas before looking for words on their rack. Examples: Triple Letter Score squares or Double Word Score squares adjacent to vowels; a single letter placed between two open Triple Word Score squares; words that take a variety of hook letters (ARE, ON, CARE).

Leave: The group of tiles on a player's rack after s/he makes a play and before s/he draws new tiles.

Open Board: During play, the board is considered "open" when there are many places to play either bingos or other high-scoring words.

Parallel Play: A word played parallel to another word. Example:

```
  M A R
L A T E
```

With MAR on the board, LATE is a parallel play that simultaneously forms MA, AT, and RE, all of which can earn points for the player.

Tracking (or Tile Tracking): The process of keeping track of the letters played on the board. This can give the astute player an advantage as the game progresses. Careful trackers can deduce an opponent's rack after there are no letters left to draw. By knowing the opponent's rack, the player can often make moves to block the opponent's best plays or set up high-scoring plays that the opponent can't block. Players are allowed to play with their own Preprinted Tracking Sheet alongside their score sheet.

Word Lists

I've tried to include only common words for the answers to every puzzle in this book. However, it would be nearly impossible to do that without assuming that readers are familiar with all the two-letter words used in club and tournament play.

The two-letter words are the building blocks of good SCRABBLE® game play. They are as important to the player as the alphabet is to a person learning our language. It's also true that some unusual and obscure three-letter words are included in some of the puzzles. In addition, a few obscure fours and fives are used. However, I've compiled a complete list of all these obscure words, taken directly from one edition or another of the Official SCRABBLE® Players Dictionary, our "bible," and listed them on the following pages. There are 97 two-letter words, most of which you already know, 87 three-letter words, 20 four-letter words, and 12 five-letter words. I don't think that's an unfair number of words to review in order to solve all 800 diagram puzzles. I hope you'll agree. By the way, in case you wonder about these words, they were all originally taken from one edition or another of one of the following five dictionaries: *Webster's Collegiate Dictionary, Webster's New World Dictionary, The Random House Collegiate Dictionary,* the *American Heritage Dictionary,* and *The Funk & Wagnall's College Dictionary.*

TWO-LETTER WORDS

AA
AB
AD
AE
AG
AH
AI
AL
AM
AN
AR
AS
AT
AW
AX
AY
BA
BE
BI
BO
BY
DA*
DE
DO
ED
EF
EH
EL
EM
EN
ER
ES
ET
EX
FA
GO
HA
HE
HI
HM
HO
ID
IF
IN
IS
IT
JO
KA
LA
LI
LO
MA
ME
MI
MM
MO
MU
MY
NA
NE
NO
NU
OD
OE
OF
OH
OM
ON
OP
OR
OS
OW
OX
OY
PA
PE
PI
RE
SH
SI
SO
TA
TI
TO
UH
UM
UN
UP
US
UT
WE
WO
XI
XU
YA
YE
YO

THREE-LETTER WORDS

AAH
ABY
ADZ
AIN
AIT
ALA
AMA
AMI
ANE
AVA
AWA
BOD

---

*As we went to press, "DA" is being removed from the National SCRABBLE® Association's official word list. The NSA and Merriam Webster agreed that this "word" had been incorrectly accepted since 1978. It is strictly a foreign word. It may be used once or twice in this book.

DAH
DEL
DOR
DOW
DUP
EAU
EDH
EME
EMU
ETA
FEM
GAR
GOA
GOB
GOX
HAE
HAO
HET
HIC
HOD
JOE
KAE
KAT
KUE
LAV
LOO
LEK
MED
MID
MIG
MOG
MOS
MUT
NAM
NEE
NOH
NOO
NTH
OBE
OBI
OHM
OHO
OKA
OPE
OVA
OXO
OXY
PER
POI
QUA
RAX
RET
REV
REX
RHO
RIN
ROE
SUQ
TAV
TAW
TET
TOD
TSK
TUN
UDO
UNS
WAB
WAE
YAH
YOM
YON
YOW
ZEE
ZIG
ZOA

FOUR-LETTER WORDS

AEON
AHEM
ALEE
CORY
DJIN
DORY
EAUX
FUTZ
JUGA
LAZE
MAYO
META
PEKE
PREX
QUAG
RYND
ULVA
VENA
ZOEA
ZORI

FIVE-LETTER WORDS

ABACI
AMIGA
AURUM
BEAUX
CUBIT
DIAZO
DJINN
ENZYM
FOOTY
GONZO
KIANG
NINJA

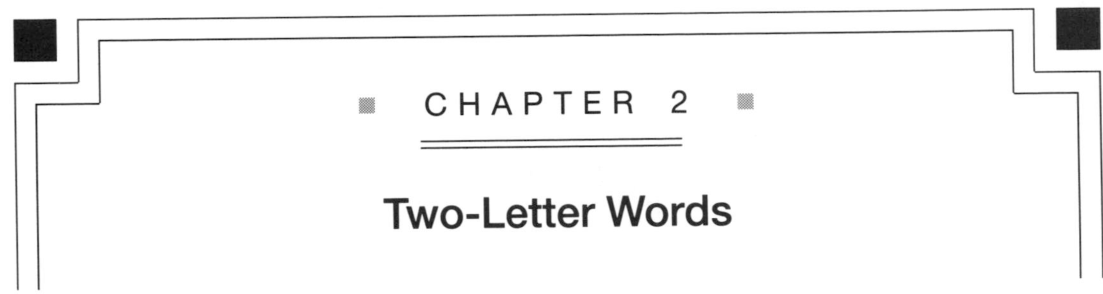

CHAPTER 2

Two-Letter Words

The two-letter words are indispensable for scoring more each turn. We've given you five two-letter words for each diagram. Find the highest-scoring placement for each of these words on the given diagram.

Make sure that for each rack: Always add TWO tiles to the board. For instance, when looking to play BA, don't use an A already on the board as the A for BA. Instead, add both letters to the configuration of letters already on the board. Then remove those two letters before trying to score with the next two-letter word.

If you can extend a letter or word you may do so. For example, if an A is on the board, you may extend it to ADO if the word you're trying to play is DO.

TWS			DLS				TWS				DLS			TWS	1
	DWS				TLS				TLS				DWS		2
		DWS				DLS		DLS				DWS			3
DLS			DWS	R	E	F	DLS A	C	E	D	DWS			DLS	4
				DWS				A		DWS					5
	TLS				TLS			L	TLS				TLS		6
		DLS				DLS		DLS I				DLS			7
TWS			DLS		F	L	O	P			DLS			TWS	8
		DLS			O	DLS		DLS H				DLS			9
	TLS				TLS X				TLS				TLS		10
				DWS	E					DWS					11
DLS			DWS		S		DLS				DWS			DLS	12
		DWS				DLS		DLS				DWS			13
	DWS				TLS				TLS				DWS		14
TWS			DLS				TWS				DLS			TWS	15
A	B	C	D	E	F	G	H	I	J	K	L	M	N	O	

DIAGRAM 2-1

Play each two-letter word on the given board position above to score the most points. Can you beat our total of 119 points?

EXPERT SCORE: 110 **GOOD SCORE: 86** **AVERAGE SCORE: 66**

1. AA
2. HI
3. PE
4. OD
5. UH

A	B	C	D	E	F	G	H	I	J	K	L	M	N	O	
TWS			DLS				TWS				DLS			TWS	1
	DWS				TLS				TLS				DWS		2
		DWS				DLS		DLS				DWS			3
DLS			DWS				DLS				DWS			DLS	4
				DWS						DWS					5
	TLS			I (1)	TLS D (2)	O (1)	L (1)	I (1)	TLS Z (10)	E (1)	S (1)		TLS		6
		DLS				DLS		DLS	I (1)		L (1)	DLS			7
TWS			DLS			R (1)	U (1)	N (1)	T (1)		DLS A (1)			TWS	8
		DLS				DLS	N (1)	DLS			N (1)	DLS			9
	TLS				TLS		D (2)		TLS		D (2)		TLS		10
				DWS			E (1)			DWS	E (1)				11
DLS			DWS				DLS R (1)				DWS R (1)			DLS	12
		DWS				DLS	D (2)	DLS				DWS			13
	DWS				TLS		O (1)		TLS				DWS		14
TWS			DLS				TWS G (2)				DLS			TWS	15

DIAGRAM 2-2

Play each two-letter word on the given board position above to score the most points. Can you beat our total of 113 points?

EXPERT SCORE: 107 GOOD SCORE: 99 AVERAGE SCORE: 77

1. AB
2. EX
3. LO
4. PI
5. YE

	A	B	C	D	E	F	G	H	I	J	K	L	M	N	O
1	TWS			DLS				TWS				DLS			TWS
2		DWS				TLS				TLS				DWS	
3			DWS				DLS		DLS				DWS		
4	DLS			DWS				DLS				DWS			DLS
5				R_1	DWS						DWS				
6		TLS		O_1		TLS				TLS				TLS	
7			DLS	O_1		I_1	DLS N_1	N_1	DLS E_1	R_1			DLS		
8	TWS		A_1	DLS M_3	A_1	T_1	E_1	U_1	R_1			DLS			TWS
9			DLS				DLS W_4		DLS G_2	L_1	I_1	T_1	DLS Z_{10}		
10		TLS				TLS				TLS				TLS	
11					DWS						DWS				
12	DLS			DWS				DLS				DWS			DLS
13			DWS				DLS		DLS				DWS		
14		DWS				TLS				TLS				DWS	
15	TWS			DLS				TWS				DLS			TWS

DIAGRAM 2-3

Play each two-letter word on the given board position above to score the most points. Can you beat our total of 106 points?

EXPERT SCORE: 96 GOOD SCORE: 90 AVERAGE SCORE: 75

1. UM
2. AD
3. BY
4. FA
5. HO

	A	B	C	D	E	F	G	H	I	J	K	L	M	N	O
1	TWS			DLS				TWS				DLS			TWS
2		DWS				TLS				TLS				DWS	
3			DWS				DLS		DLS				DWS		
4	DLS			DWS				DLS				DWS			DLS
5					DWS						DWS				
6		TLS				TLS				TLS				TLS	
7			DLS				DLS	A	DLS M	I	G	O	DLS		
8	TWS			DLS P	A	N	T	R	Y			DLS W	A	N	TWS D
9			DLS		M		DLS		DLS				DLS		
10		TLS			O	TLS				TLS				TLS	
11					DWS E						DWS				
12	DLS			DWS	B			DLS				DWS			DLS
13			DWS		A		DLS		DLS				DWS		
14		DWS C	O	P	S	TLS				TLS				DWS	
15	TWS			DLS				TWS				DLS			TWS

DIAGRAM 2-4

Play each two-letter word on the given board position above to score the most points. Can you beat our total of 94 points?

EXPERT SCORE: 83 GOOD SCORE: 78 AVERAGE SCORE: 67

1. GO
2. HM
3. ID
4. JO
5. NU

	A	B	C	D	E	F	G	H	I	J	K	L	M	N	O
1	TWS			DLS				TWS				DLS			TWS
2		DWS				TLS				TLS				DWS	
3			DWS				DLS		DLS				DWS		
4	DLS			DWS				DLS				DWS			DLS
5					DWS						DWS				
6		TLS				TLS				TLS				TLS	
7			DLS				DLS	N_1	DLS A_1	T_1	U_1	R_1	DLS A_1	L_1	
8	TWS			DLS			B_3	U_1	G_2			DLS			TWS
9			DLS R_1	A_1	T_1	I_1	DLS O_1		DLS				DLS		
10		TLS	U_1			TLS				TLS				TLS	
11			B_3		DWS						DWS				
12	DLS		I_1	DWS				DLS				DWS			DLS
13			DWS E_1				DLS		DLS				DWS		
14		DWS	S_1			TLS				TLS				DWS	
15	TWS			DLS				TWS				DLS			TWS

DIAGRAM 2-5

Play each two-letter word on the given board position above to score the most points. Can you beat our total of 92 points?

EXPERT SCORE: 88 GOOD SCORE: 85 AVERAGE SCORE: 79

1. MA
2. NE
3. OF
4. PA
5. UP

TWS			DLS				TWS				DLS			TWS	1
	DWS				TLS				TLS				DWS		2
		DWS				DLS		DLS				DWS			3
DLS			DWS				DLS				DWS			DLS	4
				DWS A_1						DWS					5
	TLS			W_4	TLS				TLS				TLS		6
		DLS		A_1		DLS		DLS				DLS			7
TWS			DLS C_3	R_1	U_1	M_3	B_3				DLS			TWS	8
		DLS	I_1	D_2		DLS		DLS				DLS			9
	TLS		L_1		TLS				TLS				TLS		10
			I_1	DWS N_1	C_3	U_1	R_1	V_4	E_1	DWS D_2					11
DLS			DWS A_1		R_1		DLS				DWS			DLS	12
		DWS			U_1	DLS		DLS				DWS			13
	DWS				TLS X_8				TLS				DWS		14
TWS			DLS				TWS				DLS			TWS	15
A	B	C	D	E	F	G	H	I	J	K	L	M	N	O	

DIAGRAM 2-6

Play each two-letter word on the given board position above to score the most points. Can you beat our total of 78 points?

EXPERT SCORE: 73 GOOD SCORE: 70 AVERAGE SCORE: 63

1. AE
2. AY
3. ED
4. IS
5. OH

	A	B	C	D	E	F	G	H	I	J	K	L	M	N	O
1	TWS			DLS				TWS				DLS			TWS
2		DWS				TLS				TLS				DWS	
3			DWS				DLS		DLS				DWS		
4	DLS			DWS				DLS				DWS			DLS
5					DWS						DWS				
6		TLS				TLS				TLS				TLS	
7			DLS				DLS		DLS				DLS		
8	TWS			DLS M_3	O_1	N_1	E_1	Y_4				DLS			TWS
9			DLS	I_1			DLS F_4	A_1	DLS N_1	G_2			DLS		
10		TLS		N_1		TLS				TLS O_1	B_3	E_1	Y_4	TLS	
11				N_1	DWS						DWS				
12	DLS			DWS O_1				DLS				DWS			DLS
13			DWS	W_4			DLS		DLS				DWS		
14		DWS				TLS				TLS				DWS	
15	TWS			DLS				TWS				DLS			TWS

DIAGRAM 2-7

Play each two-letter word on the given board position above to score the most points. Can you beat our total of 106 points?

EXPERT SCORE: **101** GOOD SCORE: **95** AVERAGE SCORE: **80**

1. BA
2. EF
3. HA
4. OE
5. SH

A	B	C	D	E	F	G	H	I	J	K	L	M	N	O	
TWS			DLS				TWS				DLS			TWS	1
	DWS				TLS				TLS				DWS		2
		DWS				DLS		DLS				DWS			3
DLS			DWS				DLS P_3				DWS			DLS	4
				DWS S_1	H_4	O_1	U_1	L_1	D_2	DWS E_1	R_1				5
	TLS				TLS		M_3		TLS				TLS		6
		DLS				DLS	P_3	DLS				DLS			7
TWS			DLS				E_1	R_1			DLS			TWS	8
		DLS				DLS	R_1	DLS E_1				DLS			9
	TLS				TLS			V_4	TLS				TLS		10
			A_1	DWS O_1	R_1	T_1	A_1	E_1		DWS					11
DLS			DWS				DLS E_1	L_1			DWS			DLS	12
		DWS				DLS	R_1	DLS				DWS			13
	DWS				TLS		I_1		TLS				DWS		14
TWS			DLS				TWS E_1				DLS			TWS	15

DIAGRAM 2-8

Play each two-letter word on the given board position above to score the most points. Can you beat our total of 69 points?

EXPERT SCORE: 65 GOOD SCORE: 60 AVERAGE SCORE: 53

1. AG
2. DO
3. MI
4. RE
5. XI

	A	B	C	D	E	F	G	H	I	J	K	L	M	N	O
1	TWS			DLS				TWS				DLS			TWS
2		DWS				TLS				TLS				DWS	
3			DWS				DLS		DLS				DWS		
4	DLS			DWS				DLS				DWS			DLS
5					DWS						DWS				
6		TLS				TLS				TLS				TLS	
7			DLS				DLS		DLS				DLS		
8	TWS			DLS W4	H4	E1	E1	L1				DLS			TWS
9			DLS		O1		DLS N1	O1	DLS B3	L1	E1	R1	DLS		
10		TLS			B3	TLS				TLS		A1		TLS	
11					DWS O1						DWS	N1			
12	DLS			DWS				DLS				DWS C3			DLS
13			DWS				DLS		DLS			I1	DWS		
14		DWS				TLS				TLS		D2		DWS	
15	TWS			DLS				TWS				DLS			TWS

DIAGRAM 2-9

Play each two-letter word on the given board position above to score the most points. Can you beat our total of 90 points?

EXPERT SCORE: 85 GOOD SCORE: 82 AVERAGE SCORE: 74

1. EH
2. KA
3. ME
4. OM
5. OX

A	B	C	D	E	F	G	H	I	J	K	L	M	N	O	
TWS			DLS				TWS				DLS			TWS	1
	DWS				TLS				TLS				DWS		2
		DWS				DLS		DLS				DWS			3
DLS			DWS				DLS				DWS			DLS	4
				DWS						DWS					5
	TLS				TLS				TLS				TLS		6
		DLS				DLS		DLS				DLS			7
TWS			DLS			D_2	O_1	G_2			DLS			TWS	8
		DLS				DLS	M_3	DLS O_1	W_4			DLS			9
	TLS				TLS				TLS O_1	D_2	D_2	L_1	TLS Y_4		10
				DWS						DWS			O_1		11
DLS			DWS				DLS				DWS		D_2	DLS	12
		DWS				DLS		DLS				DWS	L_1		13
	DWS				TLS				TLS				DWS E_1		14
TWS			DLS				TWS				DLS			TWS	15

DIAGRAM 2-10

Play each two-letter word on the given board position above to score the most points. Can you beat our total of 93 points?

EXPERT SCORE: **85** GOOD SCORE: **80** AVERAGE SCORE: **65**

1. OS
2. SI
3. XU
4. YO
5. OW

A	B	C	D	E	F	G	H	I	J	K	L	M	N	O	
TWS			DLS				TWS				DLS			TWS	1
	DWS				TLS				TLS				DWS		2
		DWS				DLS		DLS				DWS			3
DLS			DWS				DLS				DWS			DLS	4
				DWS						DWS					5
	TLS				TLS				TLS				TLS		6
		DLS		A1	R1	DLS		DLS H4	E1	I1	F4	DLS E1	R1		7
TWS		S1	DLS W4	E1	E1	T1	I1	E1			DLS A1	R1	E1	TWS A1	8
		DLS E1			A1	DLS		DLS				DLS			9
	TLS	I1			TLS D2				TLS				TLS		10
		Z10	O1	DWS O1						DWS					11
DLS		E1	DWS				DLS				DWS			DLS	12
		DWS R1				DLS		DLS				DWS			13
	DWS				TLS				TLS				DWS		14
TWS			DLS				TWS				DLS			TWS	15

DIAGRAM 2-11

Play each two-letter word on the given board position above to score the most points. Can you beat our total of 99 points?

EXPERT SCORE: 94 GOOD SCORE: 89 AVERAGE SCORE: 75

1. AH
2. BO
3. ES
4. IT
5. SO

A	B	C	D	E	F	G	H	I	J	K	L	M	N	O	
TWS			DLS				TWS				DLS			TWS	1
	DWS				TLS				TLS				DWS		2
		DWS				DLS		DLS				DWS			3
DLS			DWS				DLS				DWS			DLS	4
				DWS						DWS					5
	TLS K_5	I_1	D_2	N_1	TLS A_1	P_3			TLS				TLS		6
		DLS			G_2	DLS E_1	N_1	DLS U_1	S_1			DLS			7
TWS			DLS			H_4	U_1	M_3			DLS			TWS	8
		DLS				DLS		DLS M_3	O_1	L_1	L_1	DLS Y_4			9
	TLS				TLS				TLS				TLS		10
				DWS						DWS					11
DLS			DWS				DLS				DWS			DLS	12
		DWS				DLS		DLS				DWS			13
	DWS				TLS				TLS				DWS		14
TWS			DLS				TWS				DLS			TWS	15

DIAGRAM 2-12

Play each two-letter word on the given board position above to score the most points. Can you beat our total of 65 points?

EXPERT SCORE: 60 GOOD SCORE: 55 AVERAGE SCORE: 50

1. AI
2. LA
3. NO
4. AW
5. OP

A	B	C	D	E	F	G	H	I	J	K	L	M	N	O	
TWS			DLS				TWS				DLS			TWS	1
	DWS			O_1	TLS				TLS				DWS		2
		DWS		M_3		DLS		DLS				DWS			3
DLS			DWS	E_1			DLS				DWS			DLS	4
				DWS G_2						DWS					5
	TLS			A_1	TLS B_3				TLS				TLS		6
		DLS			L_1	DLS		DLS				DLS			7
TWS			DLS T_1	R_1	O_1	U_1	T_1				DLS			TWS	8
		DLS			O_1	DLS		DLS				DLS			9
	TLS				TLS E_1				TLS				TLS		10
				DWS	Y_4					DWS					11
DLS			DWS				DLS				DWS			DLS	12
		DWS				DLS		DLS				DWS			13
	DWS				TLS				TLS				DWS		14
TWS			DLS				TWS				DLS			TWS	15

DIAGRAM 2-13

Play each two-letter word on the given board position above to score the most points. Can you beat our total of 108 points?

EXPERT SCORE: **102** GOOD SCORE: **95** AVERAGE SCORE: **81**

1. AM
2. BE
3. EN
4. IF
5. MO

TWS			DLS				TWS				DLS			TWS	1
	DWS				TLS				TLS			R_1	DWS		2
		DWS				DLS		DLS				DWS E_1			3
DLS			DWS				DLS				DWS	A_1		DLS	4
				DWS						DWS		L_1			5
	TLS				TLS				TLS			I_1	TLS		6
		DLS				DLS		DLS J_8	A_1	B_3		DLS Z_{10}			7
TWS			DLS				N_1	O_1	T_1	I_1	DLS C_3	E_1	S_1	TWS	8
		DLS				DLS		DLS W_4	E_1	T_1		DLS	E_1		9
	TLS				TLS				TLS				TLS Q_{10}		10
				DWS						DWS			U_1		11
DLS			DWS				DLS				DWS		O_1	DLS	12
		DWS				DLS		DLS				DWS P_3	I_1		13
	DWS				TLS				TLS			A_1	DWS A_1		14
TWS			DLS			E_1	TWS X_8	P_3	O_1	U_1	DLS N_1	D_2		TWS	15
A	B	C	D	E	F	G	H	I	J	K	L	M	N	O	

DIAGRAM 2-14

Play each two-letter word on the given board position above to score the most points. Can you beat our total of 93 points?

EXPERT SCORE: 88 GOOD SCORE: 84 AVERAGE SCORE: 75

1. AL
2. EM
3. HE
4. MM
5. ON

TWS			DLS C				TWS V				DLS			TWS	1
	DWS		L		TLS		I		TLS				DWS		2
		DWS	E			DLS	N	DLS				DWS			3
DLS			DWS A				DLS A	B			DWS			DLS	4
			R	DWS	Q			U		DWS					5
	TLS		I		TLS U			S	TLS				TLS		6
		DLS	N		A	DLS		DLS H				DLS			7
TWS			DLS G	I	G	G	L	E	D		DLS			TWS	8
	A	DLS			M	DLS		DLS D	O			DLS			9
	TLS V				TLS I				TLS Z				TLS		10
	I			DWS	R				E	DWS F					11
DLS M	A	R	DWS I	N	E	S	DLS		D	O	DWS			DLS	12
	T	DWS				DLS		DLS		A		DWS			13
	DWS E				TLS				TLS	L			DWS		14
TWS			DLS				TWS				DLS			TWS	15
A	B	C	D	E	F	G	H	I	J	K	L	M	N	O	

DIAGRAM 2-15

Play each two-letter word on the given board position above to score the most points. Can you beat our total of 81 points?

EXPERT SCORE: 76 GOOD SCORE: 73 AVERAGE SCORE: 65

1. AN
2. BI
3. EL
4. YA
5. OW

	A	B	C	D	E	F	G	H	I	J	K	L	M	N	O
1	TWS			DLS				TWS				DLS			TWS
2		DWS				TLS				TLS		A		DWS	
3			DWS				DLS		DLS			X	DWS		
4	DLS			DWS				DLS				DWS I			DLS
5					DWS						DWS	A			
6		TLS				TLS W		G	O	TLS B	B	L	E	TLS	
7			DLS			H	DLS		DLS	L			DLS		
8	TWS			DLS		A	F	I	R	E		DLS			TWS
9			DLS			L	DLS A		DLS	S			DLS		
10		TLS			H	TLS E	N			TLS S				TLS	
11					DWS O		D			E	DWS				
12	DLS Y	O	G	DWS I	C		O	DLS		D		DWS			DLS
13	I		DWS		K		DLS M		DLS				DWS		
14	P	DWS				TLS				TLS				DWS	
15	TWS E			DLS				TWS				DLS			TWS

DIAGRAM 2-16

Play each two-letter word on the given board position above to score the most points. Can you beat our total of 97 points?

EXPERT SCORE: 93 GOOD SCORE: 89 AVERAGE SCORE: 79

1. AR
2. ET
3. IN
4. MY
5. OP

TWS	D_2		DLS				TWS				DLS			TWS	1
	DWS E_1				TLS				TLS	V_4			DWS		2
	N_1	DWS				DLS		DLS		E_1		DWS			3
DLS	U_1		DWS				DLS			T_1	DWS H_4	I_1	R_1	DLS D_2	4
	D_2			DWS					J_8	DWS O_1	W_4				5
P_3	TLS E_1				TLS				TLS A_1		A_1		TLS		6
U_1		DLS				DLS	B_3	DLS A_1	I_1	R_1	N_1	DLS			7
TWS F_4			DLS			B_3	O_1	W_4	L_1		DLS			TWS	8
F_4		DLS H_4	O_1	M_3	E_1	DLS Y_4		DLS				DLS			9
S_1	TLS C_3	A_1	P_3	E_1	TLS D_2				TLS				TLS		10
				DWS						DWS					11
DLS			DWS				DLS				DWS			DLS	12
		DWS				DLS		DLS				DWS			13
	DWS				TLS				TLS				DWS		14
TWS			DLS				TWS				DLS			TWS	15
A	B	C	D	E	F	G	H	I	J	K	L	M	N	O	

DIAGRAM 2-17

Play each two-letter word on the given board position above to score the most points. Can you beat our total of 103 points?

EXPERT SCORE: 95 GOOD SCORE: 90 AVERAGE SCORE: 75

1. TA
2. AS
3. AX
4. OR
5. MU

	A	B	C	D	E	F	G	H	I	J	K	L	M	N	O
1	TWS			DLS				TWS				DLS			TWS
2		DWS				TLS				TLS				DWS	
3			DWS				DLS		DLS				DWS		
4	DLS		L_1	DWS				DLS				DWS			DLS
5			A_1		DWS	E_1	L	E_1	V_4	A_1	DWS T_1	E_1			
6		TLS	M_3	Y_4	T_1	TLS H_4				TLS				TLS	
7			DLS A_1		R_1		DLS		DLS				DLS		
8	TWS			DLS	U_1			B_3	U_1	N_1	C_3	DLS H_4	I_1	N_1	TWS G_2
9			DLS L_1	O_1	C_3	A_1	DLS T_1	E_1	DLS		O_1		DLS		
10		TLS	U_1		K_5	TLS				TLS	B_3			TLS	
11			M_3		DWS E_1						DWS A_1				
12	DLS		P_3	DWS	D_2			DLS			L_1	DWS			DLS
13			DWS				DLS		DLS		T_1		DWS		
14		DWS				TLS				TLS				DWS	
15	TWS			DLS				TWS				DLS			TWS

DIAGRAM 2-18

Play each two-letter word on the given board position above to score the most points. Can you beat our total score of 98 points?

EXPERT SCORE: 93 GOOD SCORE: 88 AVERAGE SCORE: 70

1. AT
2. TA
3. OY
4. WE
5. LI

	A	B	C	D	E	F	G	H	I	J	K	L	M	N	O
1	TWS			DLS				TWS				DLS			TWS
2		DWS				TLS				TLS				DWS	
3			DWS				DLS		DLS				DWS		
4	DLS			DWS				DLS				DWS R_1			DLS
5					DWS						DWS	E_1			
6		TLS				TLS			O_1	TLS X_8	T_1	A_1	I_1	TLS L_1	
7			DLS			A_1	DLS N_1	E_1	DLS W_4			C_3	DLS		
8	TWS			DLS Z_{10}	I_1	B_3	E_1	T_1				DLS T_1			TWS
9			DLS		N_1		DLS		DLS			I_1	DLS		
10		TLS W_4	O_1	N_1	T_1	TLS				TLS		N		TLS	
11			N_1	E_1	DWS O_1	N_1					DWS	G_2			
12	DLS			DWS				DLS				DWS			DLS
13			DWS				DLS		DLS				DWS		
14		DWS				TLS				TLS				DWS	
15	TWS			DLS				TWS				DLS			TWS

DIAGRAM 2-19

Play each two-letter word on the given board position above to score the most points. Can you beat our total of 89 points?

EXPERT SCORE: 79 GOOD SCORE: 64 AVERAGE SCORE: 49

1. NA
2. TO
3. US
4. DE
5. DA

	A	B	C	D	E	F	G	H	I	J	K	L	M	N	O
1	TWS			DLS				TWS				DLS			TWS
2		DWS				TLS				TLS				DWS	
3			DWS				DLS		DLS				DWS		
4	DLS			DWS R1				DLS				DWS			DLS
5				O1	DWS						DWS				
6		TLS		U1		TLS				TLS				TLS	
7			DLS	G2			DLS		DLS				DLS		
8	TWS			DLS H4	O1	P3	E1	F4	U1	L1		DLS			TWS
9			DLS			H4	DLS		DLS	A1			DLS		
10		TLS				TLS O1				TLS X8				TLS	
11					DWS	N1					DWS				
12	DLS			DWS		I1		DLS				DWS			DLS
13			DWS			E1	DLS		DLS				DWS		
14		DWS				TLS S1				TLS				DWS	
15	TWS			DLS				TWS				DLS			TWS

DIAGRAM 2-20

Play each two-letter word on the given board position above to score the most points. Can you beat our total of 86 points?

EXPERT SCORE: 81 GOOD SCORE: 77 AVERAGE SCORE: 62

1. TI
2. AM
3. UT
4. WO
5. UN

Two-Letter Words

DIAGRAM 2-1

1. AA E10 17
2. HI E11 22
3. PE D4 40
4. OD E10 21
5. UH G10 19

TOTAL: 119 POINTS

DIAGRAM 2-2

1. AB K10 19
2. EX 5D 36
3. LO 5E 11
4. PI 5K 25
5. YE K11 22

TOTAL: 113 POINTS

DIAGRAM 2-3

1. UM 9B 14
2. ADZ M7 14
3. BY 4D 32
4. FA 6F 34
5. RHO 5D 12

TOTAL: 106 POINTS

DIAGRAM 2-4

1. GOA 13C 18
2. HM F10 32
3. ID F12 10
4. JOB 12C 24
5. NUB 12C 10

TOTAL: 94 POINTS

DIAGRAM 2-5

1. MA B10 24
2. NE 6I 12
3. OF 10E 28
4. PA B13 or 8D 16
5. UP B14 12

TOTAL: 92 POINTS

DIAGRAM 2-6

1. AE F5 13
2. AY I7 21
3. CRUMBED 8D 14
4. IS I7 15
5. OH D4 15

TOTAL: 78 POINTS

DIAGRAM 2-7

1. BA C12 or 11J 22
2. EF 11K 23
3. HA C12 25
4. OE 11J 16
5. SH 10G 20

TOTAL: 106 POINTS

DIAGRAM 2-8

1. AG 12C 12
2. DO 4K 13
3. MI 12C 12
4. RE 12D or 4K 10
5. XI 12C 22

TOTAL: 69 POINTS

DIAGRAM 2-9

1. EH F10 18
2. KAE F6 17
3. ME D11 or MED 14J 12
4. OM 7F 17
5. OX F10 26

TOTAL: 90 POINTS

DIAGRAM 2-10

1. OS 15M 12
2. SI 15N 16
3. XU O14 36
4. YO O11 15
5. OW 11I or DOW K10 or DOW L10 14

TOTAL: 93 POINTS

DIAGRAM 2-11

1. AH B9 28
2. BO 6F 24
3. ES 14B 20
4. IT 6N or AIT 9F 9
5. SO 14C 18

TOTAL: 99 POINTS

DIAGRAM 2-12

1. AI 5D 11
2. LA 7A or LAD D4 8
3. NO 10J 10
4. AW 5E 21
5. OP 10M 15

TOTAL: 65 POINTS

DIAGRAM 2-13

1. AM E10 24
2. BE E11 22
3. EN D3 12
4. IF F1 26
5. MO F2 24

TOTAL: 108 POINTS

DIAGRAM 2-14

1. AL 10H 16
2. EM N2 16
3. HE O12 23
4. MM 14J 26
5. ON 14I 12

TOTAL: 93 POINTS

DIAGRAM 2-15

1. RAN C12 12
2. BI A14 16
3. EL L12 14
4. YA C3 22
5. OW G3 or A14 17

TOTAL: 81 POINTS

DIAGRAM 2-16

1. AR N5 18
2. ET B14 14
3. IN M3 24
4. MY H12 24
5. OP H11 or K3 17

TOTAL: 97 POINTS

DIAGRAM 2-17

1. META E9 12
2. AS 9I 22
3. AX A3 36
4. OR A1 17
5. MU C2 16

TOTAL: 103 POINTS

DIAGRAM 2-18

1. AT D12 16
2. TA 6J or L11 10
3. OY 13B 34
4. WE 4L 20
5. LI 3C 18

TOTAL: 98 POINTS

DIAGRAM 2-19

1. NA 5I 17
2. TO 5I 17
3. US O5 16
4. DE 5I 19
5. DA 6F 20

TOTAL: 89 POINTS

DIAGRAM 2-20

1. TI 15F 15
2. AMA 9H 20
3. UT 15E 15
4. WO 7G 23
5. UN K10 13

TOTAL: 86 POINTS

CHAPTER 3

Placing Your Words on Hot Spots

Now that you understand how to use the two-letter words, your next step is to recognize where on the board you can place the longer words. For each diagram you're given five words. Find the highest-scoring placement for each word. Always remember to remove the previous word from the board before going on to the next word.

Unlike the previous chapter, you *may* use a letter already on the board to spell out the given word, but *not necessarily*.

A	B	C	D	E	F	G	H	I	J	K	L	M	N	O	
TWS			DLS				TWS				DLS			TWS	1
	DWS				TLS				TLS				DWS		2
		DWS	B			DLS		DLS				DWS			3
DLS			DWS A				DLS				DWS			DLS	4
			N	DWS						DWS					5
	TLS		A		TLS				TLS				TLS		6
		DLS	N			DLS		DLS				DLS			7
TWS			DLS A	I	O	L	I				DLS			TWS	8
		DLS			F	DLS I	N	DLS K	S			DLS			9
	TLS				TLS				TLS P				TLS		10
				DWS					O	DWS					11
DLS			DWS				DLS		N		DWS			DLS	12
		DWS				DLS		DLS A	G	I	L	DWS E			13
	DWS				TLS				TLS Y				DWS		14
TWS			DLS				TWS				DLS			TWS	15

DIAGRAM 3-1

Find the highest-scoring placement on the above diagram for each of the five given words. You may use a letter or two already on the board. Can you beat our total of 178 points?

EXPERT SCORE: **165** GOOD SCORE: **150** AVERAGE SCORE: **130**

1. MANANA
2. SPOOF
3. POI
4. VANMEN
5. QANAT

A	B	C	D	E	F	G	H	I	J	K	L	M	N	O	
TWS			DLS				TWS				DLS			TWS	1
	DWS				TLS				TLS				DWS		2
		DWS				DLS		DLS				DWS			3
DLS			DWS				DLS				DWS B			DLS	4
				DWS						DWS	A				5
	TLS				TLS				TLS P		W		TLS		6
	E	DLS X	O	T	I	DLS C	A	DLS	I		T	DLS			7
TWS			DLS				T	E	L	L	DLS Y			TWS	8
		DLS				DLS		DLS	A			DLS			9
	TLS				TLS				TLS F				TLS		10
				DWS			M	U	S	DWS H	Y				11
DLS			DWS				DLS				DWS			DLS	12
		DWS				DLS		DLS				DWS			13
	DWS				TLS				TLS				DWS		14
TWS			DLS				TWS				DLS			TWS	15

DIAGRAM 3-2

Find the highest-scoring placement on the above diagram for each of the five given words. You may use a letter or two already on the board. Can you beat our total of 171 points?

EXPERT SCORE: **162** GOOD SCORE: **155** AVERAGE SCORE: **140**

1. DRAMA
2. ANOA
3. ZETA
4. CAROM
5. PRIMO

TWS			DLS				TWS				DLS			TWS	1
	DWS				TLS				TLS				DWS		2
		DWS				DLS		DLS				DWS			3
DLS			DWS				DLS				DWS	R_{1}		DLS	4
				DWS						DWS		E_{1}			5
	TLS				TLS				TLS			A_{1}	TLS		6
		DLS				DLS		DLS	Q_{10}			DLS D_{2}			7
TWS			DLS				T_{1}	R_{1}	U_{1}	M_{3}	DLS P_{3}	S_{1}		TWS	8
		DLS				DLS	H_{4}	DLS	A_{1}		I_{1}	DLS			9
	TLS				TLS		R_{1}		TLS		C_{3}		TLS		10
				DWS			U_{1}			DWS	K_{5}				11
DLS			DWS				DLS S_{1}				DWS L_{1}			DLS	12
		DWS E_{1}	X_{8}	T_{1}	E_{1}	DLS N_{1}	T_{1}	DLS			E_{1}	DWS			13
	DWS				TLS		O_{1}		TLS				DWS		14
TWS			DLS				TWS R_{1}				DLS			TWS	15
A	B	C	D	E	F	G	H	I	J	K	L	M	N	O	

DIAGRAM 3-3

Find the highest-scoring placement on the above diagram for each of the five given words. You may use a letter or two already on the board. Can you beat our total of 181 points?

EXPERT SCORE: 177 GOOD SCORE: 170 AVERAGE SCORE: 155

1. ZEBRA
2. TRAGIC
3. AMEER
4. ABRADE
5. ARIA

	A	B	C	D	E	F	G	H	I	J	K	L	M	N	O
1	TWS			DLS				TWS				DLS			TWS
2		DWS				TLS				TLS				DWS	
3			DWS				DLS		DLS				DWS		
4	DLS			DWS				DLS				DWS			DLS
5					DWS						DWS				
6		TLS				TLS				TLS				TLS	
7			DLS				DLS		DLS				DLS		
8	TWS			DLS M	U	S	T	H				DLS			TWS
9			DLS			E	DLS	E	DLS X	I	T		DLS		
10		TLS				TLS Q				TLS				TLS	
11					DWS	U					DWS				
12	DLS	F	O	DWS L	L	O	W	DLS				DWS			DLS
13			DWS			I	DLS		DLS				DWS		
14		DWS				TLS A				TLS				DWS	
15	TWS			DLS		S	O	TWS D	A			DLS			TWS

DIAGRAM 3-4

Find the highest-scoring placement on the above diagram for each of the five given words. You may use a letter or two already on the board. Can you beat our total of 134 points?

EXPERT SCORE: **128** GOOD SCORE: **120** AVERAGE SCORE: **104**

1. MANA
2. NUDITY
3. ILIUM
4. VACUA
5. DATUM

	A	B	C	D	E	F	G	H	I	J	K	L	M	N	O
1	TWS			DLS				TWS				DLS			TWS
2		DWS				TLS				TLS				DWS	
3			DWS				DLS		DLS		R_1		DWS		
4	DLS			DWS				DLS			A_1	DWS			DLS
5					DWS						DWS D_2				
6		TLS				TLS				TLS	I_1			TLS	
7			DLS				DLS		DLS O_1	L_1	I_1	O_1	DLS		
8	TWS			DLS B_3	E_1	Y_4	O_1	N_1	D_2			DLS H_4	A_1	I_1	TWS L_1
9			DLS	R_1			DLS	A_1	DLS				DLS		
10		TLS		I_1		TLS		T_1	O_1	TLS Q_{10}	U_1	E_1	T_1	TLS	
11				N_1	DWS			I_1			DWS				
12	DLS			DWS K_5				DLS O_1				DWS			DLS
13			DWS				DLS	N_1	DLS				DWS		
14		DWS				TLS		A_1		TLS				DWS	
15	TWS			DLS				TWS L_1				DLS			TWS

DIAGRAM 3-5

Find the highest-scoring placement on the above diagram for each of the five given words. You may use a letter or two already on the board. Can you beat our total of 152 points?

EXPERT SCORE: 140 GOOD SCORE: 130 AVERAGE SCORE: 115

1. FOAM
2. RAIN
3. VETO
4. VOIDS
5. THAWY

A	B	C	D	E	F	G	H	I	J	K	L	M	N	O	
TWS			DLS				TWS				DLS			TWS	1
	DWS				TLS				TLS				DWS		2
		DWS				DLS		DLS				DWS			3
DLS			DWS				DLS				DWS			DLS	4
				DWS						DWS					5
	TLS				TLS				TLS				TLS		6
		DLS				DLS		DLS				DLS			7
TWS			DLS			T	O	P			DLS			TWS	8
		DLS				DLS	U	DLS				DLS			9
	TLS				TLS		T	U	TLS X	E	D	O	TLS		10
				DWS			C			DWS					11
DLS			DWS				DLS O				DWS			DLS	12
		DWS				DLS	M	DLS U	S	I	C	DWS A	L		13
	DWS				TLS		E		TLS				DWS		14
TWS S	U	B	DLS J	O	I	N	TWS S				DLS			TWS	15

DIAGRAM 3-6

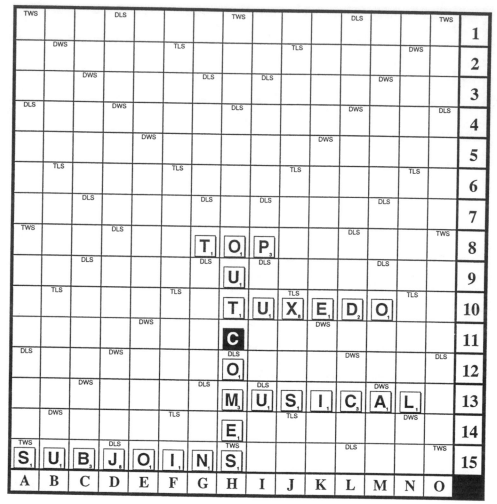

Find the highest-scoring placement on the above diagram for each of the five given words. You may use a letter or two already on the board. Can you beat our total of 164 points?

EXPERT SCORE: 155 GOOD SCORE: 145 AVERAGE SCORE: 132

1. VENA
2. AMONG
3. DICTUM
4. POACH
5. AMA

A	B	C	D	E	F	G	H	I	J	K	L	M	N	O	
TWS			DLS				TWS				DLS			TWS	1
	DWS				TLS				TLS				DWS		2
		DWS				DLS		DLS				DWS			3
DLS			DWS		H 4		DLS				DWS			DLS	4
				DWS	A 1					DWS					5
	TLS				TLS J 8				TLS				TLS		6
		DLS			E 1	DLS		DLS				DLS			7
TWS			DLS S 1	U 1	S 1	T 1	A 1	I 1	N 1		DLS			TWS	8
		DLS	W 4			DLS A 1	N 1	DLS T 1	E 1	E 1	D 2	DLS			9
	TLS		I 1		TLS				TLS				TLS		10
			N 1	DWS						DWS					11
DLS			DWS G 2				DLS				DWS			DLS	12
		DWS T 1	Y 4	P 3	E 1	DLS D 2		DLS				DWS			13
	DWS				TLS				TLS				DWS		14
TWS			DLS				TWS				DLS			TWS	15

DIAGRAM 3-7

Find the highest-scoring placement on the above diagram for each of the five given words. You may use a letter or two already on the board. Can you beat our total of 155 points?

EXPERT SCORE: 148 GOOD SCORE: 140 AVERAGE SCORE: 125

1. AORTA
2. AHOY
3. CHAOS
4. WRONG
5. AGOG

A	B	C	D	E	F	G	H	I	J	K	L	M	N	O	
TWS			DLS				TWS				DLS			TWS	1
	DWS				TLS				TLS				DWS		2
		DWS		A_1		DLS		DLS				DWS			3
DLS			DWS	W_4			DLS				DWS			DLS	4
				DWS F_4						DWS					5
	TLS			U_1	TLS P_3				TLS				TLS		6
		DLS		L_1	A_1	DLS		DLS				DLS			7
TWS			DLS		D_2	R_1	U_1	M_3			DLS			TWS	8
		DLS			D_2	DLS	N_1	DLS				DLS			9
	TLS			B_3	TLS Y_4		E_1		TLS				TLS		10
				DWS I_1			A_1			DWS					11
DLS			DWS	T_1			DLS R_1				DWS			DLS	12
		DWS		E_1		DLS	N_1	DLS O_1	T_1	I_1	C_3	DWS E_1			13
	DWS				TLS		E_1		TLS				DWS		14
TWS			DLS				TWS D_2				DLS			TWS	15

DIAGRAM 3-8

Find the highest-scoring placement on the above diagram for each of the five given words. You may use a letter or two already on the board. Can you beat our total of 213 points?

EXPERT SCORE: 200 GOOD SCORE: 185 AVERAGE SCORE: 160

1. STICKS
2. WRITHE
3. COULD
4. GAMINE
5. LAID

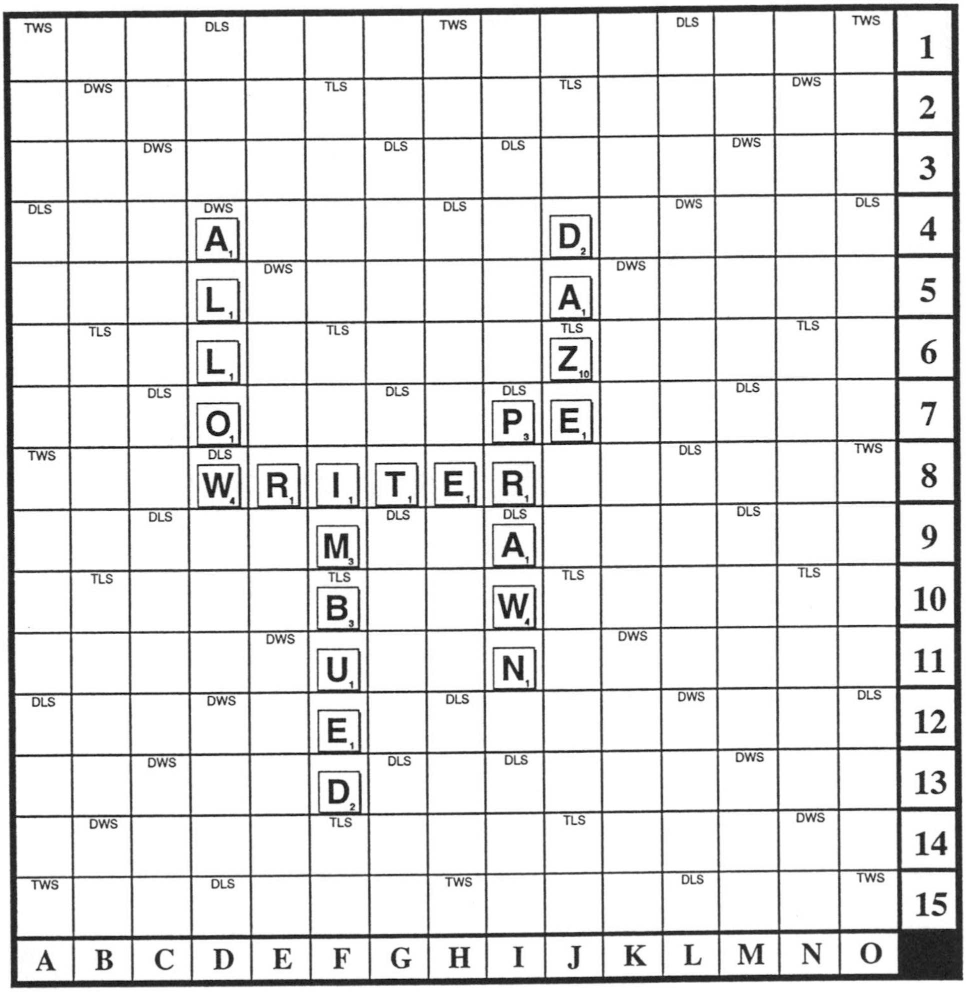

DIAGRAM 3-9

Find the highest-scoring placement on the above diagram for each of the five given words. You may use a letter or two already on the board. Can you beat our total of 138 points?

EXPERT SCORE: 131 GOOD SCORE: 123 AVERAGE SCORE: 108

1. ALIEN
2. REAM
3. ICILY
4. PAEAN
5. IDEAL

A	B	C	D	E	F	G	H	I	J	K	L	M	N	O	
TWS			DLS				TWS				DLS			TWS	1
	DWS				TLS				TLS				DWS		2
		DWS		G$_2$		DLS		DLS				DWS			3
DLS			DWS	I$_1$			DLS				DWS			DLS	4
				DWS Z$_{10}$						DWS					5
	TLS			M$_3$	TLS				TLS				TLS		6
		DLS	T$_1$	O$_1$	M$_3$	DLS A$_1$	T$_1$	DLS O$_1$				DLS			7
TWS V$_4$	I$_1$	N$_1$	DLS O$_1$	S$_1$			A$_1$	P$_3$	T$_1$	L$_1$	DLS Y$_4$			TWS	8
		DLS				DLS		DLS			O$_1$	DLS			9
	TLS				TLS				TLS		U$_1$		TLS		10
				DWS						DWS	T$_1$				11
DLS			DWS				DLS				DWS H$_4$			DLS	12
		DWS				DLS		DLS				DWS			13
	DWS				TLS				TLS				DWS		14
TWS			DLS				TWS				DLS			TWS	15

DIAGRAM 3-10

Find the highest-scoring placement on the above diagram for each of the five given words. You may use a letter or two already on the board. Can you beat our total of 160 points?

EXPERT SCORE: **150** GOOD SCORE: **140** AVERAGE SCORE: **122**

1. VEXT
2. PECTIN
3. PHIAL
4. JOINTLY
5. TOUTED

Placement

DIAGRAM 3-1

1. MANANA C2 35
2. SPOOF 10B 37
3. POI K11 20
4. VANMEN 12H 42
5. QANAT 10B 44

TOTAL: 178 POINTS

DIAGRAM 3-2

1. DRAMA K2 36
2. ANOA 12L 20
3. ZETA B6 33
4. CAROM M1 26
5. PRIMO 8A 56

TOTAL: 171 POINTS

DIAGRAM 3-3

1. ZEBRA 6F 53
2. TRAGIC 10G 31
3. AMEER 12B 40
4. ABRADE 3I 36
5. ARIA 6G or 6J 21

TOTAL: 181 POINTS

DIAGRAM 3-4

1. MANA 13A 23
2. NUDITY 10H 38
3. ILIUM 8K 26
4. VACUA 14B 20
5. DATUM 10J 27

TOTAL: 134 POINTS

DIAGRAM 3-5

1. FOAM E10 33
2. RAIN 6I 20
3. VETO L2 23
4. VOIDS N6 37
5. THAWY 11K 39

TOTAL: 152 POINTS

DIAGRAM 3-6

1. VENA O12 45
2. AMONG 9J 28
3. DICTUM 11F 35
4. POACH F6 32
5. AMA 14A 24

TOTAL: 164 POINTS

DIAGRAM 3-7

1. AORTA G5 20
2. AHOY 14E 38
3. CHAOS 7H 32
4. WRONG 10J 40
5. AGOG 8L 25

TOTAL: 155 POINTS

DIAGRAM 3-8

1. DRUMSTICKS 8F 60
2. WRITHE G7 48
3. COULD 2B 36
4. GAMINE D9 36
5. LAID D3 33

TOTAL: 213 POINTS

DIAGRAM 3-9

1. ALIEN H11 20
2. REAM E8 28
3. ICILY 3C 39
4. PAEAN C3 25
5. IDEAL H11 26

TOTAL: 138 POINTS

DIAGRAM 3-10

1. VEXT 9F 32
2. PECTIN 6G or 4A 26
3. PHIAL M9 45
4. JOINTLY K3 39
5. TOUTED 6I 18

TOTAL: 160 POINTS

CHAPTER 4

Bonus Squares, One at a Time

Using bonus squares to your advantage will give you a decided edge in scoring. For the following ten diagrams we give you a bonus square for every rack. Using only the letters in the rack, find the highest-scoring play that covers the given bonus square. Note that there may be higher-scoring plays that do *not* cover the given bonus square.

DIAGRAM 4-1

Using only the letters of each rack, find the highest-scoring play that also covers the given bonus square, either horizontally or vertically. Can you beat our total of 146 points?

EXPERT SCORE: 140 **GOOD SCORE: 130** **AVERAGE SCORE: 110**

1. K11: ADGMNOP
2. J6: ACEGHNP
3. F6: ADLRUXY
4. C9: DEHLOOT
5. H15: ADELMTU

A	B	C	D	E	F	G	H	I	J	K	L	M	N	O	
TWS			DLS				TWS				DLS			TWS	1
	DWS				TLS				TLS				DWS		2
		DWS				DLS		DLS				DWS			3
DLS			DWS				DLS				DWS			DLS	4
				DWS						DWS					5
	TLS				TLS				TLS				TLS		6
		DLS				DLS		DLS		L_1	A_1	DLS M_3	A_1		7
TWS			DLS				A_1	R_1	E_1	O_1	DLS L_1	A_1	E_1	TWS	8
		DLS				DLS		DLS				DLS			9
	TLS				TLS				TLS				TLS		10
				DWS						DWS					11
DLS			DWS				DLS				DWS			DLS	12
		DWS				DLS		DLS				DWS			13
	DWS				TLS				TLS				DWS		14
TWS			DLS				TWS				DLS			TWS	15

DIAGRAM 4-2

Using only the letters of each rack, find the highest-scoring play that also covers the given bonus square, either horizontally or vertically. Can you beat our total of 193 points?

EXPERT SCORE: **180** GOOD SCORE: **170** AVERAGE SCORE: **150**

1. N6: AGIINPW
2. K11: BEFGNOS
3. J10: CDFGIKL
4. M9: CHLMOTY
5. L4: BDFIMOR

A	B	C	D	E	F	G	H	I	J	K	L	M	N	O	
TWS			DLS				TWS				DLS			TWS	1
	DWS				TLS				TLS				DWS		2
		DWS				DLS		DLS				DWS			3
DLS			DWS				DLS				DWS			DLS	4
				DWS						DWS					5
	TLS				TLS				TLS				TLS		6
		DLS				DLS		DLS H4				DLS			7
TWS			DLS			T1	R1	I1	P3	O1	DLS D2			TWS	8
		DLS				DLS		DLS P3				DLS			9
	TLS				TLS			S1	TLS				TLS		10
				DWS				T1		DWS					11
DLS			DWS				DLS	E1			DWS			DLS	12
		DWS				DLS		DLS R1				DWS			13
	DWS				TLS				TLS				DWS		14
TWS			DLS				TWS				DLS			TWS	15

DIAGRAM 4-3

Using only the letters of each rack, find the highest-scoring play that also covers the given bonus square, either horizontally or vertically. Can you beat our total of 180 points?

EXPERT SCORE: **170** GOOD SCORE: **160** AVERAGE SCORE: **130**

1. G13: AEFHIRT
2. H12: CEELMOT
3. K11: BDEGIOR
4. J10: EHILOOT
5. L4: BBEIILM

TWS			DLS				TWS				DLS			TWS	1
	DWS				TLS				TLS				DWS		2
		DWS			M$_3$	DLS		DLS				DWS			3
DLS H$_4$	A$_1$	I$_1$	DWS R$_1$	P$_3$	I$_1$	N$_1$	DLS				DWS			DLS	4
				DWS	N$_1$					DWS					5
	TLS				TLS G$_2$				TLS				TLS		6
		DLS			L$_1$	DLS		DLS				DLS			7
TWS			DLS G$_2$	R$_1$	E$_1$	E$_1$	T$_1$				DLS			TWS	8
		DLS				DLS		DLS				DLS			9
	TLS				TLS				TLS				TLS		10
				DWS						DWS					11
DLS			DWS				DLS				DWS			DLS	12
		DWS				DLS		DLS				DWS			13
	DWS				TLS				TLS				DWS		14
TWS			DLS				TWS				DLS			TWS	15
A	B	C	D	E	F	G	H	I	J	K	L	M	N	O	

DIAGRAM 4-4

Using only the letters of each rack, find the highest-scoring play that also covers the given bonus square, either horizontally or vertically. Can you beat our total of 179 points?

EXPERT SCORE: **165** GOOD SCORE: **145** AVERAGE SCORE: **120**

1. A1: DEIMOPT
2. B6: ACFNORY
3. E5: AEGIIRT
4. G9: AEHNPSV
5. C7: CCIMPRT

TWS			DLS				TWS				DLS			TWS	1
	DWS				TLS			S_1	TLS				DWS		2
		DWS				DLS		DLS A_1				DWS			3
DLS			DWS				DLS	T_1			DWS			DLS	4
				DWS R_1	E_1	S_1	T_1	I_1	V_4	DWS E_1					5
	TLS				TLS			R_1	TLS				TLS		6
		DLS				DLS		DLS E_1				DLS			7
TWS			DLS			D_2	O_1	S_1			DLS			TWS	8
		DLS				DLS		DLS				DLS			9
	TLS				TLS				TLS				TLS		10
				DWS						DWS					11
DLS			DWS				DLS				DWS			DLS	12
		DWS				DLS		DLS				DWS			13
	DWS				TLS				TLS				DWS		14
TWS			DLS				TWS				DLS			TWS	15
A	B	C	D	E	F	G	H	I	J	K	L	M	N	O	

DIAGRAM 4-5

Using only the letters of each rack, find the highest-scoring play that also covers the given bonus square, either horizontally or vertically. Can you beat our total of 165 points?

EXPERT SCORE: **152** GOOD SCORE: **140** AVERAGE SCORE: **110**

1. J2: ABDEEGH
2. F6: BDEEEMR
3. H1: AEELOTU
4. D4: ACEEOPR
5. L4: ADDILOY

	A	B	C	D	E	F	G	H	I	J	K	L	M	N	O
1	TWS			DLS				TWS				DLS			TWS
2		DWS				TLS				TLS				DWS	
3			DWS				DLS		DLS				DWS		
4	DLS			DWS				DLS				DWS			DLS
5					DWS						DWS				
6		TLS				TLS			O_1	TLS				TLS	
7			DLS				DLS		DLS O_1				DLS		
8	TWS			DLS F_4	I_1	L_1	T_1	E_1	R_1			DLS			TWS
9			DLS				DLS		DLS I_1				DLS		
10		TLS				TLS			E_1	TLS				TLS	
11					DWS						DWS				
12	DLS			DWS				DLS				DWS			DLS
13			DWS				DLS		DLS				DWS		
14		DWS				TLS				TLS				DWS	
15	TWS			DLS				TWS				DLS			TWS

DIAGRAM 4-6

Using only the letters of each rack, find the highest-scoring play that also covers the given bonus square, either horizontally or vertically. Can you beat our total of 182 points?

EXPERT SCORE: 170 **GOOD SCORE: 160** **AVERAGE SCORE: 135**

1. H15: AGHNRUY
2. H1: FGHLOTU
3. J6: ACDILOV
4. E5: FMNOORT
5. F10: EGHIMPT

	A	B	C	D	E	F	G	H	I	J	K	L	M	N	O
1	TWS			DLS				TWS				DLS			TWS
2		DWS				TLS				TLS				DWS	
3			DWS				DLS		DLS				DWS		
4	DLS			DWS				DLS				DWS			DLS
5					DWS						DWS				
6		TLS				TLS				TLS W_4				TLS	
7			DLS				DLS		DLS	A_1			DLS		
8	TWS			DLS				H_4	E_1	R_1	T_1	DLS Z_{10}			TWS
9			DLS				DLS		DLS	D_2			DLS		
10		TLS				TLS				TLS I_1				TLS	
11					DWS					N_1	DWS				
12	DLS			DWS				DLS		G_2		DWS			DLS
13			DWS				DLS		DLS				DWS		
14		DWS				TLS				TLS				DWS	
15	TWS			DLS				TWS				DLS			TWS

DIAGRAM 4-7

Using only the letters of each rack, find the highest-scoring play that also covers the given bonus square, either horizontally or vertically. Can you beat our total of 150 points?

EXPERT SCORE: **140** GOOD SCORE: **130** AVERAGE SCORE: **110**

1. L4: AGIOPTU
2. K5: ACFNOOT
3. L12: EFHNOUU
4. I7: AIMORTU
5. L11: CDEMNOT

A	B	C	D	E	F	G	H	I	J	K	L	M	N	O	
TWS			DLS				TWS				DLS			TWS	1
	DWS				TLS				TLS				DWS		2
		DWS				DLS		DLS				DWS			3
DLS			DWS				DLS			W_4	DWS			DLS	4
				DWS						DWS H_4					5
	TLS				TLS				TLS	I_1			TLS		6
		DLS				DLS		DLS		M_3		DLS			7
TWS			DLS			D_2	U_1	M_3	P_3	S_1	DLS			TWS	8
		DLS				DLS	N_1	DLS				DLS			9
	TLS				TLS		L_1		TLS				TLS		10
				DWS			I_1			DWS					11
DLS			DWS				DLS T_1				DWS			DLS	12
		DWS				DLS		DLS				DWS			13
	DWS				TLS				TLS				DWS		14
TWS			DLS				TWS				DLS			TWS	15

DIAGRAM 4-8

Using only the letters of each rack, find the highest-scoring play that also covers the given bonus square, either horizontally or vertically. Can you beat our total of 152 points?

EXPERT SCORE: **140** GOOD SCORE: **130** AVERAGE SCORE: **110**

1. K11: ACEHILU
2. J6: AEEIOTU
3. L4: ADFIORT
4. D12: EGHILOW
5. J10: CDEHISY

A	B	C	D	E	F	G	H	I	J	K	L	M	N	O	
TWS			DLS				TWS	R_1			DLS			TWS	1
	DWS				TLS			E_1	TLS				DWS		2
		DWS				DLS		DLS L_1				DWS			3
DLS			DWS				DLS	A_1			DWS			DLS	4
				DWS				T_1		DWS					5
	TLS				TLS			I_1	TLS				TLS		6
		DLS				DLS		DLS O_1				DLS			7
TWS			DLS		C_3	O_1	R_1	N_1			DLS			TWS	8
		DLS				DLS		DLS				DLS			9
	TLS				TLS				TLS				TLS		10
				DWS						DWS					11
DLS			DWS				DLS				DWS			DLS	12
		DWS				DLS		DLS				DWS			13
	DWS				TLS				TLS				DWS		14
TWS			DLS				TWS				DLS			TWS	15

DIAGRAM 4-9

Using only the letters of each rack, find the highest-scoring play that also covers the given bonus square, either horizontally or vertically. Can you beat our total of 228 points?

EXPERT SCORE: **210** GOOD SCORE: **190** AVERAGE SCORE: **150**

1. H1: AFGILTY
2. J2: AADLMNY
3. H4: ABCEFGT
4. J6: AFINPRY
5. K5: CENORUY

	A	B	C	D	E	F	G	H	I	J	K	L	M	N	O
1	TWS			DLS				TWS				DLS			TWS
2		DWS				TLS				TLS				DWS	
3			DWS				DLS		DLS	I			DWS		
4	DLS			DWS U	R	A	N	DLS I	U	M		DWS			DLS
5	A	L	I	N	DWS E					A	DWS				
6		TLS				TLS				TLS G				TLS	
7			DLS				DLS		DLS	I			DLS		
8	TWS			DLS			T	H	I	N		DLS			TWS
9			DLS		F	L	DLS O	E	DLS	E			DLS		
10		TLS				TLS				TLS				TLS	
11					DWS						DWS				
12	DLS			DWS				DLS				DWS			DLS
13			DWS				DLS		DLS				DWS		
14		DWS				TLS				TLS				DWS	
15	TWS			DLS				TWS				DLS			TWS

DIAGRAM 4-10

Using only the letters of each rack, find the highest-scoring play that also covers the given bonus square, either horizontally or vertically. Can you beat our total of 167 points?

EXPERT SCORE: **155** GOOD SCORE: **140** AVERAGE SCORE: **120**

1. A4: DLMNORT
2. A8: DFIOORU
3. K5: ABGGNOR
4. H1: ADLMPRU
5. C3: AALNORT

One Bonus Square

DIAGRAM 4-1

1. DOGNAP 11G 25
2. PEACHY J2 30
3. LUXURY 6C 36
4. HOTROD C9 28
5. TANDEM H10 27

TOTAL: 146 POINTS

DIAGRAM 4-2

1. PAWN 6L 41
2. BELONGS K5 40
3. FLECK J6 39
4. HOLY 9J 37
5. FORBIDAL L1 36

TOTAL: 193 POINTS

DIAGRAM 4-3

1. FARTHER G13 or C13 34
2. EMOTE H11 41
3. ORBITED 11E 40
4. HOTEL J10 37
5. IMBIBED L2 28

TOTAL: 180 POINTS

DIAGRAM 4-4

1. METHOD A1 36
2. CANARY B1 38
3. INERTIA 5E 38
4. SHAVEN 9F 41
5. CRITIC C2 26

TOTAL: 179 POINTS

DIAGRAM 4-5

1. HEAVED J2 47
2. REDEEM 6A 29
3. OUTATE H1 30
4. REPEAT 4D 29
5. ODDLY 4K 30

TOTAL: 165 POINTS

DIAGRAM 4-6

1. HUNGRY H10 47
2. FOUGHT H1 47
3. VALID J2 28
4. MONITOR E5 36
5. PHLEGM F6 24

TOTAL: 182 POINTS

DIAGRAM 4-7

1. TOPAZ L4 32
2. COTTON K5 28
3. FUGUE 12H 26
4. TRAUMA 7E 24
5. CONTEND 11E 40

TOTAL: 150 POINTS

DIAGRAM 4-8

1. WHIMSICAL K4 38
2. UTOPIA J5 25
3. ADROIT L1 33
4. WEIGHT 12C 26
5. PSYCHED J8 30

TOTAL: 152 POINTS

DIAGRAM 4-9

1. GRATIFY 1H 45
2. MALADY J2 50
3. ABET H1 36
4. FRYPAN J6 49
5. COUNTRY 5E 48

TOTAL: 228 POINTS

DIAGRAM 4-10

1. DORMANT A1 39
2. FORDO 8A 38
3. BONG K5 36
4. RADIUM H1 27
5. ATONAL 3C 27

TOTAL: 167 POINTS

CHAPTER 5

Bonus Squares, Two at a Time

Your goal for the following ten diagrams is the same as in the previous chapter, except that you are offered a choice of two bonus squares and asked to find the highest scoring play that covers either one. There are more choices and more chances to be creative!

A	B	C	D	E	F	G	H	I	J	K	L	M	N	O	
TWS			DLS				TWS				DLS			TWS	1
	DWS				TLS				TLS				DWS		2
		DWS				DLS		DLS				DWS			3
DLS			DWS				DLS R1	E1	Q10	U1	DWS I1	R1	E1	DLS D2	4
				DWS					A1	DWS					5
	TLS				TLS				TLS N1				TLS		6
		DLS				DLS		DLS	A1			DLS			7
TWS			DLS			R1	U1	N1	T1		DLS			TWS	8
		DLS				DLS		DLS				DLS			9
	TLS				TLS				TLS				TLS		10
				DWS						DWS					11
DLS			DWS				DLS				DWS			DLS	12
		DWS				DLS		DLS				DWS			13
	DWS				TLS				TLS				DWS		14
TWS			DLS				TWS				DLS			TWS	15

DIAGRAM 5-1

Find the highest-scoring play for each rack on the given position that crosses either bonus square suggested, either horizontally or vertically. Can you beat our total of 161 points?

EXPERT SCORE: **149** GOOD SCORE: **136** AVERAGE SCORE: **115**

1. O1, O8: AIMNOUY
2. N2, H1: DNORRSY
3. F6, M3: BBCEIOW
4. M3, K5: EELPRSV
5. O1, I3: EILLOPW

	A	B	C	D	E	F	G	H	I	J	K	L	M	N	O
1	TWS			DLS	S (1)			TWS				DLS			TWS
2		DWS			P (3)	TLS				TLS				DWS	
3			DWS		A (1)		DLS		DLS				DWS		
4	DLS			DWS	R (1)			DLS				DWS			DLS
5					DWS S (1)						DWS				
6		TLS			I (1)	TLS				TLS				TLS	
7			DLS		T (1)		DLS		DLS				DLS		
8	TWS			DLS W (4)	Y (4)	N (1)	D (2)	S (1)				DLS			TWS
9	A (1)	J (8)	DLS E (1)	E (1)			DLS		DLS				DLS		
10		TLS				TLS				TLS				TLS	
11					DWS						DWS				
12	DLS			DWS				DLS				DWS			DLS
13			DWS				DLS		DLS				DWS		
14		DWS				TLS				TLS				DWS	
15	TWS			DLS				TWS				DLS			TWS

DIAGRAM 5-2

Find the highest-scoring play for each rack on the given position that crosses either bonus square suggested, either horizontally or vertically. Can you beat our total of 220 points?

EXPERT SCORE: **208** GOOD SCORE: **190** AVERAGE SCORE: **150**

1. A1, A8: ADHIILO
2. F10, C3: BEHLMOR
3. B2, H1: HIMNRTY
4. F10, B14: FLORTUY
5. A8, H1: CEIMTUY

A	B	C	D	E	F	G	H	I	J	K	L	M	N	O	
TWS			DLS				TWS G_2				DLS			TWS	1
	DWS				TLS		R_1		TLS				DWS		2
		DWS				DLS	A_1	DLS				DWS			3
DLS			DWS				DLS B_3	I_1			DWS			DLS	4
				DWS				L_1		DWS					5
	TLS				TLS			L_1	TLS				TLS		6
		DLS				DLS		DLS U_1				DLS			7
TWS			DLS			H_4	E_1	M_3			DLS			TWS	8
		DLS				DLS		DLS I_1				DLS			9
	TLS				TLS			N_1	TLS				TLS		10
				DWS				E_1		DWS					11
DLS			DWS				DLS				DWS			DLS	12
		DWS				DLS		DLS				DWS			13
	DWS				TLS				TLS				DWS		14
TWS			DLS				TWS				DLS			TWS	15

DIAGRAM 5-3

Find the highest-scoring play for each rack on the given position that crosses either bonus square suggested, either horizontally or vertically. Can you beat our total of 163 points?

EXPERT SCORE: 150 GOOD SCORE: 140 AVERAGE SCORE: 115

1. F6, J6: ACFIIOT
2. H15, G3: BENNORU
3. G3, F10: AFMORTU
4. E11, H15: ABDHINP
5. G7, F6: ALNSTUU

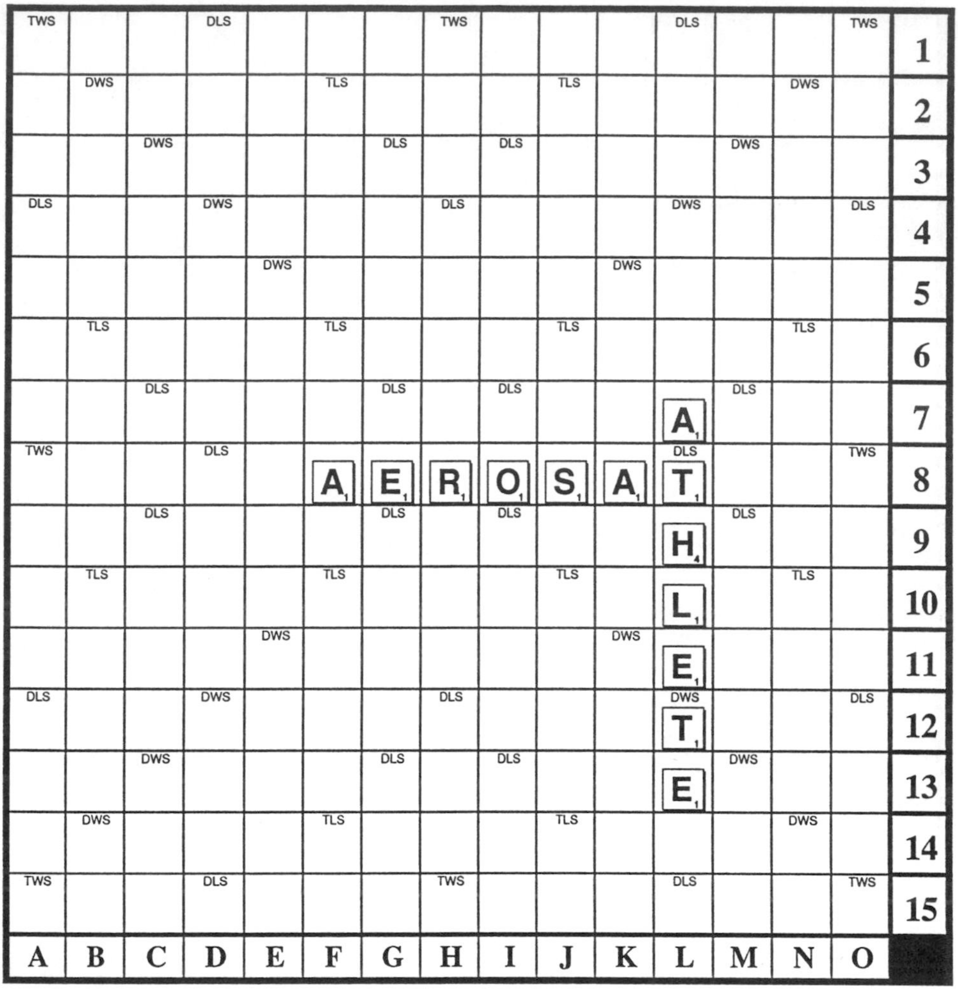

A	B	C	D	E	F	G	H	I	J	K	L	M	N	O	
TWS			DLS				TWS				DLS			TWS	1
	DWS				TLS				TLS				DWS		2
		DWS				DLS		DLS				DWS			3
DLS			DWS				DLS				DWS			DLS	4
				DWS						DWS					5
	TLS				TLS				TLS				TLS		6
		DLS				DLS		DLS			A_1	DLS			7
TWS			DLS		A_1	E_1	R_1	O_1	S_1	A_1	DLS T_1			TWS	8
		DLS				DLS		DLS			H_4	DLS			9
	TLS				TLS				TLS		L_1		TLS		10
				DWS						DWS	E_1				11
DLS			DWS				DLS				DWS T_1			DLS	12
		DWS				DLS		DLS			E_1	DWS			13
	DWS				TLS				TLS				DWS		14
TWS			DLS				TWS				DLS			TWS	15

DIAGRAM 5-4

Find the highest-scoring play for each rack on the given position that crosses either bonus square suggested, either horizontally or vertically. Can you beat our total of 163 points?

EXPERT SCORE: **150** GOOD SCORE: **135** AVERAGE SCORE: **110**

1. M3, M13: ABCILMR
2. G7, M13: ABEOPTT
3. M13, M7: AACMNOR
4. G9, J6: CEGMOPT
5. I9, M7: AFIOPSY

A	B	C	D	E	F	G	H	I	J	K	L	M	N	O	
TWS			DLS				TWS				DLS			TWS	1
	DWS				TLS				TLS				DWS		2
		DWS				DLS		DLS				DWS			3
DLS			DWS				DLS				DWS			DLS	4
				DWS						DWS					5
	TLS				TLS				TLS T				TLS		6
		DLS			R	DLS I	P	DLS	O			DLS			7
TWS			DLS				I	O	N	I	DLS C			TWS	8
		DLS				DLS		DLS	E		O	DLS			9
	TLS				TLS				TLS		M		TLS		10
				DWS						DWS	E				11
DLS			DWS				DLS				DWS T			DLS	12
		DWS				DLS		DLS				DWS			13
	DWS				TLS				TLS				DWS		14
TWS			DLS				TWS				DLS			TWS	15

DIAGRAM 5-5

Find the highest-scoring play for each rack on the given position that crosses either bonus square suggested, either horizontally or vertically. Can you beat our total of 182 points?

EXPERT SCORE: 170 **GOOD SCORE: 160** **AVERAGE SCORE: 135**

1. F10, K5: ADGIKNO
2. K11, A8: CEIINTV
3. K11, A8: BEFGIRU
4. M13, J10: ADOPRWY
5. I9, K11: ADFLMRT

A	B	C	D	E	F	G	H	I	J	K	L	M	N	O	
TWS			DLS				TWS				DLS			TWS	1
	DWS				TLS				TLS				DWS		2
		DWS				DLS		DLS				DWS			3
DLS			DWS				DLS M3		O1	I1	DWS D2	I1	A1	DLS	4
				DWS		Q10	U1	I1	P3	DWS S1					5
	TLS				TLS		D2		TLS				TLS		6
		DLS				DLS	D2	DLS				DLS			7
TWS			DLS Z10	L1	O1	T1	Y4				DLS			TWS	8
		DLS				DLS		DLS				DLS			9
	TLS				TLS				TLS				TLS		10
				DWS						DWS					11
DLS			DWS				DLS				DWS			DLS	12
		DWS				DLS		DLS				DWS			13
	DWS				TLS				TLS				DWS		14
TWS			DLS				TWS				DLS			TWS	15

DIAGRAM 5-6

Find the highest-scoring play for each rack on the given position that crosses either bonus square suggested, either horizontally or vertically. Can you beat our total of 178 points?

EXPERT SCORE: 165 GOOD SCORE: 155 AVERAGE SCORE: 130

1. E5, D4: AEEILRY
2. N2, M3: CEGLNTY
3. E11, M3: AEGLPRY
4. F10, M3: BDHLPUU
5. D12, E5: ACDIINN

	A	B	C	D	E	F	G	H	I	J	K	L	M	N	O
1	TWS			DLS				TWS				DLS			TWS
2		DWS				TLS				TLS				DWS	
3			DWS				DLS	Q_{10}	DLS				DWS		
4	DLS			DWS				DLS I_{1}				DWS			DLS
5					DWS			N_{1}			DWS				
6		TLS				TLS		T_{1}		TLS				TLS	
7			DLS		M_{3}	E_{1}	DLS N_{1}	A_{1}	DLS G_{2}	E_{1}			DLS		
8	TWS			DLS C_{3}	O_{1}	L_{1}	O_{1}	R_{1}				DLS			TWS
9			DLS	O_{1}			DLS		DLS				DLS		
10		TLS		P_{3}		TLS				TLS				TLS	
11				R_{1}	DWS						DWS				
12	DLS			DWS A_{1}				DLS				DWS			DLS
13			DWS	H_{4}			DLS		DLS				DWS		
14		DWS				TLS				TLS				DWS	
15	TWS			DLS				TWS				DLS			TWS

DIAGRAM 5-7

Find the highest-scoring play for each rack on the given position that crosses either bonus square suggested, either horizontally or vertically. Can you beat our total of 208 points?

EXPERT SCORE: 185 **GOOD SCORE: 170** **AVERAGE SCORE: 140**

1. O8, J6: BLMOOTY
2. C9, K5: ACGMOSS
3. C13, J6: AEEFORW
4. C9, O8: AFLMOOR
5. E11, E5: AADELPU

A	B	C	D	E	F	G	H	I	J	K	L	M	N	O	
TWS			DLS				TWS				DLS			TWS	1
	DWS				TLS				TLS				DWS		2
		DWS				DLS		DLS				DWS			3
DLS			DWS				DLS				DWS			DLS	4
				DWS					W	DWS					5
	TLS				TLS		Q		TLS A				TLS		6
		DLS				DLS	A	DLS	L			DLS			7
TWS			DLS			R	I	N	K		DLS			TWS	8
		DLS				DLS	D	DLS O	I	T		DLS			9
	TLS				TLS				TLS N	A			TLS		10
				DWS					G	DWS O					11
DLS			DWS				DLS				DWS			DLS	12
		DWS				DLS		DLS				DWS			13
	DWS				TLS				TLS				DWS		14
TWS			DLS				TWS				DLS			TWS	15

DIAGRAM 5-8

Find the highest-scoring play for each rack on the given position that crosses either bonus square suggested, either horizontally or vertically. Can you beat our total of 135 points?

EXPERT SCORE: **125** GOOD SCORE: **115** AVERAGE SCORE: **90**

1. F6, L12: ABBILRT
2. K5, L12: AABEIMR
3. L12, F6: ADEERTU
4. I3, L12: ABCEOTU
5. N6, L12: AEILTUY

A	B	C	D	E	F	G	H	I	J	K	L	M	N	O	
TWS			DLS				TWS				DLS			TWS	1
	DWS				TLS				TLS				DWS		2
		DWS				DLS		DLS O (1)				DWS			3
DLS			DWS				DLS	L (1)			DWS			DLS	4
				DWS				E (1)		DWS					5
	TLS				TLS			O (1)	TLS W (4)				TLS		6
		DLS				DLS		DLS	H (4)			DLS			7
TWS			DLS				P (3)	R (1)	I (1)	N (1)	DLS T (1)			TWS	8
		DLS				DLS		DLS	T (1)	O (1)	O (1)	DLS			9
	TLS				TLS				TLS				TLS		10
				DWS						DWS					11
DLS			DWS				DLS				DWS			DLS	12
		DWS				DLS		DLS				DWS			13
	DWS				TLS				TLS				DWS		14
TWS			DLS				TWS				DLS			TWS	15

DIAGRAM 5-9

Find the highest-scoring play for each rack on the given position that crosses either bonus square suggested, either horizontally or vertically. Can you beat our total of 194 points?

EXPERT SCORE: 182 **GOOD SCORE: 170** **AVERAGE SCORE: 140**

1. J10, H4: BIMOPST
2. H4, J10: EGNORRY
3. K5, H1: EHIKSTU
4. H4, J10: AFHIINS
5. E5, H1: LMRTUUV

A	B	C	D	E	F	G	H	I	J	K	L	M	N	O	
TWS			DLS				TWS				DLS			TWS	1
	DWS				TLS				TLS				DWS		2
		DWS				DLS		DLS				DWS			3
DLS			DWS				DLS				DWS			DLS	4
				DWS						DWS					5
	TLS				TLS				TLS			D_2	TLS		6
		DLS				DLS		DLS				DLS O_1			7
TWS			DLS				E_1	M_3	B_3	L_1	DLS E_1	M_3		TWS	8
		DLS				DLS		DLS				DLS E_1			9
	TLS				TLS				TLS			S_1	TLS		10
				DWS						DWS		T_1			11
DLS			DWS				DLS				DWS	I_1		DLS	12
		DWS				DLS		DLS				DWS C_3			13
	DWS				TLS				TLS				DWS		14
TWS			DLS				TWS				DLS			TWS	15

DIAGRAM 5-10

Find the highest-scoring play for each rack on the given position that crosses either bonus square suggested, either horizontally or vertically. Can you beat our total of 144 points?

EXPERT SCORE: **132** GOOD SCORE: **120** AVERAGE SCORE: **90**

1. K5, N6: AENOOPW
2. I9, L4: ACDHOTU
3. J6, K11: BINNRUW
4. L12, N6: ADILNOU
5. I7, J10: AAGHLOP

ANSWERS TO CHAPTER 5

Two Bonus Squares

Diagram 5-1

1. DYNAMO O4 36
2. ORNERY N1 34
3. COBWEB F3 or F6 30
4. RELAPSE 5G 34
5. PILLOW 3D 27

TOTAL: 161 POINTS

Diagram 5-2

1. DAHLIA A4 36
2. HOMBRE 10A 45
3. NYMPH 2B 46
4. JOYFUL B9 42
5. MYSTIC 1C 51

TOTAL: 220 POINTS

Diagram 5-3

1. COATI F6 24
2. UNBORN H10 37
3. FOURTH G3 31
4. PINHEAD 11E 52
5. SULTAN F5 19

TOTAL: 163 POINTS

Diagram 5-4

1. CLIMB M3 35
2. TEAPOT 7D 26
3. MANOR M9 40
4. COEMPTS J2 25
5. SOAPY M3 37

TOTAL: 163 POINTS

Diagram 5-5

1. KINGDOM 10F 39
2. INVITE 8A 32
3. FIGURE K7 39
4. PARODY M9 45
5. FEDORA 9I 27

TOTAL: 182 POINTS

Diagram 5-6

1. REEQUIPS 5D 38
2. LEGACY N1 40
3. GALLERY E5 44
4. BUILDUP M2 26
5. ZINNIA D8 30

TOTAL: 178 POINTS

Diagram 5-7

1. TOMBOY 8J 50
2. COSMOS 9C 44
3. WHEREOF 13C 42
4. MOOLA C9 45
5. ALAMODE E4 27

TOTAL: 208 POINTS

Diagram 5-8

1. RABBIT F6 or BARB L10 25
2. AMEBA K3 34
3. ADEQUATE 6E 22
4. BEAU I3 26
5. EQUALITY 6G 28

TOTAL: 135 POINTS

Diagram 5-9

1. STOMP 10J 36
2. ORNERY H1 46
3. HEINOUS K5 51
4. FINISH 10F 41
5. VULTURE 5C 20

TOTAL: 194 POINTS

Diagram 5-10

1. WEAPON N2 33
2. CATHODE L2 32
3. UNWIND 6H 18
4. DENIAL L7 27
5. ALPHA 7F 34

TOTAL: 144 POINTS

CHAPTER 6

Bonus Squares, Choice of Five

In a real game you won't necessarily know which bonus squares to use first, but with the practice you're getting solving these puzzles, you'll have trained yourself to look carefully at each one. In this chapter you have a choice of the same five bonus squares for all five racks. Try to find the highest-scoring play that crosses one of these bonus squares either horizontally or vertically.

TWS			DLS				TWS				DLS			TWS	1
	DWS				TLS				TLS				DWS		2
		DWS				DLS		DLS				DWS			3
DLS			DWS				DLS				DWS			DLS	4
				DWS						DWS					5
	TLS				TLS				TLS				TLS		6
		DLS	M			DLS	B (3)	DLS E (1)	T (1)			DLS			7
TWS F (4)	E (1)	T (1)	DLS A (1)	L (1)		P (3)	A (1)	L (1)			DLS			TWS	8
		DLS	G (2)	A (1)	M (3)	DLS E (1)		DLS				DLS			9
	TLS		A (1)		TLS				TLS				TLS		10
			Z (10)	DWS						DWS					11
DLS			DWS I (1)				DLS				DWS			DLS	12
		DWS	N (1)			DLS		DLS				DWS			13
	DWS		E (1)		TLS				TLS				DWS		14
TWS H (4)	I (1)	T (1)	DLS S (1)				TWS				DLS			TWS	15
A	B	C	D	E	F	G	H	I	J	K	L	M	N	O	

DIAGRAM 6-1

Bonus Squares: J6, F10, E11, C13, B14

Find the highest-scoring play that crosses one of these bonus squares either horizontally or vertically. Can you beat our total of 180 points?

EXPERT SCORE: **165** GOOD SCORE: **152** AVERAGE SCORE: **130**

1. ABEIMOU
2. AEEGRUV
3. BCHIMUY
4. CEIINPV
5. ADILORW

TWS			DLS				TWS				DLS			TWS	1
	DWS				TLS				TLS	R			DWS		2
		DWS				DLS		DLS		E		DWS			3
DLS			DWS				DLS			L	DWS			DLS	4
				DWS						DWS E					5
	TLS				TLS				TLS	A			TLS		6
		DLS				DLS		DLS		S		DLS			7
TWS A	O	R	DLS T	A			O	P	T	E	DLS D			TWS	8
		DLS		G	L	DLS A	D	DLS E				DLS			9
	TLS				TLS				TLS				TLS		10
				DWS						DWS					11
DLS			DWS				DLS				DWS			DLS	12
		DWS				DLS		DLS				DWS			13
	DWS				TLS				TLS				DWS		14
TWS			DLS				TWS				DLS			TWS	15
A	B	C	D	E	F	G	H	I	J	K	L	M	N	O	

DIAGRAM 6-2

Bonus Squares: E5, J2, J6, F10, C7

Find the highest-scoring play that crosses one of these bonus squares either horizontally or vertically. Can you beat our total of 196 points?

EXPERT SCORE: **180** GOOD SCORE: **170** AVERAGE SCORE: **140**

1. DEEGLNU
2. AEGHNOT
3. CEFNOOT
4. EKLMPRU
5. AADFGIL

TWS			DLS				TWS				DLS			TWS	1
	DWS				TLS				TLS				DWS		2
		DWS				DLS		DLS				DWS			3
DLS			DWS				DLS W4				DWS			DLS	4
				DWS			R1			DWS					5
	TLS				TLS		E1		TLS				TLS		6
		DLS				DLS	C3	DLS				DLS			7
TWS			DLS				K5	A1			DLS			TWS	8
		DLS				DLS		DLS Z10	O1	N1	A1	DLS R1	Y4		9
	TLS				TLS			O1	TLS				TLS		10
				DWS				N1		DWS					11
DLS			DWS				DLS	S1	U1	N1	DWS G2			DLS	12
		DWS				DLS		DLS				DWS			13
	DWS				TLS				TLS				DWS		14
TWS			DLS				TWS				DLS			TWS	15
A	B	C	D	E	F	G	H	I	J	K	L	M	N	O	

DIAGRAM 6-3

Bonus Squares: E5, K5, L8, J10, K11

Find the highest-scoring play that crosses one of these bonus squares either horizontally or vertically. Can you beat our total of 203 points?

EXPERT SCORE: **185** GOOD SCORE: **170** AVERAGE SCORE: **140**

1. ABCLORU
2. CEMNRTU
3. AEGILVY
4. AGHMNPT
5. AADIMNO

A	B	C	D	E	F	G	H	I	J	K	L	M	N	O	
TWS			DLS				TWS				DLS			TWS	1
	DWS				TLS				TLS				DWS		2
		DWS				DLS		DLS				DWS			3
DLS			DWS				DLS				DWS			DLS	4
				DWS						DWS					5
	TLS				TLS				TLS				TLS		6
		DLS				DLS		DLS				DLS			7
TWS			DLS			G	L	I	M	M	DLS E	R		TWS	8
		DLS		F	L	DLS O	A	DLS T				DLS			9
	TLS				TLS		B		TLS				TLS		10
				DWS			R			DWS					11
DLS			DWS				DLS A				DWS			DLS	12
		DWS				DLS	D	DLS				DWS			13
	DWS				TLS		O	R	TLS B	I	T	I	DWS N	G	14
TWS			DLS				TWS R				DLS			TWS	15

DIAGRAM 6-4

Bonus Squares: A8, O8, D12, K11, O15

Find the highest-scoring play that crosses one of these bonus squares either horizontally or vertically. Can you beat our total of 231 points?

EXPERT SCORE: **215** GOOD SCORE: **190** AVERAGE SCORE: **150**

1. AIKPRTU
2. ACDEGMO
3. EEIIPTZ
4. BEGILOU
5. DEEILPU

	A	B	C	D	E	F	G	H	I	J	K	L	M	N	O
1	TWS			DLS				TWS				DLS			TWS
2		DWS				TLS				TLS				DWS	
3			DWS	M$_3$			DLS		DLS				DWS		
4	DLS			DWS A$_1$				DLS				DWS			DLS
5				I$_1$	DWS						DWS				
6		TLS		L$_1$		TLS				TLS				TLS	
7			DLS	E$_1$			DLS		DLS				DLS		
8	TWS			DLS D$_2$	R$_1$	I$_1$	P$_3$	T$_1$				DLS			TWS
9			DLS				DLS	E$_1$	DLS				DLS		
10		TLS				TLS		N$_1$		TLS				TLS	
11					DWS			D$_2$			DWS				
12	DLS			DWS		C$_3$	O$_1$	DLS E$_1$	M$_3$	P$_3$	T$_1$	DWS S$_1$			DLS
13			DWS				DLS	R$_1$	DLS				DWS		
14		DWS				TLS		E$_1$		TLS				DWS	
15	TWS			DLS				TWS D$_2$				DLS			TWS

DIAGRAM 6-5

Bonus Squares: C3, E5, K11, B14, J14

Find the highest-scoring play that crosses one of these bonus squares either horizontally or vertically. Can you beat our total of 170 points?

EXPERT SCORE: **160** GOOD SCORE: **150** AVERAGE SCORE: **120**

1. CGORSST
2. AEHLRTV
3. ABEGIRY
4. CHLMNOO
5. AAEFLNO

TWS			DLS				TWS				DLS			TWS	1
	DWS				TLS				TLS				DWS		2
		DWS				DLS		DLS				DWS			3
DLS			DWS				DLS				DWS			DLS	4
				DWS						DWS					5
	TLS				TLS				TLS				TLS		6
		DLS				DLS		DLS				DLS			7
TWS			DLS				A1	R1	I1	A1	DLS			TWS	8
		DLS				DLS		DLS U1				DLS			9
	TLS				TLS			N1	TLS				TLS		10
				DWS				L1		DWS					11
DLS			DWS S1	E1	E1	T1	DLS H4	E1			DWS			DLS	12
		DWS				DLS	I1	DLS T1				DWS			13
	DWS				TLS		D2		TLS				DWS		14
TWS			DLS				TWS E1				DLS			TWS	15
A	B	C	D	E	F	G	H	I	J	K	L	M	N	O	

DIAGRAM 6-6

Bonus Squares: K11, F10, E11, G13, F14

Find the highest-scoring play that crosses one of these bonus squares either horizontally or vertically. Can you beat our total of 215 points?

EXPERT SCORE: **200** GOOD SCORE: **190** AVERAGE SCORE: **160**

1. CEFORUV
2. AEFHLNS
3. ABCEILZ
4. CDIMNOU
5. DLOOPRY

A	B	C	D	E	F	G	H	I	J	K	L	M	N	O	
TWS			DLS				TWS				DLS			TWS	1
	DWS				TLS				TLS				DWS		2
		DWS				DLS		DLS	E$_1$			DWS			3
DLS			DWS				DLS		L$_1$		DWS			DLS	4
				DWS					E$_1$	DWS					5
	TLS				TLS				TLS V$_4$				TLS		6
		DLS				DLS		DLS	A$_1$			DLS			7
TWS			DLS		B$_3$	E$_1$	A$_1$	U$_1$	T$_1$		DLS			TWS	8
		DLS				DLS		DLS	E$_1$			DLS			9
	TLS				TLS				TLS				TLS		10
				DWS						DWS					11
DLS			DWS				DLS				DWS			DLS	12
		DWS				DLS		DLS				DWS			13
	DWS				TLS				TLS				DWS		14
TWS			DLS				TWS				DLS			TWS	15

DIAGRAM 6-7

Bonus Squares: H4, K5, I7, J10, K11

Find the highest-scoring play that crosses one of these bonus squares either horizontally or vertically. Can you beat our total of 190 points?

EXPERT SCORE: **170** GOOD SCORE: **155** AVERAGE SCORE: **130**

1. CDELNUW
2. AADKMMS
3. HIMNRSY
4. BEHIIRS
5. AAIMRRV

A	B	C	D	E	F	G	H	I	J	K	L	M	N	O	
TWS			DLS				TWS				DLS			TWS	1
	DWS				TLS				TLS				DWS		2
		DWS				DLS		DLS				DWS			3
DLS			DWS				DLS				DWS T_{1}			DLS	4
				DWS						DWS	E_{1}				5
	TLS				TLS				TLS		L_{1}		TLS		6
		DLS				DLS		DLS			E_{1}	DLS			7
TWS			DLS				R_{1}	A_{1}	D_{2}	I_{1}	DLS X_{8}			TWS	8
		DLS F_{4}	L_{1}	E_{1}	E_{1}	DLS C_{3}	E_{1}	DLS D_{2}				DLS			9
	TLS				TLS				TLS				TLS		10
				DWS						DWS					11
DLS			DWS				DLS				DWS			DLS	12
		DWS				DLS		DLS				DWS			13
	DWS				TLS				TLS				DWS		14
TWS			DLS				TWS				DLS			TWS	15

DIAGRAM 6-8

Bonus Squares: I7, A8, K5, F10, E11

Find the highest-scoring play that crosses one of these bonus squares either horizontally or vertically. Can you beat our total of 258 points?

EXPERT SCORE: **238** GOOD SCORE: **220** AVERAGE SCORE: **160**

1. ACDFILP
2. ABCEMRY
3. ACKNOPY
4. AHIORTW
5. EIIMNNT

A	B	C	D	E	F	G	H	I	J	K	L	M	N	O	
TWS			DLS				TWS				DLS			TWS	1
	DWS				TLS				TLS				DWS		2
		DWS				DLS		DLS				DWS			3
DLS			DWS				DLS				DWS			DLS	4
				DWS						DWS					5
	TLS				TLS				TLS P_3	L_1	U_1	M_3	TLS		6
		DLS				DLS	I_1	DLS D_2	I_1	O_1	T_1	DLS			7
TWS			DLS G_2	I_1	A_1	N_1	T_1			G_2	DLS A_1	V_4	E_1	TWS L_1	8
		DLS				DLS		DLS				DLS			9
	TLS				TLS				TLS				TLS		10
				DWS						DWS					11
DLS			DWS				DLS				DWS			DLS	12
		DWS				DLS		DLS				DWS			13
	DWS				TLS				TLS				DWS		14
TWS			DLS				TWS				DLS			TWS	15

DIAGRAM 6-9

Bonus Squares: K5, N6, M13, E5, F6

Find the highest-scoring play that crosses one of these bonus squares either horizontally or vertically. Can you beat our total of 182 points?

EXPERT SCORE: 163 **GOOD SCORE: 150** **AVERAGE SCORE: 120**

1. CIILNOU
2. AINPSUU
3. AAEINSU
4. ENNOSUV
5. BEEILMV

	A	B	C	D	E	F	G	H	I	J	K	L	M	N	O
1	TWS			DLS				TWS				DLS			TWS
2		DWS				TLS				TLS				DWS	
3			DWS				DLS		DLS				DWS		
4	DLS			DWS				DLS				DWS			DLS
5					DWS						DWS				
6		TLS				TLS				TLS				TLS	
7			DLS				DLS		DLS				DLS		
8	TWS			DLS B	R	O	T	H	E	R		DLS			TWS
9			DLS		E		DLS		DLS	A			DLS		
10		TLS			E	TLS				TLS Z				TLS	
11					DWS D					O	DWS				
12	DLS			DWS	Y			DLS C	A	R	A	DWS V	A	N	DLS S
13			DWS				DLS		DLS				DWS		
14		DWS				TLS				TLS				DWS	
15	TWS			DLS				TWS				DLS			TWS

DIAGRAM 6-10

Bonus Squares: I7, D12, F10, O8, H15

Find the highest-scoring play that crosses one of these bonus squares either horizontally or vertically. Can you beat our total of 209 points?

EXPERT SCORE: 188 GOOD SCORE: 170 AVERAGE SCORE: 130

1. ABEGLMP
2. ABELNOO
3. AADELRU
4. DHILOOS
5. DHIORTU

Five Bonus Squares

Diagram 6-1

1. ZOMBIE 11D 38
2. AVERAGE 10D 32
3. BUNCHY 13B 40
4. PIECE 14B 32
5. WIZARD 11B 38

TOTAL: 180 POINTS

Diagram 6-2

1. ENGAGED E5 40
2. THRONG 2I 36
3. OCTAGON E5 40
4. PERK J3 44
5. AFRAID 2I 36

TOTAL: 196 POINTS

Diagram 6-3

1. BOAR 8L 41
2. CURRENT 5E 36
3. VOYAGE 10H 41
4. PHANTOM J4 39
5. MADONNA 11E 46

TOTAL: 203 POINTS

Diagram 6-4

1. KAPUT D8 41
2. COMRADE 11E 48
3. ITEMIZE K5 72
4. GLOBE 8A 38
5. PUERILE 11E 36

TOTAL: 235 POINTS

Diagram 6-5

1. ESCORTS 14H 30
2. LATHER C2 40
3. IMAGERY 3C 36
4. MONOCLE 14B 34
5. LEAF or LOAF E2 30

TOTAL: 170 POINTS

Diagram 6-6

1. CLOVER 11H 33
2. FLASHED 14B 44
3. BLITZ G9 51
4. NOMADIC K5 48
5. DROOPY 11A 39

TOTAL: 215 POINTS

Diagram 6-7

1. CLUED 10F 34
2. MADAMES 5E 48
3. HYMNS K7 46
4. HUBRIS I7 34
5. ARRIVAL 4D 28

TOTAL: 190 POINTS

Diagram 6-8

1. FACILE 7G 35
2. CREAMY 8A 59
3. PANICKY K5 84
4. WRAITH 10A 44
5. EMINENT E5 36

TOTAL: 258 POINTS

Diagram 6-9

1. VIOLIN M8 20
2. SUNUP N2 43
3. ANALOGUES K3 40
4. VENISON E5 40
5. BELIEVE N2 39

TOTAL: 182 POINTS

Diagram 6-10

1. GLEAM 7E 40
2. BABOON D8 39
3. ORDEAL F8 28
4. BROTHERHOODS 8D 66
5. ORCHID H10 36

TOTAL: 209 POINTS

CHAPTER 7

The J, Q, X, and Z

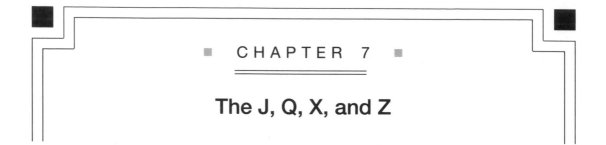

Whenever you draw one of these four tiles—the J, Q, X or Z—you have an opportunity to score really well. Here's a chance to get practice with these tiles. Each of the following 50 racks has one of these tiles. Find the highest-scoring play that uses the J, Q, X, or Z on your rack.

A	B	C	D	E	F	G	H	I	J	K	L	M	N	O	
TWS			DLS				TWS				DLS			TWS	1
	DWS				TLS				TLS				DWS		2
		DWS				DLS		DLS				DWS			3
DLS			DWS				DLS				DWS			DLS	4
				DWS						DWS					5
	TLS				TLS				TLS				TLS		6
		DLS				DLS		DLS				DLS			7
TWS			DLS I	L	I	A	C				DLS			TWS	8
		DLS				DLS	H	DLS				DLS			9
	TLS				TLS B	L	O	O	TLS M				TLS		10
				DWS			R		O	DWS D	D	L	Y		11
DLS			DWS				DLS T				DWS			DLS	12
		DWS				DLS	L	DLS				DWS			13
	DWS				TLS		E		TLS				DWS		14
TWS			DLS				TWS D				DLS			TWS	15

DIAGRAM 7-1

Using the above position, find the highest-scoring play that uses the J, Q, X, or Z on your rack. Can you beat our total of 268 points?

EXPERT SCORE: 250 **GOOD SCORE: 225** **AVERAGE SCORE: 165**

1. ABLOQRU
2. GJOORSU
3. AEGLNOX
4. AAADEIZ
5. CEHJKOR

TWS			DLS				TWS				DLS			TWS	1
	DWS				TLS				TLS				DWS		2
		DWS		O_1		DLS		DLS				DWS			3
DLS			DWS	R_1			DLS				DWS			DLS	4
				DWS A_1						DWS					5
	TLS			C_3	TLS				TLS				TLS		6
		DLS		L_1		DLS		DLS				DLS			7
TWS			DLS H_4	E_1	R_1	E_1	O_1	F_4		B_3	DLS O_1	A_1	T_1	TWS S_1	8
		DLS				DLS M_3	E_1	DLS A_1	N_1	I_1	N_1	DLS G_2			9
	TLS				TLS				TLS	N_1	E_1	O_1	TLS N_1		10
				DWS						DWS					11
DLS			DWS				DLS				DWS			DLS	12
		DWS				DLS		DLS				DWS			13
	DWS				TLS				TLS				DWS		14
TWS			DLS				TWS				DLS			TWS	15
A	B	C	D	E	F	G	H	I	J	K	L	M	N	O	

DIAGRAM 7-2

Using the above position, find the highest-scoring play that uses the J, Q, X, or Z on your rack. Can you beat our total of 232 points?

EXPERT SCORE: **218** GOOD SCORE: **200** AVERAGE SCORE: **160**

1. DHJOSTU
2. ANOQRUY
3. DEILMOX
4. EEFILOZ
5. EEHIPTX

TWS			DLS				TWS				DLS			TWS	1
	DWS				TLS				TLS				DWS		2
		DWS		K$_5$		DLS		DLS				DWS			3
DLS			DWS	O$_1$			DLS				DWS			DLS	4
				DWS T$_1$						DWS					5
	TLS			O$_1$	TLS P$_3$				TLS				TLS		6
		DLS			O$_1$	DLS		DLS				DLS			7
TWS			DLS H$_4$	Y$_4$	P$_3$	E$_1$	R$_1$				DLS			TWS	8
		DLS			U$_1$	DLS		DLS				DLS			9
	TLS				TLS L$_1$				TLS				TLS		10
				DWS	A$_1$					DWS					11
DLS			DWS	T$_1$	R$_1$	O$_1$	DLS W$_4$	S$_1$	E$_1$	R$_1$	DWS S$_1$			DLS	12
		DWS				DLS		DLS				DWS			13
	DWS				TLS				TLS				DWS		14
TWS			DLS				TWS				DLS			TWS	15
A	B	C	D	E	F	G	H	I	J	K	L	M	N	O	

DIAGRAM 7-3

Using the above position, find the highest-scoring play that uses the J, Q, X, or Z on your rack. Can you beat our total of 245 points?

EXPERT SCORE: 230 GOOD SCORE: 205 AVERAGE SCORE: 160

1. ADEIOQU
2. BEEGJMU
3. ABEHITZ
4. ABILMRX
5. ABENOUX

A	B	C	D	E	F	G	H	I	J	K	L	M	N	O	
TWS			DLS				TWS				DLS			TWS	1
	DWS				TLS				TLS	I_1			DWS		2
		DWS				DLS		DLS		V_4		DWS			3
DLS			DWS				DLS			O_1	DWS			DLS	4
				DWS						DWS R_1					5
	TLS				TLS				TLS B_3	Y_4			TLS		6
		DLS				DLS		DLS	L_1			DLS			7
TWS			DLS H_4	I_1	P_3	L_1	I_1	K_5	E_1		DLS			TWS	8
		DLS				DLS		DLS	A_1			DLS			9
	TLS				TLS				TLS T_1	O_1			TLS		10
				DWS					E_1	DWS M_3					11
DLS			DWS				DLS		R_1	E_1	DWS			DLS	12
		DWS				DLS		DLS		N_1		DWS			13
	DWS				TLS				TLS				DWS		14
TWS			DLS				TWS				DLS			TWS	15

DIAGRAM 7-4

Using the above position, find the highest-scoring play that uses the J, Q, X, or Z on your rack. Can you beat our total of 233 points?

EXPERT SCORE: **215** GOOD SCORE: **190** AVERAGE SCORE: **150**

1. ADEGINX
2. AILNOUZ
3. DEIMOQU
4. EJNOPRU
5. EILNPTZ

DIAGRAM 7-5

Using the above position, find the highest-scoring play that uses the J, Q, X, or Z on your rack. Can you beat our total of 283 points?

EXPERT SCORE: **265** GOOD SCORE: **240** AVERAGE SCORE: **190**

1. ABEJNRY
2. ACIOQTU
3. IMORTUZ
4. ADFHORX
5. DEGHISZ

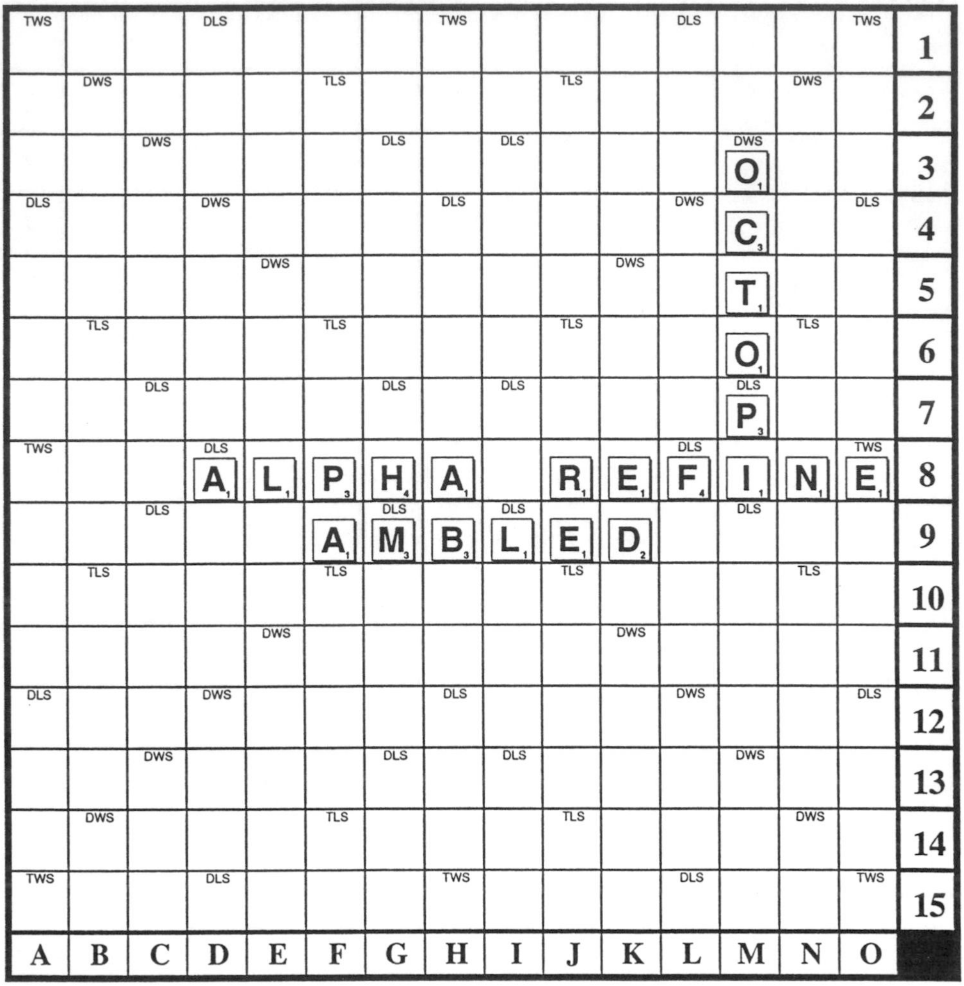

DIAGRAM 7-6

Using the above position, find the highest-scoring play that uses the J, Q, X, or Z on your rack. Can you beat our total of 219 points?

EXPERT SCORE: **195** GOOD SCORE: **175** AVERAGE SCORE: **130**

1. AEHJNOY
2. HIIRSTZ
3. ELMNOQU
4. ILOOSUX
5. ACLOTUZ

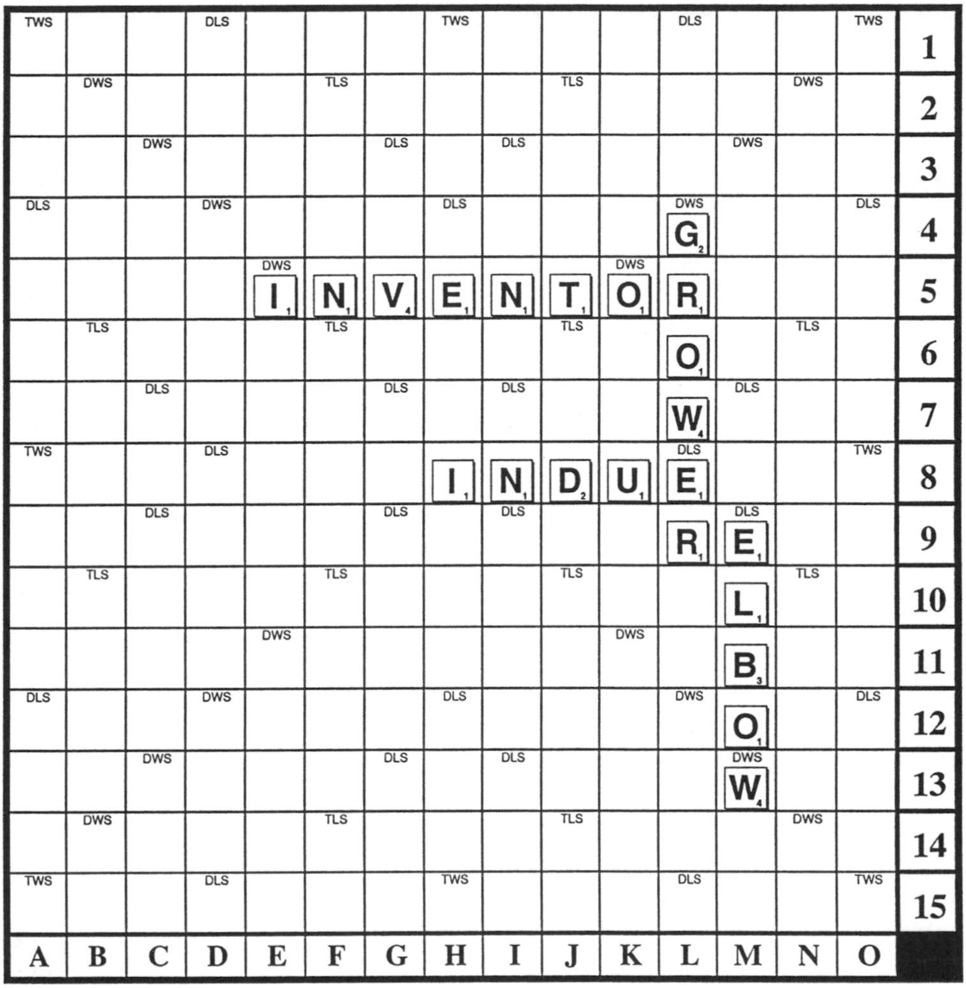

A	B	C	D	E	F	G	H	I	J	K	L	M	N	O	
TWS			DLS				TWS				DLS			TWS	1
	DWS				TLS				TLS				DWS		2
		DWS				DLS		DLS				DWS			3
DLS			DWS				DLS				DWS G_2			DLS	4
				DWS I_1	N_1	V_4	E_1	N_1	T_1	DWS O_1	R_1				5
	TLS				TLS				TLS		O_1		TLS		6
		DLS				DLS		DLS			W_4	DLS			7
TWS			DLS				I_1	N_1	D_2	U_1	DLS E_1			TWS	8
		DLS				DLS		DLS			R_1	DLS E_1			9
	TLS				TLS				TLS			L_1	TLS		10
				DWS						DWS		B_3			11
DLS			DWS				DLS				DWS	O_1		DLS	12
		DWS				DLS		DLS				DWS W_4			13
	DWS				TLS				TLS				DWS		14
TWS			DLS				TWS				DLS			TWS	15
A	B	C	D	E	F	G	H	I	J	K	L	M	N	O	

DIAGRAM 7-7

Using the above position, find the highest-scoring play that uses the J, Q, X, or Z on your rack. Can you beat our total of 300 points?

EXPERT SCORE: 270   GOOD SCORE: 220   AVERAGE SCORE: 180

1. ACILMRZ
2. AEOPQTU
3. AAEEJNR
4. AFILNPX
5. DELOPRZ

A	B	C	D	E	F	G	H	I	J	K	L	M	N	O	
TWS			DLS				TWS O				DLS			TWS	1
	DWS				TLS		R		TLS				DWS		2
		DWS				DLS	A	DLS M				DWS			3
DLS			DWS				DLS D	O			DWS			DLS	4
				DWS				V		DWS					5
	TLS				TLS W			E	TLS				TLS		6
		DLS			R	DLS		DLS R				DLS			7
TWS			DLS F	L	I	C	K	S			DLS			TWS	8
		DLS			N	DLS O		DLS				DLS			9
	TLS			A	TLS G	O			TLS				TLS		10
				DWS G		E				DWS					11
DLS			DWS	L		E	DLS L				DWS			DLS	12
		DWS		O		DLS	O	DLS				DWS			13
	DWS			W	TLS		A		TLS				DWS		14
TWS			DLS				TWS N				DLS			TWS	15

DIAGRAM 7-8

Using the above position, find the highest-scoring play that uses the J, Q, X, or Z on your rack. Can you beat our total of 246 points?

EXPERT SCORE: **230** GOOD SCORE: **210** AVERAGE SCORE: **160**

1. ELNORSZ
2. ADEGIJR
3. AFILQRU
4. EILNTXY
5. ADMNRRZ

A	B	C	D	E	F	G	H	I	J	K	L	M	N	O	
TWS			DLS				TWS				DLS			TWS	1
	DWS				TLS				TLS				DWS		2
		DWS				DLS		DLS				DWS			3
DLS			DWS				DLS				DWS			DLS	4
				DWS						DWS					5
	TLS				TLS		A_1		TLS				TLS		6
		DLS				DLS	U_1	DLS				DLS			7
TWS			DLS				D_2				DLS			TWS	8
		DLS				DLS	I_1	DLS				DLS			9
	TLS				TLS A_1	M_3	O_1	U_1	TLS N_1	T_1			TLS		10
			W_4	DWS I_1	N_1	E_1		T_1	O_1	DWS O_1	T_1	H_4			11
DLS			DWS				DLS				DWS			DLS	12
		DWS				DLS		DLS				DWS			13
	DWS				TLS				TLS				DWS		14
TWS			DLS				TWS				DLS			TWS	15

DIAGRAM 7-9

Using the above position, find the highest-scoring play that uses the J, Q, X, or Z on your rack. Can you beat our total of 194 points?

EXPERT SCORE: 182 **GOOD SCORE:** 170 **AVERAGE SCORE:** 135

1. ELNSTYZ
2. DEIJOPS
3. FIMNQST
4. AEGLNRX
5. BIJMPTU

	A	B	C	D	E	F	G	H	I	J	K	L	M	N	O
1	TWS			DLS				TWS				DLS			TWS
2		DWS				TLS T				TLS				DWS	
3			DWS			E	DLS		DLS				DWS		
4	DLS			DWS		E		DLS				DWS			DLS
5					DWS	N					DWS				
6		TLS			B	TLS Y				TLS				TLS	
7			DLS		O		DLS		DLS				DLS		
8	TWS			DLS W	R	I	S	T				DLS F			TWS
9			DLS		R		DLS	A	DLS B	L	E	R	DLS		
10		TLS			O	TLS				TLS		E		TLS	
11					DWS W						DWS	I			
12	DLS			DWS				DLS				DWS G			DLS
13			DWS				DLS		DLS			H	DWS		
14		DWS				TLS				TLS		T		DWS	
15	TWS			DLS				TWS				DLS			TWS

DIAGRAM 7-10

Using the above position, find the highest-scoring play that uses the J, Q, X, or Z on your rack. Can you beat our total of 229 points?

EXPERT SCORE: 215 GOOD SCORE: 190 AVERAGE SCORE: 150

1. CIJNOTU
2. CEFMORZ
3. AEMOQTU
4. ADEEIRX
5. AACLPRZ

The J, Q, X, and Z

Diagram 7-1

1. BAROQUE 14B 76
2. JOYOUS N9 36
3. OXYGEN N9 66
4. AZALEA M8 50
5. JOCKEY N6 40

TOTAL: 268 POINTS

Diagram 7-2

1. JUST 10F 41
2. QUARRY 4A 56
3. MIXED 11G 44
4. FRIEZE 4D 56
5. EXPECT 6A 35

TOTAL: 232 POINTS

Diagram 7-3

1. QUAKED 3B 44
2. JUMBO 4A 48
3. WHIZ H12 57
4. BORAX 4D 44
5. BEAUX 9C 52

TOTAL: 245 POINTS

Diagram 7-4

1. INDEX L8 57
2. UNZIP F4 36
3. PIQUED F8 38
4. JUNIPER E5 64
5. PRETZEL 12I 38

TOTAL: 233 POINTS

Diagram 7-5

1. JAPERY 8J 54
2. AQUATIC E5 72
3. PUTZ 8L 45
4. FAX M7 46
5. MIDSIZED H8 66

TOTAL: 283 POINTS

Diagram 7-6

1. ENJOY 10B 41
2. ZITIS 10B 43
3. OPAQUE F7 37
4. NOXIOUS N8 60
5. TOPAZ F6 38

TOTAL: 219 POINTS

Diagram 7-7

1. MAIZE H1 78
2. QUOTA 4A 50
3. AJAR L11 49
4. FLAXEN H1 72
5. ZEROED H1 51

TOTAL: 300 POINTS

Diagram 7-8

1. OZONES 13H 50
2. JADE G3 49
3. QUAIL 12A 48
4. ANXIETY 14H 66
5. ADZ 14H 33

TOTAL: 246 POINTS

Diagram 7-9

1. ZESTY L8 63
2. JOSHED M8 36
3. SQUINT 7F 26
4. RELAX G3 40
5. JUMP I4 29

TOTAL: 194 POINTS

Diagram 7-10

1. JOUNCE 4A 46
2. FEZ F10 41
3. QUALM J6 42
4. EXITED 14I 60
5. PLAZA D2 40

TOTAL: 229 POINTS

CHAPTER 8

The Highest-Scoring Play, No Hints

For the next 50 racks here's a chance to put together all that you've learned so far and see how well you're able to read the board.

A	B	C	D	E	F	G	H	I	J	K	L	M	N	O	
TWS			DLS				TWS				DLS			TWS	1
	DWS				TLS B_3				TLS C_3				DWS		2
		DWS			E_1	DLS		DLS	R_1			DWS			3
DLS			DWS		L_1		DLS		O_1		DWS			DLS	4
				DWS	L_1				W_4	DWS					5
	TLS				TLS H_4				TLS N_1				TLS		6
		DLS			O_1	DLS		DLS	I_1			DLS			7
TWS			DLS M_3	A_1	P_3	L_1	E_1		N_1		DLS			TWS	8
		DLS				DLS	F_4	DLS I_1	G_2	H_4	T_1	DLS			9
	TLS				TLS				TLS				TLS		10
				DWS						DWS					11
DLS			DWS				DLS				DWS			DLS	12
		DWS				DLS		DLS				DWS			13
	DWS				TLS				TLS				DWS		14
TWS			DLS				TWS				DLS			TWS	15

DIAGRAM 8-1

Find the highest-scoring play on the given diagram using each rack once. Can you beat our total of 164 points?

EXPERT SCORE: **155** GOOD SCORE: **145** AVERAGE SCORE: **120**

1. EEGKORW
2. DOOPRUW
3. ABMNSSU
4. BILPRVY
5. AGIOOPR

A	B	C	D	E	F	G	H	I	J	K	L	M	N	O	
TWS			DLS				TWS				DLS			TWS	1
	DWS				TLS				TLS				DWS		2
		DWS				DLS		DLS				DWS			3
DLS			DWS				DLS				DWS			DLS	4
				DWS						DWS					5
	TLS				TLS				TLS				TLS		6
		DLS				DLS L	A	DLS B	O	R		DLS			7
TWS			DLS V	A	N	I	T	Y			DLS			TWS	8
		DLS	I			DLS		DLS				DLS			9
	TLS		R		TLS				TLS				TLS		10
			I	DWS						DWS					11
DLS			DWS L				DLS W				DWS			DLS	12
		DWS M	E	D	I	DLS C	A	DLS L				DWS			13
	DWS				TLS		R		TLS				DWS		14
TWS			DLS				TWS K				DLS			TWS	15

DIAGRAM 8-2

Find the highest-scoring play on the given diagram using each rack once. Can you beat our total of 222 points?

EXPERT SCORE: 210 GOOD SCORE: 185 AVERAGE SCORE: 145

1. EHIIRSU
2. BDEEFLM
3. ACEFGRS
4. AADEGLV
5. ACEEGMO

	A	B	C	D	E	F	G	H	I	J	K	L	M	N	O
1	TWS			DLS				TWS				DLS			TWS
2		DWS				TLS				TLS				DWS	
3			DWS				DLS		DLS				DWS		
4	DLS			DWS				DLS				DWS			DLS
5					O	V	E	R	C	A	S	T			
6		TLS				O				TLS				TLS	E
7			DLS			C	DLS	T	R	U	M	P	E	T	S
8	TWS			DLS		A	H	O	Y			DLS			T
9			DLS			L	DLS	M	A	J	O	R	DLS		R
10		TLS				TLS				TLS				TLS	A
11					DWS						DWS				Y
12	DLS			DWS				DLS				DWS			DLS
13			DWS				DLS		DLS				DWS		
14		DWS				TLS				TLS				DWS	
15	TWS			DLS				TWS				DLS			TWS

DIAGRAM 8-3

Find the highest-scoring play on the given diagram using each rack once. Can you beat our total of 170 points?

EXPERT SCORE: **160** GOOD SCORE: **145** AVERAGE SCORE: **120**

1. EGGLNOU
2. ADEEIOP
3. DLOOTUW
4. ABIOPRU
5. EIIORRS

	A	B	C	D	E	F	G	H	I	J	K	L	M	N	O
1	TWS			DLS				TWS				DLS			TWS
2		DWS				TLS				TLS				DWS	
3			DWS				DLS		DLS				DWS		
4	DLS			DWS				DLS				DWS			DLS
5					DWS A_1						DWS				
6		TLS			U_1	TLS				TLS				TLS	
7			DLS		R_1		DLS	O_1	DLS D_2	I_1	O_1	U_1	DLS S_1		
8	TWS			DLS F_4	U_1	L_1	L_1	Y_4				DLS H_4	O_1	L_1	TWS Y_4
9			DLS	E_1	M_3		DLS		DLS				DLS		
10		TLS		W_4		TLS				TLS				TLS	
11				E_1	DWS						DWS				
12	DLS			DWS R_1				DLS				DWS			DLS
13			DWS				DLS		DLS				DWS		
14		DWS				TLS				TLS				DWS	
15	TWS			DLS				TWS				DLS			TWS

DIAGRAM 8-4

Find the highest-scoring play on the given diagram using each rack once. Can you beat our total of 253 points?

EXPERT SCORE: 225 **GOOD SCORE: 195** **AVERAGE SCORE: 150**

1. AHMNOOP
2. EEGNORZ
3. EGHIMUW
4. AFGMORY
5. BEGHLSU

TWS			DLS				TWS				DLS			TWS	1
	DWS				TLS				TLS				DWS		2
		DWS				DLS		DLS				DWS			3
DLS			DWS				DLS				DWS			DLS	4
				DWS						DWS					5
	TLS				TLS				TLS				TLS		6
		DLS				DLS		DLS				DLS			7
TWS			DLS S	A	T	I	R	E	S		DLS			TWS	8
		DLS				DLS		DLS				DLS			9
	TLS				TLS				TLS				TLS		10
				DWS						DWS					11
DLS			DWS				DLS				DWS			DLS	12
		DWS				DLS		DLS				DWS			13
	DWS				TLS				TLS				DWS		14
TWS			DLS				TWS				DLS			TWS	15
A	B	C	D	E	F	G	H	I	J	K	L	M	N	O	

DIAGRAM 8-5

Find the highest-scoring play on the given diagram using each rack once. Can you beat our total of 172 points?

EXPERT SCORE: 160 GOOD SCORE: 150 AVERAGE SCORE: 120

1. AADILNW
2. BCEIOTU
3. DIORSVW
4. FGLNRTU
5. CEILOTX

TWS			DLS				TWS				DLS			TWS	1
	DWS				TLS	R_1			TLS				DWS		2
		DWS				DLS E_1		DLS				DWS			3
DLS			DWS			A_1	DLS				DWS			DLS	4
				DWS		C_3				DWS					5
	TLS				TLS	T_1			TLS				TLS		6
		DLS				DLS I_1		DLS K_5				DLS			7
TWS			DLS D_2	R_1	I_1	V_4	E_1	N_1			DLS			TWS	8
		DLS				DLS E_1		DLS E_1				DLS			9
	TLS				TLS		A_1	W_4	TLS				TLS		10
				DWS			M_3			DWS					11
DLS			DWS				DLS A_1				DWS			DLS	12
		DWS				DLS	Z_{10}	DLS				DWS			13
	DWS				TLS		E_1		TLS				DWS		14
TWS			DLS				TWS D_2				DLS			TWS	15
A	B	C	D	E	F	G	H	I	J	K	L	M	N	O	

DIAGRAM 8-6

Find the highest-scoring play on the given diagram using each rack once. Can you beat our total of 207 points?

EXPERT SCORE: 185 GOOD SCORE: 170 AVERAGE SCORE: 140

1. AEHILRV
2. ADINTUY
3. BILORTU
4. CDEGNTY
5. ABCGORT

TWS			DLS				TWS				DLS			TWS	1
	DWS				TLS				TLS				DWS		2
		DWS				DLS		DLS				DWS			3
DLS			DWS				DLS				DWS			DLS	4
				DWS						DWS					5
	TLS				TLS			M	TLS				TLS		6
		DLS				DLS E	P	DLS A	U	L	E	DLS T			7
TWS			DLS			T	E	X	T		DLS F	O	U	TWS R	8
		DLS				DLS		DLS I				DLS			9
	TLS				TLS			M	TLS				TLS		10
				DWS				A		DWS					11
DLS			DWS				DLS	L			DWS			DLS	12
		DWS				DLS		DLS				DWS			13
	DWS				TLS				TLS				DWS		14
TWS			DLS				TWS				DLS			TWS	15
A	B	C	D	E	F	G	H	I	J	K	L	M	N	O	

DIAGRAM 8-7

Find the highest-scoring play on the given diagram using each rack once. Can you beat our total of 182 points?

EXPERT SCORE: **165** GOOD SCORE: **150** AVERAGE SCORE: **130**

1. BDEEOPV
2. DFORPUV
3. ACFILLO
4. ABEPRST
5. BLLOPUW

A	B	C	D	E	F	G	H	I	J	K	L	M	N	O	
TWS			DLS				TWS				DLS			TWS	1
	DWS				TLS				TLS				DWS		2
		DWS				DLS		DLS				DWS			3
DLS			DWS				DLS				DWS			DLS	4
				DWS						DWS					5
	TLS				TLS				TLS G2				TLS		6
		DLS				DLS		DLS	O1			DLS			7
TWS			DLS			Z10	E1	A1	L1		DLS			TWS	8
		DLS				DLS O1		DLS	E1			DLS			9
	TLS				TLS	E1			TLS M3	A1			TLS		10
				DWS		A1				DWS P3					11
DLS			DWS			E1	DLS L1			A1	DWS			DLS	12
		DWS				DLS	O1	DLS		R1		DWS			13
	DWS				TLS		W4		TLS	T1			DWS		14
TWS			DLS				TWS N1				DLS			TWS	15

DIAGRAM 8-8

Find the highest-scoring play on the given diagram using each rack once. Can you beat our total of 215 points?

EXPERT SCORE: **195** GOOD SCORE: **175** AVERAGE SCORE: **150**

1. AEGLTWY
2. ACGNOUW
3. AFGMOST
4. CFMPRTU
5. AILOSUY

	A	B	C	D	E	F	G	H	I	J	K	L	M	N	O
1	TWS			DLS				TWS				DLS			TWS
2		DWS				TLS				TLS				DWS	
3			DWS				DLS	T	DLS				DWS		
4	DLS			DWS				DLS R				DWS			DLS
5		P	O	L	DWS K	A		I			DWS				
6		TLS				TLS M	O	P		TLS				TLS	
7			DLS				DLS	O	DLS				DLS		
8	TWS			DLS				D				DLS			TWS
9			DLS				DLS	S	DLS W	E	R	V	DLS E	D	
10		TLS				TLS				TLS		A		TLS	
11					DWS						DWS M	U			
12	DLS			DWS				DLS			E	DWS L			DLS
13			DWS				DLS		DLS		A	T	DWS		
14		DWS				TLS				TLS	T			DWS	
15	TWS			DLS				TWS				DLS			TWS

DIAGRAM 8-9

Find the highest-scoring play on the given diagram using each rack once. Can you beat our total of 186 points?

EXPERT SCORE: **170** GOOD SCORE: **150** AVERAGE SCORE: **120**

1. EFILOTT
2. CDEEFLN
3. EELNRVW
4. ABIITUY
5. ACHOTVY

A	B	C	D	E	F	G	H	I	J	K	L	M	N	O	
TWS			DLS				TWS				DLS			TWS	1
	DWS				TLS				TLS				DWS		2
		DWS				DLS		DLS				DWS			3
DLS			DWS				DLS				DWS			DLS	4
			T	DWS						DWS					5
	TLS		E		TLS	P	I	N	TLS A	T	A		TLS		6
		DLS	N			DLS O		DLS				DLS			7
TWS			DLS F	R	O	N	T				DLS			TWS	8
		DLS	O			DLS Y		DLS				DLS			9
	TLS		L		TLS				TLS				TLS		10
			D	DWS						DWS					11
DLS			DWS S				DLS				DWS			DLS	12
		DWS				DLS		DLS				DWS			13
	DWS				TLS				TLS				DWS		14
TWS			DLS				TWS				DLS			TWS	15

DIAGRAM 8-10

Find the highest-scoring play on the given diagram using each rack once. Can you beat our total of 250 points?

EXPERT SCORE: 231 GOOD SCORE: 206 AVERAGE SCORE: 181

1. AEGIOSV
2. BDGIILN
3. BEJLNSS
4. AEIMNRS
5. ACHLOSV

ANSWERS TO CHAPTER 8

The Highest-Scoring Play, No Hints

DIAGRAM 8-1

1. LEGWORK 4F 34
2. WOOD K4 36
3. NUMBS 9B 35
4. PRIVY 3I 32
5. GOOP I4 27

TOTAL: 164 POINTS

DIAGRAM 8-2

1. HURRIES K5 40
2. EMBED 8K 41
3. CARAFES E5 59
4. RAVAGED 14H 42
5. CAMEO 6H 40

TOTAL: 222 POINTS

DIAGRAM 8-3

1. LOUNGE N10 27
2. PODIA N10 43
3. WOULD 4A 29
4. ABRUPT N2 42
5. SORER 10I 29

TOTAL: 170 POINTS

DIAGRAM 8-4

1. MANFULLY 8A 48
2. LOZENGE N8 74
3. WEIGH F2 44
4. FORAY C9 51
5. BUSHEL F3 36

TOTAL: 253 POINTS

DIAGRAM 8-5

1. LAW 7G 25
2. CUBIT 7C 24
3. DISAVOW E5 56
4. FRUGAL E4 20
5. EXOTIC 9H 47

TOTAL: 172 POINTS

DIAGRAM 8-6

1. ARCHIVE 5E 60
2. DAINTY J9 31
3. OUTDRIVEN 8A 39
4. DENY H1 49
5. ACROBAT 4G 28

TOTAL: 207 POINTS

DIAGRAM 8-7

1. BELOVED 12G 28
2. ROMP 6G 33
3. CALLIOPE H1 43
4. STAMPER 6F 46
5. BLOWUP 12H 32

TOTAL: 182 POINTS

DIAGRAM 8-8

1. GETAWAY I3 45
2. WAGON F10 38
3. ATOMS K4 35
4. CRAFT 11E 31
5. ZEALOUSLY 8G 66

TOTAL: 215 POINTS

DIAGRAM 8-9

1. FETTLE M8 34
2. FLEECED J6 36
3. TWELVE 3H 32
4. ABILITY D2 32
5. YACHT 15K 52

TOTAL: 186 POINTS

DIAGRAM 8-10

1. SEAFRONT 8A 33
2. BIDING 5H 35
3. JOBLESS F7 34
4. FRONTIERSMAN 8D 104
5. VOCALIST H1 44

TOTAL: 250 POINTS

PART TWO

Balancing Your Rack

"Rack balancing," or "balancing your rack," is making a play that keeps a good combination of the letters.

There are two ways to approach balancing your rack of letters. The first is to look for your high-scoring plays and decide upon which rack leave is best. The second is to decide which letters you want to keep and find a play that uses the remaining tiles.

The following chapters are devoted to practicing this second method. You are given a set of three, four, or five letters to play for the most possible points.

This second method for rack balancing is often useful when you need a bingo and also are short of time. It's a quick way to get a good play.

CHAPTER 9

Three-Tile Plays

Often the best strategy is to save your best tiles and "fish" away others in the hopes of drawing a bingo next time. This chapter and the following two are devoted to practicing playing off those three, four, or five unwanted tiles. We're not going to show you what those saved tiles are. You don't need to know them to solve the puzzles. Perhaps they are the ES, ERS, EST, ENR, ANT, AEST, EIRT, AENR, or even EIRT. Maybe they're one of a hundred other somewhat less potent combinations. Whatever they are, they're what you've decided to keep while trying to find the best way to use the others.

A	B	C	D	E	F	G	H	I	J	K	L	M	N	O	
TWS			DLS				TWS				DLS			TWS	1
	DWS				TLS				TLS				DWS		2
		DWS				DLS		DLS				DWS			3
DLS			DWS				DLS			M3	DWS			DLS	4
				DWS						DWS A1					5
	TLS				TLS				TLS	N1			TLS		6
		DLS				DLS		DLS		I1		DLS			7
TWS			DLS				P3	U1	N1	C3	DLS H4			TWS	8
		DLS	T1	O1	U1	DLS C3	A1	DLS N1			O1	DLS			9
	TLS				TLS				TLS		T1		TLS		10
				DWS						DWS	T1				11
DLS			DWS				DLS				DWS E1			DLS	12
		DWS				DLS		DLS			D2	DWS			13
	DWS				TLS				TLS				DWS		14
TWS			DLS				TWS				DLS			TWS	15

DIAGRAM 9-1

Find the highest-scoring play using ALL three given tiles. Can you beat our total of 93 points?

EXPERT SCORE: 85 GOOD SCORE: 80 AVERAGE SCORE: 68

1. AEP
2. IKT
3. AIO
4. KST
5. HNT

A	B	C	D	E	F	G	H	I	J	K	L	M	N	O	
TWS			DLS				TWS				DLS			TWS	1
	DWS				TLS				TLS				DWS		2
		DWS				DLS		DLS				DWS			3
DLS			DWS				DLS				DWS			DLS	4
				DWS						DWS					5
	TLS				TLS				TLS				TLS		6
		DLS				DLS		DLS W_4				DLS			7
TWS			DLS			B_3	O_1	I_1	L_1		DLS			TWS	8
		DLS				DLS		DLS L_1				DLS			9
	TLS				TLS		A_1	D_2	TLS				TLS		10
				DWS			M_3			DWS					11
DLS			DWS				DLS O_1				DWS			DLS	12
		DWS				DLS	U_1	DLS				DWS			13
	DWS				TLS		N_1		TLS				DWS		14
TWS			DLS				TWS T_1				DLS			TWS	15

DIAGRAM 9-2

Find the highest-scoring play using ALL three given tiles. Can you beat our total of 100 points?

EXPERT SCORE: 92 GOOD SCORE: 83 AVERAGE SCORE: 70

1. INO
2. ALM
3. AHO
4. BOO
5. BEY

TWS			DLS				TWS				DLS			TWS	1
	DWS				TLS				TLS				DWS		2
		DWS				DLS		DLS				DWS			3
DLS			DWS				DLS				DWS			DLS	4
				DWS						DWS					5
	TLS				TLS				TLS B3				TLS		6
		DLS		F4		DLS		DLS	L1			DLS			7
TWS			DLS	I1		H4	O1	L1	E1		DLS			TWS	8
		DLS	C3	L1	U1	DLS M3	P3	DLS	W4			DLS			9
	TLS			A1	TLS				TLS				TLS		10
				DWS M3						DWS					11
DLS			DWS	E1			DLS				DWS			DLS	12
		DWS		N1		DLS		DLS				DWS			13
	DWS			T1	TLS				TLS				DWS		14
TWS G2	O1	O1	DLS D2	S1			TWS				DLS			TWS	15
A	B	C	D	E	F	G	H	I	J	K	L	M	N	O	

DIAGRAM 9-3

Find the highest-scoring play using ALL three given tiles. Can you beat our total of 123 points?

EXPERT SCORE: 115 GOOD SCORE: 108 AVERAGE SCORE: 90

1. LOP
2. OOT
3. AIP
4. AOV
5. ASW

A	B	C	D	E	F	G	H	I	J	K	L	M	N	O	
TWS			DLS				TWS				DLS			TWS	1
	DWS				TLS				TLS				DWS		2
		DWS				DLS		DLS				DWS			3
DLS			DWS				DLS				DWS B_{3}			DLS	4
				DWS						DWS P_{3}	A_{1}				5
	TLS				TLS				TLS	I_{1}	T_{1}		TLS		6
		DLS				DLS		DLS		A_{1}	I_{1}	DLS			7
TWS			DLS				P_{3}	R_{1}	I_{1}	N_{1}	DLS K_{5}			TWS	8
		DLS F_{4}	R_{1}	E_{1}	E_{1}	DLS Z_{10}	E_{1}	DLS		O_{1}		DLS			9
	TLS				TLS				TLS				TLS		10
				DWS						DWS					11
DLS			DWS				DLS				DWS			DLS	12
		DWS				DLS		DLS				DWS			13
	DWS				TLS				TLS				DWS		14
TWS			DLS				TWS				DLS			TWS	15

DIAGRAM 9-4

Find the highest-scoring play using ALL three given tiles. Can you beat our total of 119 points?

EXPERT SCORE: **110** GOOD SCORE: **100** AVERAGE SCORE: **80**

1. ABS
2. EFL
3. BIJ
4. HRY
5. EOR

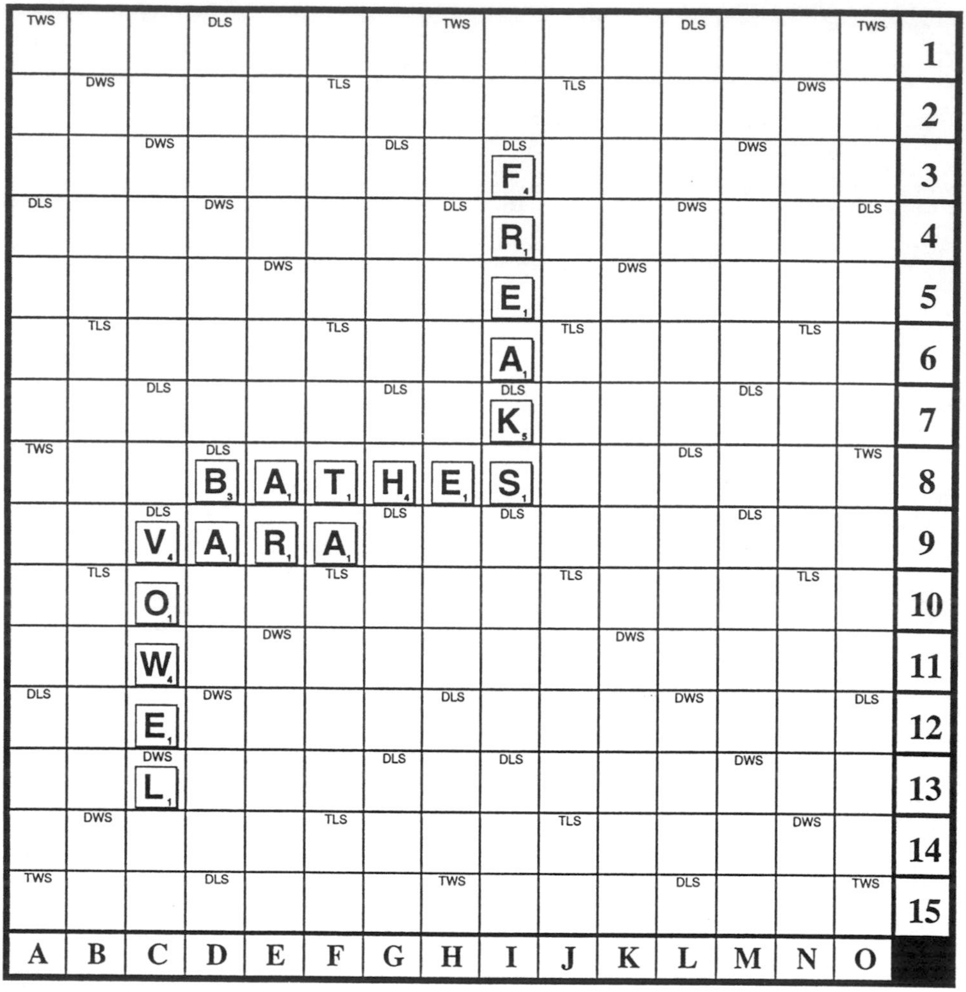

DIAGRAM 9-5

Find the highest-scoring play using ALL three given tiles. Can you beat our total of 130 points?

EXPERT SCORE: **117** GOOD SCORE: **108** AVERAGE SCORE: **92**

1. MRY
2. AMP
3. EHT
4. HOO
5. ILV

TWS			DLS				TWS				DLS			TWS	1
	DWS				TLS				TLS				DWS		2
		DWS				DLS		DLS				DWS			3
DLS			DWS		C$_{3}$		DLS				DWS			DLS	4
				DWS	O$_{1}$					DWS					5
	TLS				TLS Z$_{10}$				TLS				TLS		6
		DLS			I$_{1}$	DLS		DLS				DLS			7
TWS			DLS W$_{4}$	H$_{4}$	E$_{1}$	L$_{1}$	M$_{3}$				DLS			TWS	8
		DLS				DLS	E$_{1}$	DLS X$_{8}$	P$_{3}$	O$_{1}$	S$_{1}$	DLS E$_{1}$	D$_{2}$		9
	TLS				TLS				TLS				TLS		10
				DWS						DWS					11
DLS			DWS				DLS				DWS			DLS	12
		DWS				DLS		DLS				DWS			13
	DWS				TLS				TLS				DWS		14
TWS			DLS				TWS				DLS			TWS	15
A	B	C	D	E	F	G	H	I	J	K	L	M	N	O	

DIAGRAM 9-6

Find the highest-scoring play using ALL three given tiles. Can you beat our total of 123 points?

EXPERT SCORE: 115 GOOD SCORE: 105 AVERAGE SCORE: 85

1. AOR
2. EIT
3. IOR
4. DEH
5. CHI

TWS			DLS				TWS				DLS			TWS	1
	DWS				TLS				TLS			G_2	DWS		2
		DWS				DLS		DLS				DWS L_1			3
DLS			DWS				DLS				DWS	O_1		DLS	4
				DWS						DWS		B_3			5
	TLS				TLS				TLS		R_1	E_1	TLS X_8		6
		DLS				DLS	P_3	DLS A_1	R_1	T_1	Y_4	DLS			7
TWS			DLS			A_1	I_1	D_2			DLS A_1	M_3	E_1	TWS N_1	8
		DLS				DLS		DLS				DLS			9
	TLS				TLS				TLS				TLS		10
				DWS						DWS					11
DLS			DWS				DLS				DWS			DLS	12
		DWS				DLS		DLS				DWS			13
	DWS				TLS				TLS				DWS		14
TWS			DLS				TWS				DLS			TWS	15
A	B	C	D	E	F	G	H	I	J	K	L	M	N	O	

DIAGRAM 9-7

Find the highest-scoring play using ALL three given tiles. Can you beat our total of 144 points?

EXPERT SCORE: 132 GOOD SCORE: 120 AVERAGE SCORE: 105

1. AFO
2. DEW
3. QSU
4. APR
5. AEP

A	B	C	D	E	F	G	H	I	J	K	L	M	N	O	
TWS			DLS				TWS				DLS			TWS	1
	DWS				TLS				TLS B_3				DWS		2
		DWS				DLS		DLS	L_1			DWS			3
DLS			DWS		D_2	E_1	DLS F_4	L_1	E_1	C_3	DWS T_1			DLS	4
				DWS					N_1	DWS					5
	TLS				TLS				TLS D_2				TLS		6
		DLS				DLS		DLS	E_1			DLS			7
TWS			DLS P_3	E_1	N_1	C_3	I_1	L_1	S_1		DLS			TWS	8
		DLS	E_1			DLS		DLS				DLS			9
	TLS		N_1		TLS				TLS				TLS		10
			A_1	DWS						DWS					11
DLS			DWS L_1				DLS				DWS			DLS	12
		DWS	T_1			DLS		DLS				DWS			13
	DWS		Y_4		TLS				TLS				DWS		14
TWS			DLS				TWS				DLS			TWS	15

DIAGRAM 9-8

Find the highest-scoring play using ALL three given tiles. Can you beat our total of 111 points?

EXPERT SCORE: 100 GOOD SCORE: 90 AVERAGE SCORE: 70

1. AEL
2. DEO
3. EEM
4. ALN
5. ABY

	A	B	C	D	E	F	G	H	I	J	K	L	M	N	O
1	TWS			DLS				TWS				DLS			TWS
2		DWS				TLS				TLS				DWS	
3			DWS				DLS		DLS				DWS		
4	DLS			DWS M3				DLS				DWS			DLS
5				I1	DWS						DWS				
6		TLS		R1		TLS				TLS				TLS Q10	
7			DLS	T1			DLS		DLS				DLS	U1	
8	TWS			DLS H4	O1	R1	S1	Y4			A1	DLS V4	O1	I1	TWS D2
9			DLS				DLS O1	A1	DLS K5	E1	N1		DLS	T1	
10		TLS				TLS				TLS				TLS	
11					DWS						DWS				
12	DLS			DWS				DLS				DWS			DLS
13			DWS				DLS		DLS				DWS		
14		DWS				TLS				TLS				DWS	
15	TWS			DLS				TWS				DLS			TWS

DIAGRAM 9-9

Find the highest-scoring play using ALL three given tiles. Can you beat our total of 138 points?

EXPERT SCORE: 130 GOOD SCORE: 120 AVERAGE SCORE: 100

1. ACS
2. AHM
3. ERV
4. OXY
5. CHR

	A	B	C	D	E	F	G	H	I	J	K	L	M	N	O
1	TWS			DLS				TWS				DLS			TWS
2		DWS				TLS				TLS				DWS	
3			DWS				DLS		DLS				DWS		
4	DLS			DWS				DLS				DWS			DLS
5					DWS						DWS R_1				
6		TLS P_3	R_1	O_1	V_4	TLS E_1				TLS	A_1			TLS	
7			DLS			M_3	DLS A_1	N_1	DLS Y_4		N_1		DLS		
8	TWS			DLS			A_1	E_1	O_1	N_1	S_1	DLS			TWS
9			DLS				DLS		DLS		O_1		DLS		
10		TLS				TLS				TLS	M_3			TLS	
11					DWS						DWS S_1				
12	DLS			DWS				DLS				DWS			DLS
13			DWS				DLS		DLS				DWS		
14		DWS				TLS				TLS				DWS	
15	TWS			DLS				TWS				DLS			TWS

DIAGRAM 9-10

Find the highest-scoring play using ALL three given tiles. Can you beat our total of 123 points?

EXPERT SCORE: **115** GOOD SCORE: **105** AVERAGE SCORE: **85**

1. AEU
2. EHN
3. OTW
4. AGY
5. DOW

Three-Tile Plays

DIAGRAM 9-1

1. APE K11 21
2. KIT L3 24
3. IOTA 11J 8
4. TSK 10H 25
5. NTH J2 15

TOTAL: 93 POINTS

DIAGRAM 9-2

1. LION J8 14
2. BALM G8 19
3. HAO I13 23
4. BOLO J6 19
5. BEADY 10F 25

TOTAL: 100 POINTS

DIAGRAM 9-3

1. CLOP D9 30
2. FOOT 7E 22
3. PAID D12 26
4. OVA F5 19
5. SWAT 14B 26

TOTAL: 123 POINTS

DIAGRAM 9-4

1. BARS I6 28
2. ELF 10D 31
3. JIBE F6 29
4. HAIRY 7J 17
5. ORE 8A 14

TOTAL: 119 POINTS

DIAGRAM 9-5

1. MARRY E7 20
2. MAP B10 32
3. ETH J4 31
4. OHO D11 29
5. VITAL F6 18

TOTAL: 130 POINTS

DIAGRAM 9-6

1. OAR 9D 30
2. TIE 10H 25
3. ZORI 6F 13
4. EDH 10J 23
5. HIC 8M 32

TOTAL: 123 POINTS

DIAGRAM 9-7

1. OAF N2 25
2. WED 9G 34
3. SUQ F8 37
4. RAPT K4 25
5. APEX N3 23

TOTAL: 144 POINTS

DIAGRAM 9-8

1. LEAF H1 21
2. COED K4 24
3. EME 3F 23
4. ELAN E8 16
5. ABY C13 27

TOTAL: 111 POINTS

DIAGRAM 9-9

1. ACQUITS N4 20
2. HAM 10H 39
3. REV 10M 24
4. OXY 10E 35
5. RANCH K7 20

TOTAL: 138 POINTS

DIAGRAM 9-10

1. EAU J10 13
2. HEN 9G 31
3. TOW or TWO 4K 22
4. GAY J4 30
5. WOOD 9I 27

TOTAL: 123 POINTS

CHAPTER 10

Four-Tile Plays

It's not often that a veteran player will call a four-tile play a "fishing" play. However, that's essentially what many of them are when the other three tiles are extremely "bingo-prone." Here are 50 racks that will give you a chance to extend your skills even more.

A	B	C	D	E	F	G	H	I	J	K	L	M	N	O	
TWS			DLS				TWS				DLS			TWS	1
	DWS				TLS	M_3			TLS				DWS		2
		DWS				DLS O_1		DLS				DWS			3
DLS			DWS			R_1	DLS				DWS			DLS	4
				DWS		T_1				DWS					5
	TLS				TLS	U_1			TLS				TLS		6
		DLS				DLS A_1		DLS				DLS			7
TWS			DLS			R_1	I_1	P_3	O_1	F_4	DLS F_4			TWS	8
		DLS			A_1	DLS Y_4		DLS			I_1	DLS			9
	TLS				TLS X_8				TLS		E_1		TLS		10
				DWS	I_1					DWS	L_1				11
DLS			DWS		A_1		DLS				DWS D_2			DLS	12
		DWS			L_1	DLS		DLS				DWS			13
	DWS				TLS				TLS				DWS		14
TWS			DLS				TWS				DLS			TWS	15

DIAGRAM 10-1

Find your highest-scoring play using all four given tiles. Can you beat our total of 195 points?

EXPERT SCORE: 180 GOOD SCORE: 170 AVERAGE SCORE: 150

1. AEHT
2. AGMY
3. EPTY
4. CSTY
5. ACKU

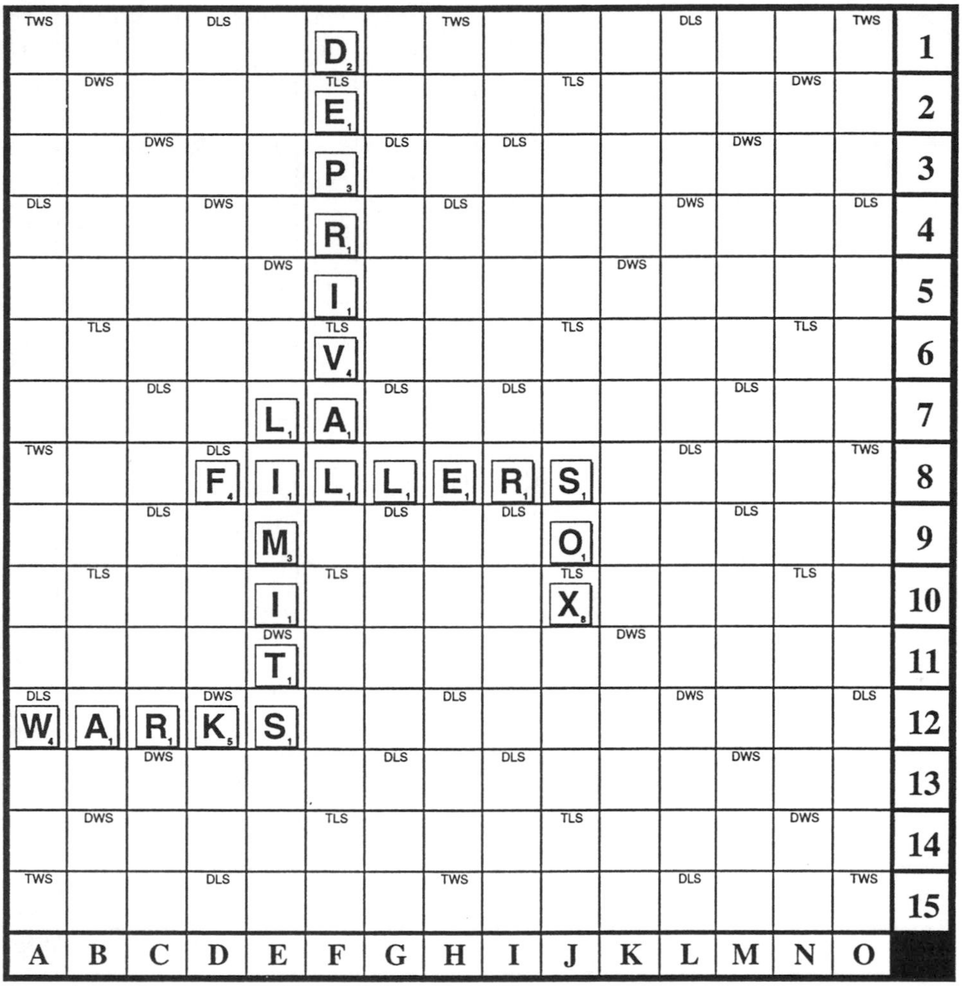

DIAGRAM 10-2

Find your highest-scoring play using all four given tiles. Can you beat our total of 154 points?

EXPERT SCORE: 147 GOOD SCORE: 140 AVERAGE SCORE: 110

1. AGNT
2. IPSW
3. HLMY
4. ELTW
5. AEWY

A	B	C	D	E	F	G	H	I	J	K	L	M	N	O	
TWS			DLS				TWS G	A	L	A	DLS			TWS	1
	DWS				TLS				TLS	L			DWS		2
		DWS				DLS		DLS		T		DWS			3
DLS			DWS				DLS			I	DWS			DLS	4
				DWS						DWS T					5
	TLS				TLS				TLS	U			TLS		6
		DLS				DLS		DLS		D		DLS			7
TWS			DLS				O	B	O	E	DLS			TWS	8
		DLS		L	O	DLS O	N	DLS Y				DLS			9
	TLS				TLS			E	TLS P	I	C	S	TLS		10
				DWS						DWS		O			11
DLS			DWS				DLS				DWS	F		DLS	12
		DWS				DLS		DLS				DWS A			13
	DWS				TLS				TLS				DWS		14
TWS			DLS				TWS				DLS			TWS	15

DIAGRAM 10-3

Find your highest-scoring play using all four given tiles. Can you beat our total of 172 points?

EXPERT SCORE: **160** GOOD SCORE: **140** AVERAGE SCORE: **110**

1. EISX
2. EFLT
3. AORY
4. ANPT
5. ANNO

A	B	C	D	E	F	G	H	I	J	K	L	M	N	O	
TWS			DLS				TWS				DLS			TWS	1
	DWS				TLS				TLS				DWS		2
		DWS				DLS		DLS		B (3)		DWS			3
DLS			DWS				DLS J (8)	E (1)	L (1)	L (1)	DWS Y (4)			DLS	4
				DWS			I (1)			DWS O (1)					5
	TLS				TLS		N (1)		TLS	W (4)			TLS		6
		DLS				DLS	G (2)	DLS				DLS			7
TWS			DLS F (4)	O (1)	L (1)	I (1)	O (1)				DLS			TWS	8
		DLS			I (1)	DLS		DLS				DLS			9
	TLS				TLS Z (10)				TLS				TLS		10
				DWS	A (1)					DWS					11
DLS			DWS		R (1)		DLS				DWS			DLS	12
		DWS			D (2)	DLS		DLS				DWS			13
	DWS				TLS				TLS				DWS		14
TWS			DLS				TWS				DLS			TWS	15

DIAGRAM 10-4

Find your highest-scoring play using all four given tiles. Can you beat our total of 123 points?

EXPERT SCORE: 112 GOOD SCORE: 100 AVERAGE SCORE: 80

1. INOT
2. BEOP
3. DOOV
4. DIIM
5. EOPT

A	B	C	D	E	F	G	H	I	J	K	L	M	N	O	
TWS			DLS				TWS				DLS			TWS	1
	DWS				TLS				TLS				DWS		2
		DWS				DLS		DLS				DWS			3
DLS			DWS				DLS Y_4				DWS			DLS	4
				DWS			O_1			DWS					5
	TLS				TLS		G_2		TLS				TLS		6
		DLS				DLS	I_1	DLS				DLS			7
TWS			DLS				C_3	O_1	M_3	P_3	DLS			TWS	8
		DLS				DLS		DLS		O_1	A_1	DLS F_4			9
	TLS				TLS T_1	A_1	U_1	G_2	TLS H_4	T_1			TLS		10
				DWS R_1	A_1	I_1	N_1			DWS T_1					11
DLS			DWS				DLS			E_1	DWS			DLS	12
		DWS				DLS		DLS		D_2		DWS			13
	DWS				TLS				TLS				DWS		14
TWS			DLS				TWS				DLS			TWS	15
A	B	C	D	E	F	G	H	I	J	K	L	M	N	O	

DIAGRAM 10-5

Find your highest-scoring play using all four given tiles. Can you beat our total of 167 points?

EXPERT SCORE: **155** GOOD SCORE: **140** AVERAGE SCORE: **120**

1. EMNO
2. DIKN
3. GRUU
4. DENV
5. EELT

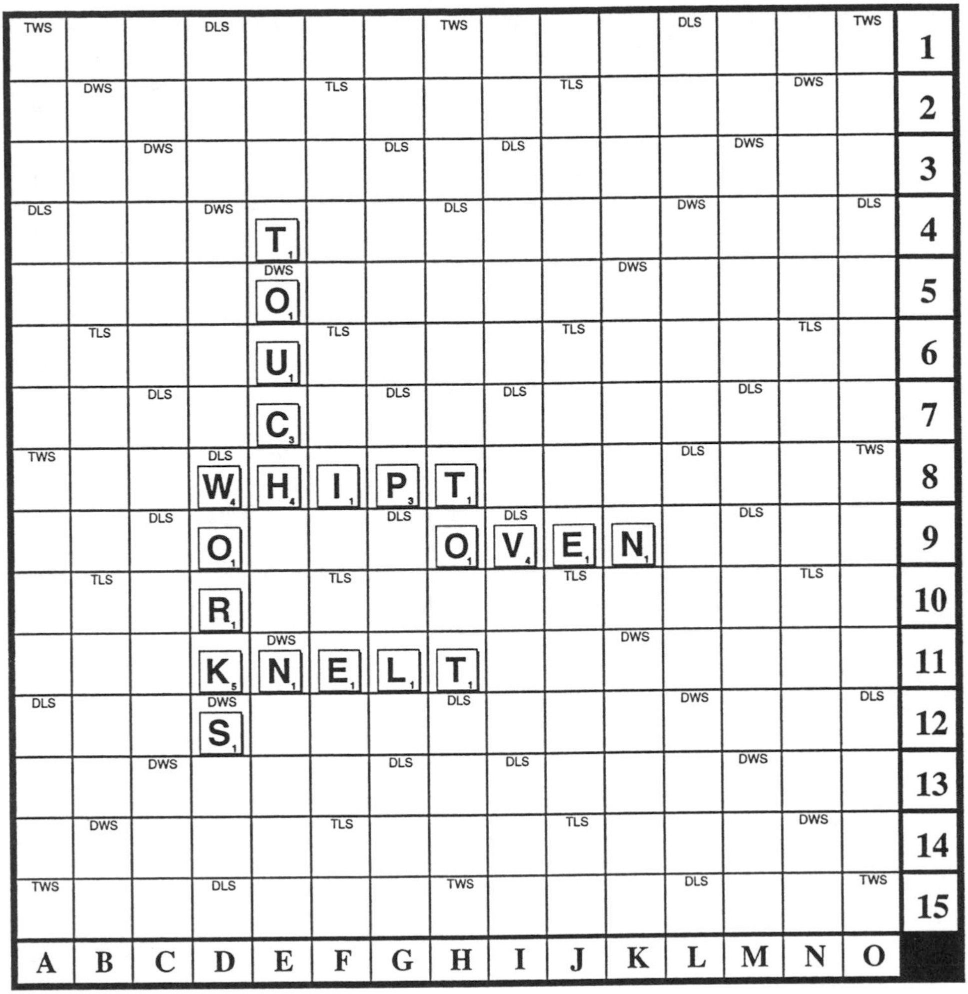

DIAGRAM 10-6

Find your highest-scoring play using all four given tiles. Can you beat our total of 130 points?

EXPERT SCORE: 122 GOOD SCORE: 115 AVERAGE SCORE: 90

1. ENVY
2. EIPR
3. EMOP
4. DIOV
5. NSTV

A	B	C	D	E	F	G	H	I	J	K	L	M	N	O	
TWS			DLS F_4	L_1	U_1	T_1	TWS E_1				DLS			TWS	1
	DWS				TLS	R_1			TLS				DWS		2
		DWS				DLS A_1		DLS				DWS			3
DLS			DWS			N_1	DLS				DWS			DLS	4
				DWS	E_1	Q_{10}	U_1	A_1	T_1	DWS E_1					5
	TLS				TLS	U_1			TLS				TLS		6
		DLS				DLS I_1		DLS				DLS			7
TWS			DLS V_4	O_1	I_1	L_1	A_1				DLS			TWS	8
		DLS	I_1			DLS		DLS				DLS			9
	TLS		L_1		TLS				TLS				TLS		10
			L_1	DWS						DWS					11
DLS			DWS A_1				DLS				DWS			DLS	12
		DWS				DLS		DLS				DWS			13
	DWS				TLS				TLS				DWS		14
TWS			DLS				TWS				DLS			TWS	15

DIAGRAM 10-7

Find your highest-scoring play using all four given tiles. Can you beat our total of 133 points?

EXPERT SCORE: **120** GOOD SCORE: **110** AVERAGE SCORE: **85**

1. AGMT
2. ABEG
3. GNST
4. DEIZ
5. ADIN

	A	B	C	D	E	F	G	H	I	J	K	L	M	N	O
1	TWS			DLS				TWS				DLS			TWS
2		DWS				TLS				TLS				DWS	
3			DWS				DLS		DLS				DWS		
4	DLS			DWS	R_1			DLS				DWS			DLS
5					DWS A_1						DWS				
6		TLS			D_2	TLS				TLS				TLS	
7			DLS		I_1		DLS		DLS				DLS		
8	TWS			DLS O_1	O_1	R_1	A_1	L_1	I_1			DLS			TWS
9			DLS	M_3			DLS W_4	I_1	DLS N_1	E_1	S_1		DLS C_3		
10		TLS		E_1		TLS				TLS	I_1		U_1	TLS	
11				L_1	DWS						DWS Z_{10}		D_2		
12	DLS			DWS E_1				DLS	F_4	R_1	E_1	DWS M_3	D_2		DLS
13			DWS	T_1			DLS		DLS		S_1		DWS Y_4		
14		DWS				TLS				TLS				DWS	
15	TWS			DLS				TWS				DLS			TWS

DIAGRAM 10-8

Find your highest-scoring play using all four given tiles. Can you beat our total of 119 points?

EXPERT SCORE: 110 **GOOD SCORE: 100** **AVERAGE SCORE: 75**

1. EEIS
2. EEKP
3. DEIO
4. DESS
5. CEIP

	A	B	C	D	E	F	G	H	I	J	K	L	M	N	O
1	TWS			DLS				TWS H4				DLS			TWS
2		DWS				TLS		O1		TLS				DWS	
3			DWS				DLS	A1	DLS				DWS		
4	DLS	F4	E1	DWS E1	L1	I1	N1	DLS G2	S1			DWS			DLS
5					DWS			I1			DWS				
6		TLS				TLS	P3	E1		TLS				TLS	
7			DLS				DLS A1		DLS				DLS		
8	TWS			DLS			V4	I1	N1	Y4		DLS			TWS
9			DLS			B3	DLS E1		DLS				DLS		
10		TLS				TLS O1	D2			TLS				TLS	
11					DWS	W4					DWS				
12	DLS			DWS		L1		DLS				DWS			DLS
13			DWS				DLS		DLS				DWS		
14		DWS				TLS				TLS				DWS	
15	TWS			DLS				TWS				DLS			TWS

DIAGRAM 10-9

Find your highest-scoring play using all four given tiles. Can you beat our total of 116 points?

EXPERT SCORE: 108 GOOD SCORE: 100 AVERAGE SCORE: 75

1. ORTT
2. ABIL
3. AAPT
4. BEOO
5. ABOU

A	B	C	D	E	F	G	H	I	J	K	L	M	N	O	
TWS			DLS				TWS				DLS			TWS	1
	DWS				TLS				TLS		W		DWS		2
		DWS				DLS		DLS			E	DWS			3
DLS			DWS				DLS				DWS I			DLS	4
				DWS						DWS	G				5
	TLS				TLS F	L	A	Y	TLS		H		TLS		6
		DLS				DLS	P	DLS A	I	N	T	DLS E	D		7
TWS			DLS	D	A	T	E				DLS			TWS	8
		DLS				DLS		DLS				DLS			9
	TLS				TLS				TLS				TLS		10
				DWS						DWS					11
DLS			DWS				DLS				DWS			DLS	12
		DWS				DLS		DLS				DWS			13
	DWS				TLS				TLS				DWS		14
TWS			DLS				TWS				DLS			TWS	15

DIAGRAM 10-10

Find your highest-scoring play using all four given tiles. Can you beat our total of 140 points?

EXPERT SCORE: **130** GOOD SCORE: **120** AVERAGE SCORE: **95**

1. AILV
2. OSTY
3. AMOT
4. DIOW
5. NOOT

Four-Tile Plays

DIAGRAM 10-1

1. HEAT E9 38
2. GAMY E9 49
3. TYPE H1 44
4. CYST M6 32
5. CAULK 13C 32

TOTAL: 195 POINTS

DIAGRAM 10-2

1. TWANG A11 27
2. WISP K9 32
3. LYMPH 3C 38
4. DWELT 1F 27
5. WEARY C9 30

TOTAL: 154 POINTS

DIAGRAM 10-3

1. GALAXIES 1H 72
2. CLEFT L10 37
3. ROYAL 2G 22
3. PANT N11 23
5. ANON L3 18

TOTAL: 172 POINTS

DIAGRAM 10-4

1. INTO 7J 15
2. BEBOP 3I 42
3. OVOID 5E 21
4. IDIOM E5 20
5. POET E11 25

TOTAL: 123 POINTS

DIAGRAM 10-5

1. OMEN L11 25
2. UNKIND H10 48
3. GURU D11 16
4. VEND 12D 25
5. COMPLETE 8H 53

TOTAL: 167 POINTS

DIAGRAM 10-6

1. ENVOY 9A 29
2. RIPER 10D 31
3. TEMPO H11 30
4. VOID D2 23
5. INVEST F8 17

TOTAL: 130 POINTS

DIAGRAM 10-7

1. GAMUT 6D 26
2. BEGAN 4C 18
3. STUNG 6E 17
4. TRANQUILIZED G1 32
5. INADEQUATE 5B 40

TOTAL: 133 POINTS

DIAGRAM 10-8

1. SEIZED 11H 27
2. PEKE D3 33
3. DIODE 6B 13
4. DISUSE 10J 20
5. EPIC C11 26

TOTAL: 119 POINTS

DIAGRAM 10-9

1. TROT 5C 18
2. BAIL K5 23
3. PASTA I2 22
4. OBOE E9 35
5. BAYOU J6 18

TOTAL: 116 POINTS

DIAGRAM 10-10

1. VALIDATE 8A 39
2. TOYS 8J 38
3. MOAT 5E 25
4. WIDOW 2H 16
5. ONTO M2 22

TOTAL: 140 POINTS

CHAPTER 11

Five-Tile Plays

Among the better players, five-tile plays number a significant percentage of turns. There are often several ways to use five tiles. My advice is to see which two tiles you'd most like to save for your next rack; then try to find a decent play with the remaining five. Failing that, try saving the second-best set of two tiles and looking for a word that includes all the remaining tiles. While this procedure won't always work, if you have no obvious bonus squares to use or other strategic goals, this can be another useful method for searching for your best play.

The following 100 racks should give you plenty of practice using this searching technique. With other things being equal, it's generally better to play five tiles than four, since you're giving yourself a better chance to draw the S's and blanks.

A	B	C	D	E	F	G	H	I	J	K	L	M	N	O	
TWS			DLS				TWS				DLS			TWS	1
	DWS				TLS				TLS				DWS		2
		DWS				DLS		DLS				DWS			3
DLS			DWS				DLS				DWS			DLS	4
				DWS						DWS					5
	TLS				TLS				TLS N	O	R	T	TLS H		6
		DLS				DLS		DLS V				DLS	I		7
TWS			DLS		D	O	G	E		W	DLS H	I	T	TWS E	8
		DLS				DLS M	O	DLS X	I	E		DLS			9
K	TLS I	D	N	A	TLS P	S			TLS				TLS		10
I				DWS						DWS					11
DLS T			DWS				DLS				DWS			DLS	12
T		DWS				DLS		DLS				DWS			13
E	DWS				TLS				TLS				DWS		14
TWS N			DLS				TWS				DLS			TWS	15

DIAGRAM 11-1

Find the highest-scoring play using all five tiles of each rack. In some cases, there may be only one way to use the five tiles. Can you beat our total of 212 points?

EXPERT SCORE: **195** GOOD SCORE: **180** AVERAGE SCORE: **150**

1. BDNSU
2. ARSTZ
3. CDEEI
4. FOSTU
5. EMNOV

	A	B	C	D	E	F	G	H	I	J	K	L	M	N	O
1	TWS			DLS				TWS				DLS			TWS
2		DWS				TLS				TLS				DWS	
3			DWS				DLS		DLS				DWS		
4	DLS			DWS				DLS				DWS			DLS
5					DWS	N (1)					DWS				
6		TLS				TLS I (1)				TLS				TLS	
7			DLS			B (3)	DLS	A (1)	DLS R (1)	M (3)	Y (4)		DLS		
8	TWS			DLS H (4)	A (1)	B (3)	I (1)	T (1)				DLS			TWS
9			DLS			L (1)	DLS		DLS				DLS		
10		TLS			O (1)	TLS E (1)				TLS				TLS	
11					DWS O (1)	D (2)					DWS				
12	DLS			DWS	Z (10)			DLS				DWS			DLS
13			DWS		E (1)		DLS		DLS				DWS		
14		DWS			D (2)	TLS				TLS				DWS	
15	TWS			DLS				TWS				DLS			TWS

DIAGRAM 11-2

Find the highest-scoring play using all five tiles of each rack. In some cases, there may be only one way to use the five tiles. Can you beat our total of 163 points?

EXPERT SCORE: **148** GOOD SCORE: **135** AVERAGE SCORE: **105**

1. DEOPT
2. CMOST
3. LPRUY
4. ACKPS
5. CPTUU

A	B	C	D	E	F	G	H	I	J	K	L	M	N	O	
TWS			DLS				TWS				DLS			TWS	1
	DWS				TLS				TLS				DWS		2
		DWS				DLS		DLS				DWS			3
DLS			DWS				DLS		B_3		DWS			DLS	4
				DWS					R_1	DWS					5
	TLS				TLS				TLS O_1				TLS		6
		DLS				DLS		DLS D_2	O_1			DLS			7
TWS			DLS C_3	H_4	A_1	R_1	G_2	E_1	D_2		DLS			TWS	8
		DLS	Y_4			DLS		DLS V_4				DLS			9
	TLS		A_1		TLS			E_1	TLS				TLS		10
			N_1	DWS				L_1		DWS				E_1	11
DLS			DWS I_1				DLS	O_1			DWS			DLS N_1	12
		DWS	D_2			DLS		DLS P_3	I_1	N_1	I_1	DWS O_1	N_1	S_1	13
	DWS		E_1		TLS			S_1	TLS				DWS	U_1	14
TWS			DLS				TWS				DLS			TWS E_1	15

DIAGRAM 11-3

Find the highest-scoring play using all five tiles of each rack. In some cases, there may be only one way to use the five tiles. Can you beat our total of 204 points?

EXPERT SCORE: **185** GOOD SCORE: **170** AVERAGE SCORE: **140**

1. AMORU
2. AIMRU
3. AIMMX
4. HILPS
5. ACEGU

A	B	C	D	E	F	G	H	I	J	K	L	M	N	O	
TWS			DLS				TWS G_2				DLS			TWS	1
	DWS				TLS		I_1		TLS				DWS		2
		DWS				DLS	Z_{10}	DLS				DWS			3
DLS D_2	E_1	W_4	DWS A_1	X_8			DLS M_3				DWS			DLS	4
				DWS I_1	C_3	H_4	O_1	R_1		DWS					5
	TLS				TLS H_4				TLS				TLS		6
		DLS			U_1	DLS		DLS				DLS			7
TWS			DLS N_1	U_1	M_3	B_3	E_1	R_1			DLS			TWS	8
		DLS			P_3	DLS Y_4	R_1	DLS E_1				DLS			9
	TLS				TLS			D_2	TLS J_8	I_1	N_1		TLS		10
				DWS						DWS					11
DLS			DWS				DLS				DWS			DLS	12
		DWS				DLS		DLS				DWS			13
	DWS				TLS				TLS				DWS		14
TWS			DLS				TWS				DLS			TWS	15

DIAGRAM 11-4

Find the highest-scoring play using all five tiles of each rack. In some cases, there may be only one way to use the five tiles. Can you beat our total of 172 points?

EXPERT SCORE: 160 GOOD SCORE: 145 AVERAGE SCORE: 110

1. AELOT
2. AFLOO
3. IQSSU
4. ADPRU
5. GOTUU

A	B	C	D	E	F	G	H	I	J	K	L	M	N	O	
TWS			DLS				TWS				DLS			TWS	1
	DWS				TLS				TLS				DWS		2
		DWS				DLS		DLS				DWS O			3
DLS			DWS				DLS				DWS	P		DLS	4
				DWS						DWS		T			5
	TLS				TLS				TLS			I	TLS		6
		DLS				DLS		DLS				DLS C			7
TWS			DLS				G	R	O	O	DLS M	S		TWS	8
		DLS				DLS	O	DLS				DLS			9
	TLS				TLS		L		TLS				TLS		10
		B	E	DWS H	O	W	L			DWS					11
DLS			DWS				DLS I				DWS			DLS	12
		DWS				DLS	W	DLS I	D	G	E	DWS T			13
	DWS				TLS		O		TLS				DWS		14
TWS			DLS				TWS G				DLS			TWS	15

DIAGRAM 11-5

Find the highest-scoring play using all five tiles of each rack. In some cases, there may be only one way to use the five tiles. Can you beat our total of 178 points?

EXPERT SCORE: 160 **GOOD SCORE:** 145 **AVERAGE SCORE:** 110

1. AJOPY
2. EGLOT
3. FINOT
4. AKMRU
5. FLOTU

A	B	C	D	E	F	G	H	I	J	K	L	M	N	O	
TWS			DLS				TWS				DLS			TWS	1
	DWS				TLS				TLS				DWS		2
		DWS S$_1$				DLS		DLS				DWS			3
DLS		E$_1$	DWS				DLS				DWS			DLS	4
		N$_1$		DWS						DWS					5
	TLS H$_4$	A$_1$	L$_1$	V$_4$	TLS A$_1$				TLS				TLS		6
		DLS T$_1$			B$_3$	DLS A$_1$	L$_1$	DLS M$_3$	Y$_4$			DLS			7
TWS		O$_1$	DLS			E$_1$	A$_1$	U$_1$			DLS			TWS	8
		DLS R$_1$				DLS		DLS G$_2$	A$_1$	U$_1$	G$_2$	DLS E$_1$			9
	TLS	S$_1$			TLS				TLS				TLS		10
				DWS						DWS					11
DLS			DWS				DLS				DWS			DLS	12
		DWS				DLS		DLS				DWS			13
	DWS				TLS				TLS				DWS		14
TWS			DLS				TWS				DLS			TWS	15

DIAGRAM 11-6

Find the highest-scoring play using all five tiles of each rack. In some cases, there may be only one way to use the five tiles. Can you beat our total of 145 points?

EXPERT SCORE: 130 **GOOD SCORE: 120** **AVERAGE SCORE: 90**

1. DENPU
2. AANOT
3. ABORV
4. EMNYZ
5. BDEGR

	A	B	C	D	E	F	G	H	I	J	K	L	M	N	O
1	TWS			DLS				TWS				DLS			TWS
2		DWS				TLS				TLS				DWS	
3			DWS				DLS		DLS	P3			DWS		
4	DLS			DWS				DLS		R1		DWS			DLS
5					DWS					O1	DWS				
6		TLS				TLS				TLS V4				TLS	
7			DLS				DLS		DLS	E1			DLS		
8	TWS T1	I1	B3	DLS I1	A1		W4	I1	N1	D2		DLS			TWS
9			DLS		G2	L1	DLS E1	N1	DLS				DLS		
10		TLS				TLS		K5	E1	TLS P3	T1			TLS	
11					DWS						DWS				
12	DLS			DWS				DLS				DWS			DLS
13			DWS				DLS		DLS				DWS		
14		DWS				TLS				TLS				DWS	
15	TWS			DLS				TWS				DLS			TWS

DIAGRAM 11-7

Find the highest-scoring play using all five tiles of each rack. In some cases, there may be only one way to use the five tiles. Can you beat our total of 201 points?

EXPERT SCORE: **184** GOOD SCORE: **170** AVERAGE SCORE: **140**

1. MORST
2. BLOST
3. DEIOV
4. ABDER
5. DEGMO

	A	B	C	D	E	F	G	H	I	J	K	L	M	N	O
1	TWS			DLS				TWS				DLS			TWS
2		DWS				TLS				TLS		A		DWS	
3			DWS				DLS B	E	DLS L	I	E	V	DWS E		
4	DLS			DWS C	A	D	E	DLS T				DWS I			DLS
5					DWS						DWS P	A			
6		TLS				TLS				TLS	O	N		TLS	
7			DLS				DLS		DLS		N		DLS		
8	TWS P			DLS				A	W	R	Y	DLS			TWS
9	U		DLS				DLS F	L	DLS E	E			DLS		
10	B	TLS O	N	A	N	TLS Z	A			TLS				TLS	
11					DWS						DWS				
12	DLS			DWS				DLS				DWS			DLS
13			DWS				DLS		DLS				DWS		
14		DWS				TLS				TLS				DWS	
15	TWS			DLS				TWS				DLS			TWS

DIAGRAM 11-8

Find the highest-scoring play using all five tiles of each rack. In some cases, there may be only one way to use the five tiles. Can you beat our total of 194 points?

EXPERT SCORE: **180** GOOD SCORE: **165** AVERAGE SCORE: **130**

1. AILST
2. CILLY
3. EEHNT
4. AEIRT
5. CHINU

	A	B	C	D	E	F	G	H	I	J	K	L	M	N	O
1	TWS			DLS				TWS U				DLS			TWS
2		DWS				TLS S		N		TLS				DWS	
3			DWS B	E	D	I	DLS M	S	DLS				DWS		
4	DLS			DWS		L		DLS U				DWS			DLS
5					DWS	I		R			DWS				
6		TLS				TLS Q		E		TLS				TLS	
7			DLS			U	DLS		DLS				DLS		
8	TWS			DLS P	L	A	C	E				DLS			TWS
9			DLS				DLS	X	DLS				DLS		
10		TLS				TLS		T		TLS				TLS	
11					DWS			E			DWS				
12	DLS			DWS				DLS R				DWS			DLS
13			DWS G	O	T	T	DLS E	N	DLS				DWS		
14		DWS				TLS		A		TLS				DWS	
15	TWS			DLS				TWS L				DLS			TWS

DIAGRAM 11-9

Find the highest-scoring play using all five tiles of each rack. In some cases, there may be only one way to use the five tiles. Can you beat our total of 170 points?

EXPERT SCORE: **160** GOOD SCORE: **145** AVERAGE SCORE: **120**

1. CMNOT
2. CMNOS
3. DIIOT
4. AAIRT
5. ELSSU

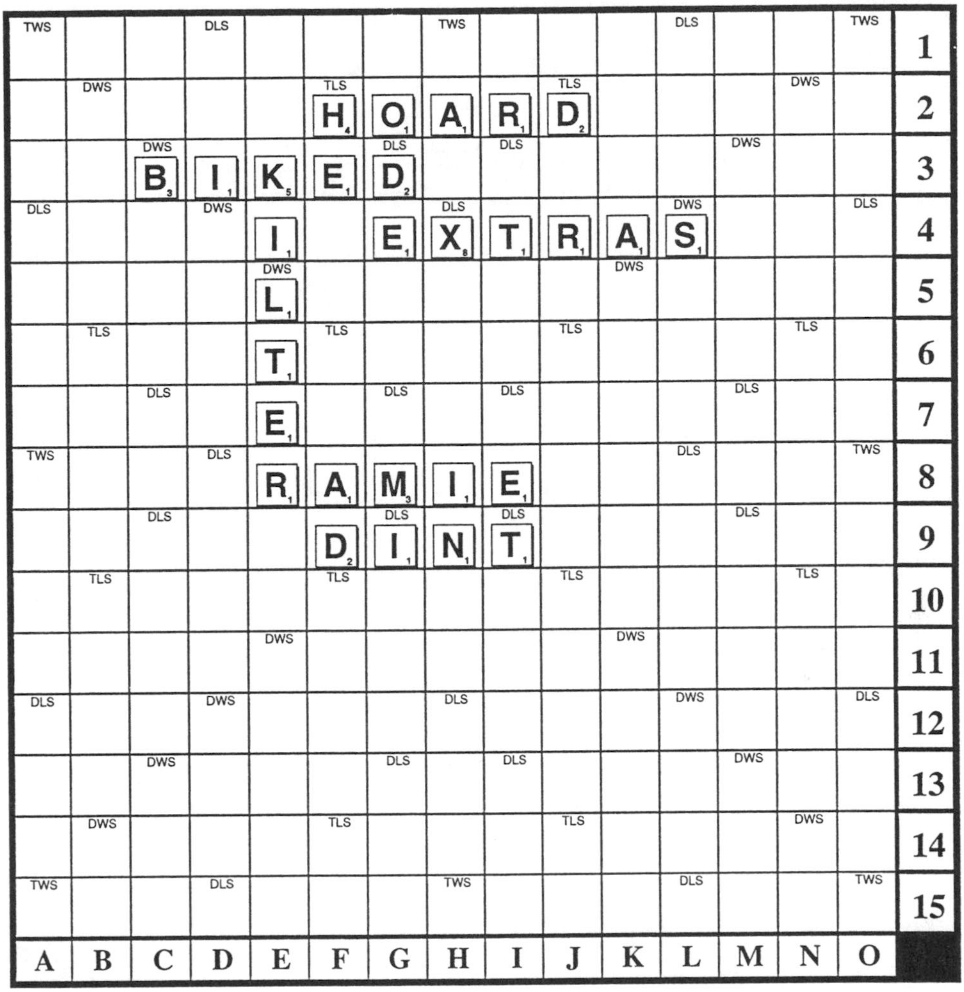

	A	B	C	D	E	F	G	H	I	J	K	L	M	N	O
1	TWS			DLS				TWS				DLS			TWS
2		DWS				TLS H	O	A	R	TLS D				DWS	
3			DWS B	I	K	E	DLS D		DLS				DWS		
4	DLS			DWS	I		E	DLS X	T	R	A	DWS S			DLS
5					DWS L						DWS				
6		TLS			T	TLS				TLS				TLS	
7			DLS		E		DLS		DLS				DLS		
8	TWS			DLS	R	A	M	I	E			DLS			TWS
9			DLS			D	DLS I	N	DLS T				DLS		
10		TLS				TLS				TLS				TLS	
11					DWS						DWS				
12	DLS			DWS				DLS				DWS			DLS
13			DWS				DLS		DLS				DWS		
14		DWS				TLS				TLS				DWS	
15	TWS			DLS				TWS				DLS			TWS

DIAGRAM 11-10

Find the highest-scoring play using all five tiles of each rack. In some cases, there may be only one way to use the five tiles. Can you beat our total of 243 points?

EXPERT SCORE: 225 **GOOD SCORE: 200** **AVERAGE SCORE: 150**

1. GILTZ
2. ACHLT
3. DEHOO
4. ABORR
5. INOSY

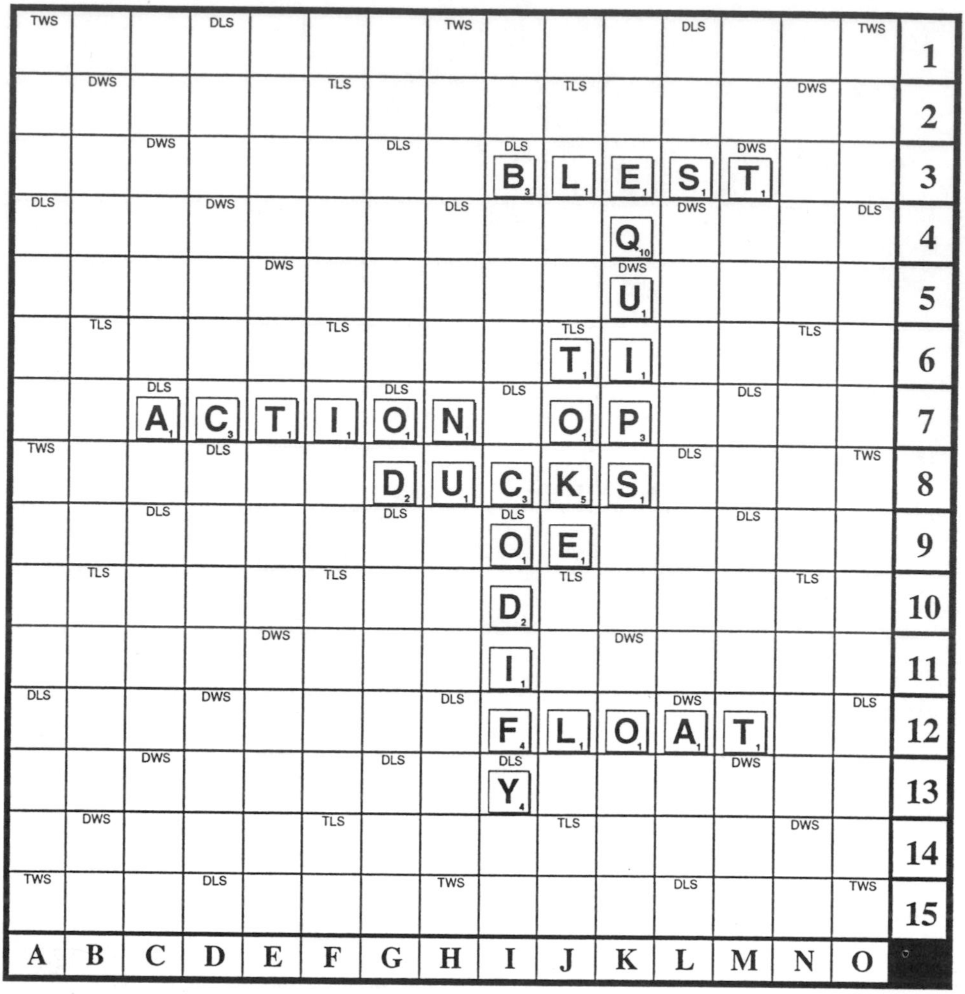

DIAGRAM 11-11

Find the highest-scoring play using all five tiles of each rack. In some cases, there may be only one way to use the five tiles. Can you beat our total of 168 points?

EXPERT SCORE: **150** GOOD SCORE: **135** AVERAGE SCORE: **110**

1. AABET
2. AABMS
3. ERSVY
4. DEILM
5. EHIRT

A	B	C	D	E	F	G	H	I	J	K	L	M	N	O	
TWS			DLS				TWS				DLS			TWS	1
	DWS				TLS				TLS				DWS		2
		DWS				DLS		DLS				DWS			3
DLS			DWS				DLS				DWS			DLS	4
				DWS				M$_3$		DWS					5
	TLS				TLS			E$_1$	TLS				TLS		6
		DLS				DLS		DLS A$_1$				DLS			7
TWS			DLS			F$_4$	E$_1$	L$_1$	L$_1$	O$_1$	DLS W$_4$			TWS	8
		DLS		P$_3$	E$_1$	DLS A$_1$		DLS T$_1$		D$_2$	O$_1$	DLS X$_8$	Y$_4$		9
	TLS C$_3$	R$_1$	U$_1$	E$_1$	TLS T$_1$			I$_1$	TLS		M$_3$		TLS		10
				DWS				M		DWS	B$_3$				11
DLS			DWS				DLS O$_1$	E$_1$			DWS A$_1$			DLS	12
		DWS				DLS	V$_4$	DLS			T$_1$	DWS			13
	DWS				TLS		E$_1$		TLS				DWS		14
TWS			DLS				TWS R$_1$				DLS			TWS	15

DIAGRAM 11-12

Find the highest-scoring play using all five tiles of each rack. In some cases, there may be only one way to use the five tiles. Can you beat our total of 211 points?

EXPERT SCORE: 188 GOOD SCORE: 173 AVERAGE SCORE: 128

1. BCNOU
2. EERST
3. AADEH
4. ABEOV
5. AAHJR

A	B	C	D	E	F	G	H	I	J	K	L	M	N	O	
TWS			DLS				TWS				DLS			TWS	1
	DWS				TLS				TLS				DWS		2
		DWS				DLS		DLS				DWS			3
DLS			DWS				DLS				DWS			DLS	4
				DWS						DWS					5
	TLS				TLS H$_4$	A$_1$	F$_4$	I$_1$	TLS Z$_{10}$				TLS		6
		DLS				DLS		DLS	I$_1$			DLS			7
TWS			DLS		T$_1$	H$_4$	I$_1$	N$_1$	G$_2$	S$_1$	DLS			TWS	8
		DLS				DLS	M$_3$	DLS		T$_1$		DLS			9
	TLS				TLS		P$_3$		TLS	R$_1$			TLS		10
				DWS			L$_1$			DWS I$_1$					11
DLS			DWS				DLS O$_1$			N$_1$	DWS			DLS	12
		DWS				DLS	D$_2$	DLS		G$_2$		DWS			13
	DWS				TLS		E$_1$		TLS	S$_1$			DWS		14
TWS			DLS				TWS S$_1$				DLS			TWS	15

DIAGRAM 11-13

Find the highest-scoring play using all five tiles of each rack. In some cases, there may be only one way to use the five tiles. Can you beat our total of 167 points?

EXPERT SCORE: **150** GOOD SCORE: **140** AVERAGE SCORE: **120**

1. EILST
2. EIMRT
3. BGIPR
4. DEIMS
5. ADEJS

A	B	C	D	E	F	G	H	I	J	K	L	M	N	O	
TWS			DLS				TWS				DLS			TWS	1
	DWS				TLS				TLS F_4				DWS		2
		DWS				DLS		DLS	I_1			DWS			3
DLS			DWS			I_1	DLS M_3	A_1	G_2	E_1	DWS R_1			DLS	4
				DWS					U_1	DWS					5
	TLS				TLS				TLS R_1				TLS		6
		DLS				DLS		DLS	E_1			DLS			7
TWS T_1	E_1	A_1	DLS K_5			B_3	O_1	Y_4	S_1		DLS			TWS	8
		DLS R_1	A_1	D_2	I_1	DLS I_1		DLS				DLS			9
	TLS				TLS				TLS				TLS		10
				DWS						DWS					11
DLS			DWS				DLS				DWS			DLS	12
		DWS				DLS		DLS				DWS			13
	DWS				TLS				TLS				DWS		14
TWS			DLS				TWS				DLS			TWS	15

DIAGRAM 11-14

Find the highest-scoring play using all five tiles of each rack. In some cases, there may be only one way to use the five tiles. Can you beat our total of 216 points?

EXPERT SCORE: 195 GOOD SCORE: 170 AVERAGE SCORE: 140

1. DEEMR
2. GNOOZ
3. FOSTY
4. BMORS
5. DEINX

A	B	C	D	E	F	G	H	I	J	K	L	M	N	O	
TWS			DLS				TWS				DLS P_3			TWS	1
	DWS				TLS				TLS		O_1		DWS		2
		DWS				DLS		DLS			U_1	DWS			3
DLS			DWS				DLS				DWS R_1			DLS	4
				DWS						DWS	E_1				5
	TLS			R_1	TLS E_1	A_1	L_1	I_1	TLS Z_{10}	E_1	D_2		TLS		6
		DLS				DLS		DLS	I_1			DLS			7
TWS			DLS		M_3	A_1	K_5	E_1	R_1		DLS			TWS	8
		DLS				DLS		DLS	C_3			DLS			9
	TLS				TLS				TLS O_1				TLS		10
				DWS					N_1	DWS					11
DLS			DWS				DLS				DWS			DLS	12
		DWS				DLS		DLS				DWS			13
	DWS				TLS				TLS				DWS		14
TWS			DLS				TWS				DLS			TWS	15

DIAGRAM 11-15

Find the highest-scoring play using all five tiles of each rack. In some cases, there may be only one way to use the five tiles. Can you beat our total of 223 points?

EXPERT SCORE: **205** GOOD SCORE: **180** AVERAGE SCORE: **140**

1. EEFUY
2. ADMNU
3. ALMTU
4. ACHMT
5. DEELV

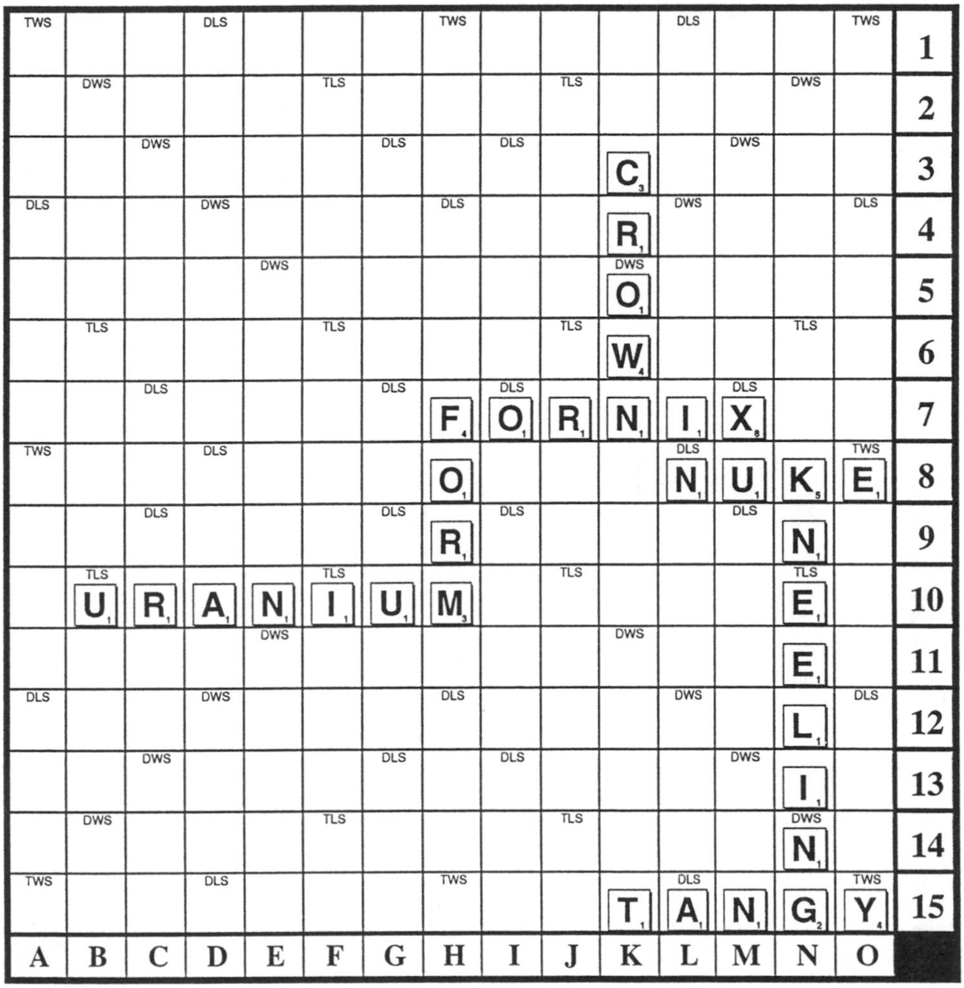

DIAGRAM 11-16

Find the highest-scoring play using all five tiles of each rack. In some cases, there may be only one way to use the five tiles. Can you beat our total of 172 points?

EXPERT SCORE: 160 GOOD SCORE: 145 AVERAGE SCORE: 120

1. AILTY
2. AAFIL
3. EGNST
4. AEHTT
5. DEMST

A	B	C	D	E	F	G	H	I	J	K	L	M	N	O	
TWS			DLS				TWS				DLS			TWS	1
	DWS				TLS				TLS				DWS		2
		DWS				DLS		DLS				DWS			3
DLS			DWS				DLS				DWS			DLS	4
				DWS						DWS					5
	TLS				TLS				TLS				TLS		6
		DLS				DLS		DLS A				DLS			7
TWS			DLS C	A	N	T	O	N			DLS			TWS	8
		DLS				DLS		DLS X				DLS			9
	TLS				TLS			I	TLS				TLS		10
				DWS				O		DWS					11
DLS			DWS				DLS Q	U	A	I	DWS N	T		DLS	12
		DWS				DLS	U	DLS S				DWS			13
	DWS				TLS		I		TLS				DWS		14
TWS			DLS				TWS D				DLS			TWS	15

DIAGRAM 11-17

Find the highest-scoring play using all five tiles of each rack. In some cases, there may be only one way to use the five tiles. Can you beat our total of 167 points?

EXPERT SCORE: **152** GOOD SCORE: **140** AVERAGE SCORE: **120**

1. ACERS
2. AMNRS
3. AIOSS
4. EMOTV
5. EEJRT

A	B	C	D	E	F	G	H	I	J	K	L	M	N	O	
TWS			DLS				TWS				DLS			TWS	1
	DWS				TLS				TLS				DWS		2
		DWS	F$_4$			DLS		DLS				DWS			3
DLS			DWS E$_1$				DLS				DWS			DLS	4
			D$_2$	DWS						DWS					5
	TLS		O$_1$		TLS				TLS				TLS		6
		DLS	R$_1$			DLS		DLS				DLS			7
TWS			DLS A$_1$	B$_3$	O$_1$	U$_1$	T$_1$			N$_1$	DLS O$_1$	V$_4$	E$_1$	TWS L$_1$	8
		DLS			R$_1$	DLS H$_4$	O$_1$	DLS M$_3$	B$_3$	U$_1$	S$_1$	DLS			9
	TLS				TLS				TLS				TLS		10
				DWS						DWS					11
DLS			DWS				DLS				DWS			DLS	12
		DWS				DLS		DLS				DWS			13
	DWS				TLS				TLS				DWS		14
TWS			DLS				TWS				DLS			TWS	15

DIAGRAM 11-18

Find the highest-scoring play using all five tiles of each rack. In some cases, there may be only one way to use the five tiles. Can you beat our total of 138 points?

EXPERT SCORE: **125** GOOD SCORE: **115** AVERAGE SCORE: **95**

1. EINOP
2. ABCOR
3. AEEST
4. DIMNO
5. AADIR

	A	B	C	D	E	F	G	H	I	J	K	L	M	N	O
1	TWS			DLS				TWS				DLS			TWS
2		DWS				TLS				TLS				DWS	
3			DWS				DLS		DLS				DWS		
4	DLS			DWS				DLS				DWS			DLS
5					DWS						DWS				
6		TLS				TLS				TLS				TLS	
7			DLS				DLS	C_3	DLS O_1	R_1	K_5		DLS		
8	TWS			DLS H_4	Y_4	D_2	R_1	O_1				DLS			TWS
9			DLS T_1	O_1	E_1	A_1	DLS	M_3	DLS				DLS		
10		TLS				TLS		F_4		TLS P_3				TLS	
11					DWS			O_1		I_1	DWS				
12	DLS			DWS				DLS R_1		L_1		DWS			DLS
13			DWS				DLS	T_1	DLS W_4	E_1	N_1	T_1	DWS Y_4		
14		DWS				TLS		S_1		TLS D_2				DWS	
15	TWS			DLS				TWS				DLS			TWS

DIAGRAM 11-19

Find the highest-scoring play using all five tiles of each rack. In some cases, there may be only one way to use the five tiles. Can you beat our total of 211 points?

EXPERT SCORE: 195 **GOOD SCORE: 180** **AVERAGE SCORE: 150**

1. ACDRT
2. DHITW
3. ACORT
4. ALPRS
5. ACEIN

	A	B	C	D	E	F	G	H	I	J	K	L	M	N	O
1	TWS			DLS				TWS				DLS			TWS
2		DWS				TLS				TLS				DWS	
3			DWS				DLS		DLS				DWS		
4	DLS			DWS				DLS O	U	R	E	DWS B	I		DLS
5					DWS D	I	L	U	T	E	DWS D				
6		TLS P	A	G	O	TLS D		T		TLS				TLS	
7			DLS				DLS	M	DLS				DLS		
8	TWS			DLS				A				DLS			TWS
9			DLS				DLS	N	DLS				DLS		
10		TLS		R	A	TLS V	E	S		TLS				TLS	
11					DWS						DWS				
12	DLS			DWS				DLS				DWS			DLS
13			DWS				DLS		DLS				DWS		
14		DWS				TLS				TLS				DWS	
15	TWS			DLS				TWS				DLS			TWS

DIAGRAM 11-20

Find the highest-scoring play using all five tiles of each rack. In some cases, there may be only one way to use the five tiles. Can you beat our total of 156 points?

EXPERT SCORE: 140 **GOOD SCORE: 125** **AVERAGE SCORE: 90**

1. ACLOR
2. GHLOU
3. LOTUY
4. HORTW
5. DMRUU

Five-Tile Plays

DIAGRAM 11-1

1. DUSTBIN M3 35
2. ERSATZ 14A 70
3. DEICE 5K 35
4. FOURTHS L3 41
5. VENOM 7C 31

TOTAL: 212 POINTS

DIAGRAM 11-2

1. OPTED 8K 38
2. SITCOM 6E 35
3. PURELY 13B 30
4. SKYCAP K5 34
5. CUTUP E2 26

TOTAL: 163 POINTS

DIAGRAM 11-3

1. AMOUR H11 51
2. BARIUM 4J 26
3. MAXIM C10 57
4. POLISH 12H 41
5. GAUCHE E4 29

TOTAL: 204 POINTS

DIAGRAM 11-4

1. ZEALOT 3H 32
2. ALOOF 11G 40
3. SQUISH 6A 48
4. UPWARD C2 28
5. DUGOUT A4 24

TOTAL: 172 POINTS

DIAGRAM 11-5

1. JALOPY 10F 70
2. GOBLET C9 22
3. FOOTING K7 22
4. MARKUP 4H 34
5. FLOUT L2 30

TOTAL: 178 POINTS

DIAGRAM 11-6

1. UPEND N5 23
2. ATONAL D1 22
3. BRAVO 6J 31
4. ENZYM B10 46
5. GRABBED F4 23

TOTAL: 145 POINTS

DIAGRAM 11-7

1. WINDSTORM 8G 48
2. INKBLOTS H8 45
3. VIDEO 10B 27
4. BREAD 7D 33
5. DEMAGOG E5 48

TOTAL: 201 POINTS

DIAGRAM 11-8

1. PONYTAILS K5 36
2. PUBLICLY A8 54
3. ETHANE 2I 35
4. IRATE N2 27
5. UNETHICAL H1 42

TOTAL: 194 POINTS

DIAGRAM 11-9

1. COMPLACENT 8A 54
2. MICRONS 5E 44
3. IDIOT I7 33
4. TIARAS 2A 21
5. SEQUELS 6D 18

TOTAL: 170 POINTS

DIAGRAM 11-10

1. GLITZ 10B 72
2. LATCH 1D 61
3. OOHED 3I 35
4. ARBOR 7G 28
5. NOISY 1H 47

TOTAL: 243 POINTS

DIAGRAM 11-11

1. ABATE H1 32
2. SAMBA H11 49
3. VESTRY M9 32
4. MIDDLE 10G 28
5. THEIR 11K 27

TOTAL: 168 POINTS

DIAGRAM 11-12

1. BUNCO 8A 41
2. STEEPER E5 36
3. AHEAD K11 33
4. ABOVE H1 46
5. RAJAH H1 55

TOTAL: 211 POINTS

DIAGRAM 11-13

1. ITSELF H1 30
2. REMIT 5E 30
3. PROBING 12F 24
4. DIMMEST 9E 45
5. JADES 5E 41

TOTAL: 170 POINTS

DIAGRAM 11-14

1. DEMURE 5G 35
2. GONZO 10G 41
3. SOFTY 10D 47
4. SOMBER 7F 34
5. INDEX 3C 59

TOTAL: 216 POINTS

DIAGRAM 11-15

1. EYEFUL H1 48
2. UNMADE K1 36
3. TALCUM 9G 24
4. MATCHMAKER 8A 78
5. DELVE 7D 37

TOTAL: 223 POINTS

DIAGRAM 11-16

1. FORMALITY H7 54
2. FACIAL 3I 30
3. GENTS D11 33
4. THETA 11A 29
5. MODEST I6 26

TOTAL: 172 POINTS

DIAGRAM 11-17

1. REACQUAINTS 12D 44
2. RANSOM 11E 35
3. OASIS J6 33
4. MOTIVE 10F 25
5. REJECT D4 30

TOTAL: 167 POINTS

DIAGRAM 11-18

1. OPINE C3 38
2. CAROB 10B 32
3. TEASE 10H 26
4. DOMINOS L3 20
5. AFRAID 3C 22

TOTAL: 138 POINTS

DIAGRAM 11-19

1. CAROTID 11E 40
2. WIDTH 10B 58
3. ACTOR 8K 36
4. PLAYERS E5 48
5. CANINE K9 29

TOTAL: 211 POINTS

DIAGRAM 11-20

1. CORAL 3I 43
2. GHOUL C10 28
3. OUTLAY C2 26
4. THROW 6J 33
5. DURUM 4B 26

TOTAL: 156 POINTS

PART THREE

Playing All Seven Tiles

By far the most number of bingos you'll play are those that have common beginning or ending letter combinations. If you learn the most common of these and look for them on your rack, I guarantee that you'll find more bingos.

Enjoy the practice!

CHAPTER 12

Bingos: Beginnings and Endings, the Key to Success

There is no doubt: find more bingos and you'll win more games. For the following 150 racks, we've given you the beginnings and endings. Your task is simply to find the bingos that play in the diagrams and that either start or end with certain letter combinations. We suggest you create the positions and racks in front of you and take your time looking for the bingos. You may find the extra time spent will be well worth it when you find more bingos during your competitive games. In each case we estimate that in a 30-minute time limit, an expert player will find all five words of each diagram, a good player will find four while an average player will find three of the plays.

Please note that in some cases, other bingos, scoring more points, are available. You can have some extra fun looking for them, but they're not listed in the answers, since they're not what you're asked to find.

A	B	C	D	E	F	G	H	I	J	K	L	M	N	O	
TWS			DLS				TWS				DLS			TWS	1
	DWS				TLS				TLS				DWS		2
		DWS				DLS		DLS				DWS			3
DLS			DWS				DLS J	E	T	T	DWS Y			DLS	4
				DWS					I	DWS					5
	TLS				TLS				TLS B				TLS		6
		DLS				DLS		DLS	I			DLS			7
TWS			DLS P	O	L	E	N	T	A		DLS			TWS	8
		DLS			I	DLS		DLS				DLS			9
	TLS				TLS Q				TLS				TLS		10
				DWS	U					DWS					11
DLS			DWS		I		DLS				DWS			DLS	12
		DWS			D	DLS		DLS				DWS			13
	DWS				TLS				TLS				DWS		14
TWS			DLS				TWS				DLS			TWS	15

DIAGRAM 12-1

Beginnings: AIR, DE, CON **Endings:** TION, ED, IAL

Find the highest-scoring, playable bingo with each rack that either begins or ends with one of the above combinations of letters. Can you beat our total of 374 points?

1. AAEILNR
2. FIINORT
3. ACNOSTT
4. DEEMNRU
5. BCDEERS

	A	B	C	D	E	F	G	H	I	J	K	L	M	N	O
1								L							
2								I							
3								K							
4				U			N	E							
5				N			O	D							
6				F	I	X	T								
7				I			I								
8				T			F	I	G						
9							I	N							
10							E	N							
11							S	O							
12								C							
13								E							
14								N							
15								T							

DIAGRAM 12-2

Beginnings: BE, EN, OUT **Endings:** ING, IC, IUM

Find the highest-scoring, playable bingo with each rack that either begins or ends with one of the above combinations of letters. Can you beat our total of 361 points?

1. ABGIILN
2. DEIIMRU
3. AACDMRT
4. HIKNOTU
5. EEINNSV

	A	B	C	D	E	F	G	H	I	J	K	L	M	N	O
1	TWS			DLS				TWS R				DLS			TWS
2		DWS			C	TLS		E		TLS				DWS	
3			DWS		A		DLS	P	DLS				DWS		
4	DLS			DWS	N			DLS A				DWS			DLS
5					DWS O			I			DWS				
6		TLS			E	TLS F		R	E	TLS V	E	R	T	TLS	
7			DLS			A	DLS	E	DLS				DLS		
8	TWS			DLS T	H	I	R	D				DLS			TWS
9			DLS			R	DLS		DLS				DLS		
10		TLS W	O	O	D	TLS Y				TLS				TLS	
11					DWS						DWS				
12	DLS			DWS				DLS				DWS			DLS
13			DWS				DLS		DLS				DWS		
14		DWS				TLS				TLS				DWS	
15	TWS			DLS				TWS				DLS			TWS

DIAGRAM 12-3

Beginnings: FOR, IN, MIS **Endings:** ATE, NT, ER

Find the highest-scoring, playable bingo with each rack that either begins or ends with one of the above combinations of letters. Can you beat our total of 356 points?

1. AEFLOPY
2. ADILNRY
3. IMNPSST
4. AEEORRT
5. ABENRRT

A	B	C	D	E	F	G	H	I	J	K	L	M	N	O	
TWS			DLS				TWS				DLS			TWS	1
	DWS				TLS				TLS				DWS		2
		DWS				DLS		DLS				DWS			3
DLS			DWS				DLS				DWS			DLS	4
				DWS						DWS					5
	TLS				TLS				TLS				TLS		6
		DLS				DLS	P	DLS O	I			DLS			7
TWS T	R	O	DLS O	P			A	N	T	I	DLS C			TWS	8
		DLS	R	I	T	DLS Z	Y	DLS			R	DLS			9
	TLS				TLS				TLS		O		TLS		10
				DWS						DWS	W				11
DLS			DWS				DLS				DWS E			DLS	12
		DWS				DLS		DLS			D	DWS			13
	DWS				TLS				TLS				DWS		14
TWS			DLS				TWS				DLS			TWS	15

DIAGRAM 12-4

Beginnings: OVER, RE, UN **Endings:** IUM, FUL, OUS

Find the highest-scoring, playable bingo with each rack that either begins or ends with one of the above combinations of letters. Can you beat our total of 369 points?

1. FHILMRU
2. ENOORSU
3. AEMNSUU
4. AAIMQUU
5. AEORSVW

A	B	C	D	E	F	G	H	I	J	K	L	M	N	O	
TWS			DLS				TWS				DLS			TWS	1
	DWS				TLS				TLS				DWS		2
		DWS				DLS		DLS				DWS			3
DLS			DWS				DLS				DWS			DLS	4
				DWS						DWS					5
	TLS				TLS	C$_3$	R$_1$	E$_1$	TLS A$_1$	T$_1$	O$_1$	R$_1$	TLS		6
		DLS			T$_1$	DLS O$_1$	I$_1$	DLS L$_1$				DLS			7
TWS			DLS B$_3$	L$_1$	O$_1$	W$_4$	N$_1$				DLS			TWS	8
		DLS	O$_1$			DLS		DLS				DLS			9
	TLS		U$_1$		TLS				TLS				TLS		10
			Q$_{10}$	DWS						DWS					11
DLS			DWS U$_1$				DLS				DWS			DLS	12
		DWS	E$_1$			DLS		DLS				DWS			13
	DWS		T$_1$		TLS				TLS				DWS		14
TWS			DLS				TWS				DLS			TWS	15

DIAGRAM 12-5

Beginnings: AB, UN, SUB **Endings:** LIKE, ARD, CH

Find the highest-scoring, playable bingo with each rack that either begins or ends with one of the above combinations of letters. Can you beat our total of 400 points?

1. AABEISV
2. BNNOTTU
3. DEGIKLO
4. ACDRSTU
5. AACHPPR

DIAGRAM 12-6

Beginnings: PRO, RE, NON **Endings:** INE, OR, IC

Find the highest-scoring, playable bingo with each rack that either begins or ends with one of the above combinations of letters. Can you beat our total of 412 points?

1. ACOPRRT
2. AEEFNST
3. ENNORTV
4. NOOPRSS
5. CGIIOST

A	B	C	D	E	F	G	H	I	J	K	L	M	N	O	
TWS			DLS				TWS				DLS			TWS	1
	DWS				TLS				TLS				DWS		2
		DWS				DLS M$_3$		DLS				DWS			3
DLS			DWS			A$_1$	DLS				DWS			DLS	4
				DWS		N$_1$				DWS					5
	TLS				TLS	N$_1$			TLS				TLS		6
		DLS				DLS E$_1$		DLS				DLS			7
TWS			DLS		G$_2$	R$_1$	E$_1$	E$_1$			DLS			TWS	8
		DLS			A$_1$	DLS		DLS				DLS			9
	TLS				TLS Z$_{10}$				TLS				TLS		10
				DWS	I$_1$					DWS					11
DLS			DWS		N$_1$		DLS				DWS			DLS	12
	K$_5$	DWS L$_1$	O$_1$	N$_1$	G$_2$	DLS		DLS				DWS			13
	DWS				TLS				TLS				DWS		14
TWS			DLS				TWS				DLS			TWS	15

DIAGRAM 12-7

Beginnings: OUT, RE, DIS **Endings:** IES, AL, BLE

Find the highest-scoring, playable bingo with each rack that either begins or ends with one of the above combinations of letters. Can you beat our total of 377 points?

1. ABEORTU
2. DRSSTTU
3. EIIPRRS
4. AAILRRV
5. ABEELNT

A	B	C	D	E	F	G	H	I	J	K	L	M	N	O	
TWS			DLS				TWS				DLS			TWS	1
	DWS				TLS				TLS				DWS		2
		DWS				DLS		DLS				DWS			3
DLS			DWS				DLS				DWS			DLS	4
				DWS						DWS					5
	TLS				TLS				TLS				TLS		6
		DLS				DLS		DLS				DLS			7
TWS			DLS P_3	I_1	N_1	T_1	O_1		B_3	O_1	DLS A_1	R_1	D_2	TWS S_1	8
		DLS				DLS	D_2	DLS W_4	A_1	R_1	F_4	DLS			9
	TLS				TLS				TLS		F_4		TLS		10
				DWS						DWS	E_1				11
DLS			DWS				DLS				DWS C_3			DLS	12
		DWS				DLS		DLS			T_1	DWS			13
	DWS				TLS				TLS				DWS		14
TWS			DLS				TWS				DLS			TWS	15

DIAGRAM 12-8

Beginnings: COM, HEAD, OUT **Endings:** CH, ING, AGE

Find the highest-scoring, playable bingo with each rack that either begins or ends with one of the above combinations of letters. Can you beat our total of 403 points?

1. CHNOOPT
2. GILNOOS
3. AABDEHN
4. AEGHORT
5. ACEMOOT

A	B	C	D	E	F	G	H	I	J	K	L	M	N	O	
TWS			DLS				TWS				DLS			TWS	1
	DWS				TLS				TLS				DWS		2
		DWS				DLS		DLS		C_3		DWS			3
DLS			DWS				DLS			H_4	DWS			DLS	4
				DWS						DWS A_1					5
	TLS				TLS				TLS J_8	O_1			TLS		6
		DLS				DLS		DLS	U_1			DLS			7
TWS			DLS C_3	H_4	A_1	P_3	T_1	E_1	R_1		DLS			TWS	8
		DLS				DLS	O_1	DLS	Y_4			DLS			9
	TLS				TLS		T_1		TLS				TLS		10
				DWS			A_1			DWS					11
DLS			DWS				DLS L_1				DWS			DLS	12
		DWS				DLS	I_1	DLS				DWS			13
	DWS				TLS		Z_{10}		TLS				DWS		14
TWS			DLS				TWS E_1				DLS			TWS	15

DIAGRAM 12-9

Beginnings: RE, MIS, PRE **Endings:** ION, IER, ILE

Find the highest-scoring, playable bingo with each rack that either begins or ends with one of the above combinations of letters. Can you beat our total of 419 points?

1. EINOORS
2. AELLOTV
3. EGIPRST
4. EIKMNST
5. AEMRRRY

	A	B	C	D	E	F	G	H	I	J	K	L	M	N	O
1	TWS			DLS				TWS				DLS D			TWS
2		DWS				TLS				TLS		E		DWS	
3			DWS				DLS		DLS			F	DWS		
4	DLS			DWS				DLS			S	DWS I			DLS
5					DWS						DWS W	E			
6		TLS				TLS				TLS	O	S		TLS	
7			DLS				DLS		DLS		O		DLS		
8	TWS			DLS			E	R	R	I	N	DLS G			TWS
9			DLS				DLS		DLS			R	DLS		
10		TLS				TLS				TLS		A		TLS	
11					DWS						DWS	D			
12	DLS			DWS				DLS				DWS E			DLS
13			DWS				DLS		DLS				DWS		
14		DWS				TLS				TLS				DWS	
15	TWS			DLS				TWS				DLS			TWS

DIAGRAM 12-10

Beginnings: TRI, IM, STR **Endings:** ORT, ANT, ICE

Find the highest-scoring, playable bingo with each rack that either begins or ends with one of the above combinations of letters. Can you beat our total of 521 points?

1. HIMPRTU
2. AILMNPT
3. AGRSTTY
4. AIOPRRT
5. ACEIJNU

	A	B	C	D	E	F	G	H	I	J	K	L	M	N	O
1	TWS			DLS				TWS				DLS			TWS
2		DWS				TLS				TLS				DWS	
3			DWS		W		DLS		DLS				DWS		
4	DLS			DWS	I			DLS				DWS			DLS
5					DWS D						DWS				
6		TLS			I	TLS				TLS				TLS	
7			DLS		S		DLS		DLS				DLS		
8	TWS			DLS W	H	I	P	T				DLS			TWS
9			DLS	R			DLS		DLS				DLS		
10		TLS		A		TLS				TLS				TLS	
11				N	DWS						DWS				
12	DLS			DWS G				DLS				DWS			DLS
13			DWS I	L	I	A	DLS C		DLS				DWS		
14		DWS		E		TLS				TLS				DWS	
15	TWS			DLS D	Y	V	O	TWS U	R			DLS			TWS

DIAGRAM 12-11

Beginnings: DE, UN, ANTI **Endings:** IVE, MAN, IEST

Find the highest-scoring, playable bingo with each rack that either begins or ends with one of the above combinations of letters. Can you beat our total of 400 points?

1. EEILRVY
2. ADEKNSU
3. ACEHIRV
4. AMNNSTU
5. CEIKLSU

A	B	C	D	E	F	G	H	I	J	K	L	M	N	O	
TWS			DLS				TWS				DLS			TWS	1
	DWS				TLS				TLS				DWS		2
		DWS				DLS		DLS				DWS			3
DLS			DWS				DLS				DWS			DLS	4
				DWS						DWS					5
	TLS				TLS				TLS H$_4$				TLS		6
	C$_3$	DLS H$_4$	A$_1$	P$_3$	E$_1$	DLS A$_1$	U$_1$	DLS	E$_1$			DLS			7
TWS			DLS				P$_3$	A$_1$	R$_1$	T$_1$	DLS Y$_4$			TWS	8
		DLS				DLS		DLS	E$_1$			DLS			9
	TLS				TLS				TLS T$_1$				TLS		10
				DWS				N$_1$	I$_1$	DWS X$_8$	E$_1$				11
DLS			DWS				DLS L$_1$	O$_1$	C$_3$	U$_1$	DWS M$_3$			DLS	12
		DWS				DLS		DLS				DWS			13
	DWS				TLS				TLS				DWS		14
TWS			DLS				TWS				DLS			TWS	15

DIAGRAM 12-12

Beginnings: RE, UN, UP **Endings:** ENT, ND, WN

Find the highest-scoring, playable bingo with each rack that either begins or ends with one of the above combinations of letters. Can you beat our total of 390 points?

1. DNOSTUW
2. AEEMNTV
3. ADGLNNO
4. ABEILLR
5. GIINRSU

	A	B	C	D	E	F	G	H	I	J	K	L	M	N	O
1	TWS			DLS				TWS				DLS			TWS
2		DWS				TLS				TLS				DWS	
3			DWS				DLS		DLS				DWS		
4	DLS			DWS				DLS				DWS			DLS
5					DWS						DWS				
6		TLS				TLS				TLS				TLS	
7			DLS				DLS		DLS				DLS		
8	TWS			DLS			D_2	E_1	I_1	F_4	I_1	DLS C_3			TWS
9			DLS				DLS		DLS		M_3		DLS		
10		TLS				TLS				TLS	P_3			TLS	
11					DWS						DWS E_1				
12	DLS			DWS				DLS			A_1	DWS			DLS
13			DWS				DLS		DLS		C_3		DWS		
14		DWS				TLS		M_3	I_1	TLS G_2	H_4	T_1	I_1	DWS E_1	R_1
15	TWS			DLS				TWS				DLS			TWS

DIAGRAM 12-13

Beginnings: EN, HY, MID **Endings:** EE, ED, ITE

Find the highest-scoring, playable bingo with each rack that either begins or ends with one of the above combinations of letters. Can you beat our total of 507 points?

1. EEEGINN
2. DGHNORY
3. DIOSTY?
4. EGHISST
5. DEEIRTU

A	B	C	D	E	F	G	H	I	J	K	L	M	N	O	
TWS			DLS				TWS				DLS			TWS	1
	DWS				TLS				TLS				DWS		2
		DWS				DLS		DLS				DWS			3
DLS			DWS				DLS				DWS			DLS	4
				DWS						DWS					5
	TLS				TLS				TLS B3				TLS		6
		DLS				DLS		DLS	R1			DLS			7
TWS			DLS			N1	A1	T1	I1	O1	DLS N1			TWS	8
		DLS				DLS		DLS	N1			DLS			9
	TLS				TLS				TLS K5	A1	U1	R1	TLS Y4		10
				DWS						DWS					11
DLS			DWS				DLS				DWS			DLS	12
		DWS				DLS		DLS				DWS			13
	DWS				TLS				TLS				DWS		14
TWS			DLS				TWS				DLS			TWS	15

DIAGRAM 12-14

Beginnings: OUT, UP, SUB **Endings:** OUR, OUS, OUT

Find the highest-scoring, playable bingo with each rack that either begins or ends with one of the above combinations of letters. Can you beat our total of 374 points?

1. AGLMORU
2. EHINOSU
3. AADGOTU
4. ALOSTTU
5. AENOPSU

TWS			DLS				TWS				DLS			TWS	1
	DWS				TLS				TLS				DWS		2
		DWS				DLS		DLS				DWS H			3
DLS			DWS				DLS				DWS	O		DLS	4
				DWS						DWS		V			5
	TLS				TLS				TLS		P	E	TLS		6
		DLS				DLS		DLS	C		A	DLS L			7
TWS			DLS				G	L	O	G	DLS G			TWS	8
		DLS	R	A	D	DLS I	O	DLS	O		E	DLS			9
	TLS				TLS				TLS F		B		TLS		10
				DWS						DWS	O				11
DLS			DWS				DLS				DWS Y			DLS	12
		DWS				DLS		DLS				DWS			13
	DWS				TLS				TLS				DWS		14
TWS			DLS				TWS				DLS			TWS	15
A	B	C	D	E	F	G	H	I	J	K	L	M	N	O	

DIAGRAM 12-15

Beginnings: BI, DI, PL **Endings:** BLE, DLE, TLE

Find the highest-scoring, playable bingo with each rack that either begins or ends with one of the above combinations of letters. Can you beat our total of 380 points?

1. AABELPR
2. EEIKLNR
3. BIILMNO
4. ADEILMM
5. AEELPSU

DIAGRAM 12-16

Beginnings: GL, IN, UN **Endings:** ER, CH, TH

Find the highest-scoring, playable bingo with each rack that either begins or ends with one of the above combinations of letters. Can you beat our total of 438 points?

1. CEGLOSU
2. AEILNRY
3. ADEHINR
4. ACHINPS
5. ABHINST

TWS			DLS				TWS				DLS			TWS	1
	DWS				TLS				TLS				DWS		2
		DWS				DLS		DLS				DWS			3
DLS			DWS				DLS				DWS			DLS	4
				DWS U						DWS					5
	TLS			N	TLS				TLS				TLS		6
		DLS		B		DLS	O	DLS A	S	I	S	DLS			7
TWS			DLS C	I	P	H	E	R			DLS H	A	B	TWS U	8
		DLS		T		DLS		DLS				DLS			9
	TLS			T	TLS				TLS				TLS		10
				DWS E						DWS					11
DLS			DWS	N			DLS				DWS			DLS	12
		DWS				DLS		DLS				DWS			13
	DWS				TLS				TLS				DWS		14
TWS			DLS				TWS				DLS			TWS	15
A	B	C	D	E	F	G	H	I	J	K	L	M	N	O	

DIAGRAM 12-17

Beginnings: BE, CON, PRE **Endings:** ER, ICE, OW

Find the highest-scoring, playable bingo with each rack that either begins or ends with one of the above combinations of letters. Can you beat our total of 390 points?

1. DEEFINR
2. CEEGORV
3. ABELMPR
4. EEIJLNR
5. CEFIIRT

	A	B	C	D	E	F	G	H	I	J	K	L	M	N	O
1	TWS			DLS				TWS				DLS			TWS
2		DWS				TLS				TLS				DWS	
3			DWS				DLS		DLS				DWS		
4	DLS			DWS				DLS				DWS			DLS
5					DWS						DWS				
6		TLS				TLS				TLS				TLS	
7			DLS				DLS A1	L1	DLS P3	A1	C3	A1	DLS		
8	TWS			DLS D2	A1	H4	L1	I1	A1			DLS I1	D2	E1	TWS A1
9			DLS			E1	DLS		DLS				DLS		
10		TLS				TLS X8				TLS				TLS	
11					DWS	A1					DWS				
12	DLS			DWS		D2		DLS				DWS			DLS
13			DWS			E1	DLS		DLS				DWS		
14		DWS				TLS S1				TLS				DWS	
15	TWS			DLS				TWS				DLS			TWS

DIAGRAM 12-18

Beginnings: THR, NON, OVER **Endings:** FUL, HEAD, WN

Find the highest-scoring, playable bingo with each rack that either begins or ends with one of the above combinations of letters. Can you beat our total of 374 points?

1. EEHNRTT
2. AFLNNOY
3. EEORSVY
4. ACEFNOW
5. CEFHLRU

	A	B	C	D	E	F	G	H	I	J	K	L	M	N	O
1	TWS			DLS				TWS				DLS			TWS
2		DWS				TLS				TLS				DWS	
3			DWS				DLS		DLS				DWS		
4	DLS			DWS				DLS				DWS			DLS
5					DWS						DWS				
6		TLS				TLS				TLS				TLS	
7			DLS				DLS		DLS				DLS		
8	TWS			DLS Z10	E1	P3	H4	Y4	R1			DLS			TWS
9			DLS				DLS M3	E1	DLS E1	T1			DLS		
10		TLS				TLS				TLS W4				TLS	
11					DWS					I1	DWS				
12	DLS			DWS				DLS		N1		DWS			DLS
13			DWS				DLS		DLS	E1			DWS		
14		DWS				TLS				TLS D2				DWS	
15	TWS			DLS				TWS				DLS			TWS

DIAGRAM 12-19

Beginnings: CH, EX, IN **Endings:** AL, IA, LY

Find the highest-scoring, playable bingo with each rack that either begins or ends with one of the above combinations of letters. Can you beat our total of 384 points?

1. CHKMNPU
2. AEELRTX
3. GINNORW
4. AGIILOR
5. ADEIILR

A	B	C	D	E	F	G	H	I	J	K	L	M	N	O	
TWS			DLS				TWS				DLS			TWS	1
	DWS				TLS				TLS				DWS		2
		DWS				DLS		DLS				DWS			3
DLS			DWS				DLS				DWS			DLS	4
				DWS		B$_{3}$				DWS					5
	TLS				TLS	O$_{1}$			TLS				TLS		6
		DLS				DLS M$_{3}$		DLS				DLS			7
TWS			DLS T$_{1}$	R$_{1}$	I$_{1}$	B$_{3}$	A$_{1}$	L$_{1}$			DLS			TWS	8
		DLS	O$_{1}$			DLS	M$_{3}$	DLS A$_{1}$	N$_{1}$	H$_{4}$	U$_{1}$	DLS N$_{1}$	T$_{1}$		9
	TLS		P$_{3}$		TLS				TLS				TLS		10
			I$_{1}$	DWS						DWS					11
DLS			DWS C$_{3}$				DLS				DWS			DLS	12
		DWS				DLS		DLS				DWS			13
	DWS				TLS				TLS				DWS		14
TWS			DLS				TWS				DLS			TWS	15

DIAGRAM 12-20

Beginnings: PRE, RE, TW **Endings:** IA, AIL, OUS

Find the highest-scoring, playable bingo with each rack that either begins or ends with one of the above combinations of letters. Can you beat our total of 428 points?

1. AAIMORS
2. AAGHILN
3. DIOSSTU
4. DENORSU
5. GHIILTW

A	B	C	D	E	F	G	H	I	J	K	L	M	N	O	
TWS			DLS				TWS				DLS V			TWS	1
	DWS				TLS				TLS		I		DWS		2
		DWS				DLS		DLS			O	DWS			3
DLS			DWS				DLS				DWS L			DLS	4
				DWS						DWS M	A				5
	TLS				TLS				TLS	U			TLS		6
		DLS	B	O	L	DLS L	O	DLS X		R		DLS			7
TWS			DLS				R	I	S	K	DLS Y			TWS	8
		DLS				DLS		DLS			A	DLS			9
	TLS				TLS				TLS		W		TLS		10
				DWS						DWS	N				11
DLS			DWS				DLS				DWS E			DLS	12
		DWS				DLS		DLS			D	DWS			13
	DWS				TLS				TLS				DWS		14
TWS			DLS				TWS				DLS			TWS	15

DIAGRAM 12-21

Beginnings: SUB, MIS, DIS **Endings:** ISM, IST, ITY

Find the highest-scoring, playable bingo with each rack that either begins or ends with one of the above combinations of letters. Can you beat our total of 478 points?

1. BEILMSU
2. AIMNPSS
3. DEEHILS
4. AEGLRTY
5. ACIISTT

A	B	C	D	E	F	G	H	I	J	K	L	M	N	O	
TWS			DLS				TWS				DLS			TWS	1
	DWS				TLS				TLS				DWS		2
		DWS				DLS		DLS				DWS			3
DLS			DWS				DLS				DWS			DLS	4
				DWS						DWS					5
	TLS				TLS				TLS V$_4$				TLS		6
		DLS				DLS		DLS	I$_1$			DLS			7
TWS			DLS S$_1$	I$_1$	G$_2$	N$_1$	A$_1$	L$_1$	S$_1$		DLS			TWS	8
		DLS				DLS	R$_1$	DLS	I$_1$	F$_4$		DLS			9
	TLS				TLS		R$_1$		TLS T$_1$	O$_1$			TLS		10
				DWS			I$_1$			DWS R$_1$					11
DLS			DWS				DLS V$_4$			G$_2$	DWS O$_1$	W$_4$	K$_5$	DLS	12
		DWS				DLS	I$_1$	DLS		O$_1$		DWS			13
	DWS				TLS		N$_1$		TLS	T$_1$			DWS		14
TWS			DLS				TWS G$_2$				DLS			TWS	15

DIAGRAM 12-22

Beginnings: RE, PRO, UN **Endings:** ISH, BLE, AL

Find the highest-scoring, playable bingo with each rack that either begins or ends with one of the above combinations of letters. Can you beat our total of 442 points?

1. FHILOOS
2. ABEILTU
3. AAEENRW
4. OOPRSSV
5. AEHNNSU

A	B	C	D	E	F	G	H	I	J	K	L	M	N	O	
TWS			DLS				TWS				DLS			TWS	1
	DWS				TLS B$_3$				TLS				DWS		2
		DWS			I$_1$	DLS		DLS				DWS			3
DLS			DWS		O$_1$		DLS				DWS			DLS	4
				DWS	N$_1$					DWS					5
	TLS				TLS I$_1$				TLS P$_3$				TLS		6
		DLS			C$_3$	DLS A$_1$	M$_3$	DLS	U$_1$			DLS			7
TWS			DLS			W$_4$	Y$_4$	N$_1$	D$_2$		DLS			TWS	8
		DLS				DLS		DLS	D$_2$			DLS			9
	TLS				TLS				TLS I$_1$				TLS		10
				DWS					N$_1$	DWS					11
DLS			DWS				DLS		G$_2$		DWS			DLS	12
		DWS				DLS		DLS				DWS			13
	DWS				TLS				TLS				DWS		14
TWS			DLS				TWS				DLS			TWS	15

DIAGRAM 12-23

Beginnings: DE, AB, EM **Endings:** NCE, ER, ING

Find the highest-scoring, playable bingo with each rack that either begins or ends with one of the above combinations of letters. Can you beat our total of 421 points?

1. ACDDEET
2. ALPRTUY
3. ABCEEMR
4. ABCEIRV
5. ADEENNR

TWS			DLS				TWS				DLS			TWS	1
	DWS				TLS				TLS				DWS		2
		DWS				DLS		DLS				DWS			3
DLS			DWS				DLS				DWS			DLS	4
				DWS						DWS					5
	TLS				TLS				TLS				TLS		6
		DLS				DLS		DLS				DLS			7
TWS			DLS N	I	G	H	T			A	DLS X	O	N	TWS E	8
		DLS				DLS O	O	DLS Z	E	D		DLS			9
	TLS				TLS Y	E	P		TLS				TLS		10
			A	DWS D	O					DWS					11
DLS			DWS				DLS				DWS			DLS	12
		DWS				DLS		DLS				DWS			13
	DWS				TLS				TLS				DWS		14
TWS			DLS				TWS				DLS			TWS	15
A	B	C	D	E	F	G	H	I	J	K	L	M	N	O	

DIAGRAM 12-24

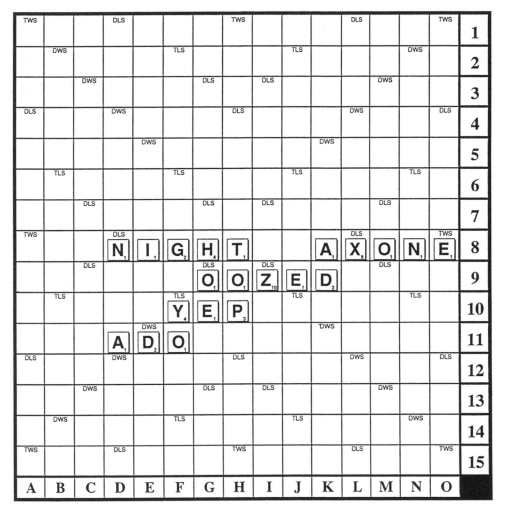

Beginnings: BR, TH, WH **Endings:** GNT, NGE, TH

Find the highest-scoring, playable bingo with each rack that either begins or ends with one of the above combinations of letters. Can you beat our total of 426 points?

1. BDEIMOR
2. EGHINRT
3. EEHNSTV
4. AGHRTTU
5. AAEGNRR

A	B	C	D	E	F	G	H	I	J	K	L	M	N	O	
TWS			DLS				TWS				DLS			TWS	1
	DWS				TLS				TLS				DWS		2
		DWS				DLS		DLS				DWS			3
DLS			DWS				DLS G				DWS			DLS	4
				DWS			L	A	U	DWS G	H				5
	TLS				TLS		I		TLS				TLS		6
		DLS				DLS	M	DLS				DLS			7
TWS			DLS				P				DLS			TWS	8
		DLS				DLS	S	DLS				DLS			9
	TLS		O	U	TLS R	I	E		TLS				TLS		10
				DWS			D	E	V	DWS O	I	D			11
DLS			DWS				DLS				DWS			DLS	12
		DWS				DLS		DLS				DWS			13
	DWS				TLS				TLS				DWS		14
TWS			DLS				TWS				DLS			TWS	15

DIAGRAM 12-25

Beginnings: PRO, THR, UN **Endings:** ANE, IUM, OR

Find the highest-scoring, playable bingo with each rack that either begins or ends with one of the above combinations of letters. Can you beat our total of 371 points?

1. AHRSTWY
2. DFNOPRU
3. AEHINNU
4. AEOORRT
5. AIINTTU

	A	B	C	D	E	F	G	H	I	J	K	L	M	N	O
1	TWS			DLS				TWS				DLS			TWS
2		DWS				TLS				TLS				DWS	
3			DWS				DLS		DLS				DWS		
4	DLS			DWS				DLS				DWS			DLS
5					DWS						DWS				
6		TLS				TLS				TLS				TLS	
7			DLS				DLS A1		DLS				DLS		
8	TWS			DLS H4	U1	L1	L1	O1				DLS			TWS
9			DLS			A1	DLS E1	R1	DLS O1				DLS		
10		TLS				TLS			H4	TLS Y4	P3	E1	D2	TLS	
11					DWS						DWS				
12	DLS			DWS				DLS				DWS			DLS
13			DWS				DLS		DLS				DWS		
14		DWS				TLS				TLS				DWS	
15	TWS			DLS				TWS				DLS			TWS

DIAGRAM 12-26

Beginnings: SUB, RE, DE **Endings:** ENT, LY, OUS

Find the highest-scoring, playable bingo with each rack that either begins or ends with one of the above combinations of letters. Can you beat our total of 392 points?

1. ELNOSTV
2. EEILLSY
3. LOOPSUU
4. BEGMRSU
5. EEIRSTV

A	B	C	D	E	F	G	H	I	J	K	L	M	N	O	
TWS			DLS				TWS				DLS			TWS	1
	DWS				TLS				TLS				DWS		2
		DWS				DLS		DLS				DWS			3
DLS			DWS				DLS				DWS			DLS	4
				DWS						DWS					5
	TLS				TLS				TLS				TLS		6
		DLS				DLS	Q_{10}	DLS				DLS			7
TWS			DLS				U_1	N_1	O_1	P_3	DLS E_1	N_1	E_1	TWS D_2	8
		DLS				DLS	A_1	DLS				DLS			9
	TLS A_1	I_1	R_1	H_4	TLS E_1	A_1	D_2		TLS				TLS		10
				DWS						DWS					11
DLS			DWS				DLS				DWS			DLS	12
		DWS				DLS		DLS				DWS			13
	DWS				TLS				TLS				DWS		14
TWS			DLS				TWS				DLS			TWS	15

DIAGRAM 12-27

Beginnings: CH, IN, MIS **Endings:** AGE, IER, LE

Find the highest-scoring, playable bingo with each rack that either begins or ends with one of the above combinations of letters. Can you beat our total of 406 points?

1. AABLLPY
2. AAEGIMR
3. EGIOORV
4. DEINNOU
5. ACIMMST

TWS			DLS				TWS				DLS			TWS	1
	DWS				TLS				TLS				DWS		2
		DWS				DLS		DLS		M		DWS			3
DLS			DWS				DLS			E	DWS			DLS	4
				DWS						DWS T					5
	TLS				TLS				TLS	R			TLS		6
		DLS				DLS		DLS		I		DLS			7
TWS			DLS				T	R	I	C	DLS K			TWS	8
		DLS	H	E	L	DLS L	O	DLS E	D		N	DLS			9
	TLS				TLS				TLS	B	E		TLS		10
				DWS						DWS A	L				11
DLS			DWS				DLS			I	DWS T			DLS	12
		DWS				DLS		DLS		T		DWS			13
	DWS				TLS				TLS	H			DWS		14
TWS			DLS				TWS				DLS			TWS	15
A	B	C	D	E	F	G	H	I	J	K	L	M	N	O	

DIAGRAM 12-28

Beginnings: AB, FOR, TRI **Endings:** EST, IC, ITY

Find the highest-scoring, playable bingo with each rack that either begins or ends with one of the above combinations of letters. Can you beat our total of 374 points?

1. ABIILTY
2. FGINORV
3. IILNORT
4. ABDLNST
5. ACEIMTT

A	B	C	D	E	F	G	H	I	J	K	L	M	N	O	
TWS			DLS				TWS				DLS			TWS	1
	DWS				TLS				TLS				DWS		2
		DWS				DLS		DLS				DWS			3
DLS			DWS				DLS		O		DWS			DLS	4
				DWS					U	DWS					5
	TLS				TLS				TLS Z				TLS		6
		DLS				DLS		DLS	E			DLS			7
TWS		U	DLS			P	I	L	L	O	DLS W			TWS	8
		DLS V	A	G	U	DLS E		DLS				DLS			9
	TLS	U			TLS				TLS				TLS		10
		L		DWS						DWS					11
DLS		A	DWS				DLS				DWS			DLS	12
		DWS E				DLS		DLS				DWS			13
	DWS				TLS				TLS				DWS		14
TWS			DLS				TWS				DLS			TWS	15

DIAGRAM 12-29

Beginnings: DIS, IM, MON **Endings:** ARD, MAN, TON

Find the highest-scoring, playable bingo with each rack that either begins or ends with one of the above combinations of letters. Can you beat our total of 422 points?

1. AKMMNRS
2. EEKLNST
3. ABDGOPR
4. AILMMRT
5. AMMNOOR

A	B	C	D	E	F	G	H	I	J	K	L	M	N	O	
TWS			DLS				TWS				DLS			TWS	1
	DWS				TLS				TLS				DWS		2
		DWS	D_2			DLS		DLS				DWS			3
DLS			DWS E_1				DLS				DWS			DLS	4
			F_4	DWS						DWS					5
	TLS		L_1		TLS				TLS				TLS		6
		DLS	E_1		V_4	DLS		DLS				DLS			7
TWS			DLS C_3	O_1	U_1	R_1	T_1				DLS			TWS	8
		DLS	T_1		G_2	DLS		DLS				DLS			9
	TLS				TLS H_4				TLS				TLS		10
				DWS						DWS					11
DLS			DWS				DLS				DWS			DLS	12
		DWS				DLS		DLS				DWS			13
	DWS				TLS				TLS				DWS		14
TWS			DLS				TWS				DLS			TWS	15

DIAGRAM 12-30

Beginnings: CH, PRE, UP **Endings:** OUT, RE, RM

Find the highest-scoring, playable bingo with each rack that either begins or ends with one of the above combinations of letters. Can you beat our total of 364 points?

1. ADFPRTU
2. AEPPRRR
3. EFHOORS
4. AEMNRRU
5. CENSTTU

Bingos

DIAGRAM 12-1

1. AIRPLANE D5 70
2. FRUITION 11D 94
3. CONSTANT H6 61
4. NUMBERED 6G 67
5. DESCRIBE 12A 82

TOTAL: 374 POINTS

DIAGRAM 12-2

1. BAILING C7 87
2. DELIRIUM 1F 62
3. DRAMATIC 2B 80
4. OUTTHINK 15E 70
5. ENLIVENS 1F 62

TOTAL: 361 POINTS

DIAGRAM 12-3

1. FOREPLAY 1F 67
2. INWARDLY B8 80
3. MISSPENT K1 74
4. OVERRATE J5 63
5. ABERRANT 4H 72

TOTAL: 356 POINTS

DIAGRAM 12-4

1. MIRTHFUL A5 67
2. ONEROUS M2 74
3. UNAMUSED 13E 63
4. AQUARIUM B4 73
5. REAVOWS M2 92

TOTAL: 369 POINTS

DIAGRAM 12-5

1. ABRASIVE M4 65
2. UNBUTTON 10D 68
3. DOGLIKE 9H 74
4. CUSTARD 15B 103
5. APPROACH L2 90

TOTAL: 400 POINTS

DIAGRAM 12-6

1. PROTRACT C1 80
2. REFASTEN A8 86
3. NONVOTER N7 88
4. SPONSOR 5D 72
5. LOGISTIC 08 86

TOTAL: 412 POINTS

DIAGRAM 12-7

1. OUTBREAK B6 68
2. DISTRUST 11E 86
3. PRAIRIES 4E 72
4. ARRIVAL E3 78
5. TENABLE J6 73

TOTAL: 377 POINTS

DIAGRAM 12-8

1. TOPNOTCH 13G 88
2. SOLOING 7C 77
3. HEADBAND N1 84
4. SHORTAGE O8 89
5. COMATOSE O2 65

TOTAL: 403 POINTS

DIAGRAM 12-9

1. EROSION L6 76
2. VOLATILE 13C 76
3. PRESTIGE 15A 86
4. MISTAKEN 11D 106
5. REMARRY L5 75

TOTAL: 419 POINTS

DIAGRAM 12-10

1. TRIUMPH F2 83
2. IMPLANT 9A 68
3. STRATEGY 2G 78
4. AIRPORT 13G 80
5. JAUNDICE 1H 212

TOTAL: 521 POINTS

DIAGRAM 12-11

1. DELIVERY 5E 80
2. UNASKED 7H 66
3. ARCHIVE 14I 86
4. STUNTMAN H4 61
5. LUCKIEST H1 107

TOTAL: 400 POINTS

DIAGRAM 12-12

1. SHUTDOWN C6 82
2. PAVEMENT E7 80
3. LONGHAND C3 78
4. RELIABLY L1 78
5. UPRISING E6 72

TOTAL: 390 POINTS

DIAGRAM 12-13

1. ENGINEER O7 80
2. HYDROGEN 11E 82
3. MIDSTORY O8 158
4. SIGHTSEE H1 98
5. ERUDITE 15B 89

TOTAL: 507 POINTS

DIAGRAM 12-14

1. GLAMOUR 9B 67
2. HEINOUS M2 79
3. GADABOUT 6F 66
4. OUTLAST 11E 94
5. SUBPOENA 6H 64

TOTAL: 370 POINTS

DIAGRAM 12-15

1. PARABLE N6 89
2. REKINDLE F4 75
3. BINOMIAL E3 74
4. DILEMMA 7B 70
5. PLEASURE D3 72

TOTAL: 380 POINTS

DIAGRAM 12-16

1. GLUCOSE 11E 99
2. INLAYER 11F 82
3. HANDIER K9 87
4. SPINACH F5 85
5. ABSINTH L3 85

TOTAL: 438 POINTS

DIAGRAM 12-17

1. BEFRIEND N8 94
2. CONVERGE 6C 85
3. PREAMBLE 11C 64
4. JETLINER 10C 69
5. ARTIFICE M8 78

TOTAL: 390 POINTS

DIAGRAM 12-18

1. THREATEN 11B 72
2. NONLEAFY 13B 88
3. OVEREASY J2 79
4. FACEDOWN 12B 92
5. CHEERFUL 13C 86

TOTAL: 417 POINTS

DIAGRAM 12-19

1. CHIPMUNK 11H 92
2. EXTERNAL 12E 82
3. INGROWN 7I 67
4. ORIGINAL 12E 72
5. DELIRIA 7H 71

TOTAL: 384 POINTS

DIAGRAM 12-20

1. AMBROSIA 5E 98
2. HANGNAIL M7 82
3. STUDIOUS L7 70
4. REBOUNDS 5E 94
5. TWILIGHT N2 84

TOTAL: 428 POINTS

DIAGRAM 12-21

1. SUBLIME 9B 68
2. MISPLANS F3 70
3. DISHEVEL 1G 95
4. REGALITY 2G 78
5. ACTIVIST 1H 167

TOTAL: 478 POINTS

DIAGRAM 12-22

1. FOOLISH O7 106
2. SUITABLE D8 72
3. REAWAKEN N7 96
4. PROVISOS E4 102
5. UNSHAVEN 6E 66

TOTAL: 442 POINTS

DIAGRAM 12-23

1. DECADENT 11D 98
2. ABRUPTLY 2E 67
3. EMBRACE 9A 74
4. VIBRANCE 11E 110
5. ENDANGER 12E 72

TOTAL: 421 POINTS

DIAGRAM 12-24

1. BROMIDE 12C 93
2. THREADING K4 106
3. SEVENTH 11H 82
4. RETAUGHT O7 64
5. ARRANGE 12B 81

TOTAL: 426 POINTS

DIAGRAM 12-25

1. THRUWAYS E7 84
2. PROFOUND D8 88
3. INHUMANE 7D 65
4. TOREADOR M6 72
5. TITANIUM 7A 62

TOTAL: 371 POINTS

DIAGRAM 12-26

1. SOLVENT 6G 72
2. SLEEPILY K6 76
3. POPULOUS K8 74
4. SUBMERGE L6 82
5. RESTIVE 10A 88

TOTAL: 392 POINTS

DIAGRAM 12-27

1. PLAYABLE N1 92
2. MARRIAGE D8 80
3. GROOVIER D3 76
4. INNUENDO M3 74
5. MISMATCH E3 84

TOTAL: 406 POINTS

DIAGRAM 12-28

1. ABILITY M2 91
2. FORGIVEN 4E 84
3. TRILLION F6 or F5 62
4. BLANDEST E4 94
5. THEMATIC D8 88

TOTAL: 419 POINTS

DIAGRAM 12-29

1. MARKSMAN D3 97
2. SKELETON 4D 76
3. PEGBOARD 13B 67
4. IMMORTAL 4G 80
5. MONOGRAM E5 102

TOTAL: 422 POINTS

DIAGRAM 12-30

1. UPDRAFT 7H 72
2. PREPARER 4B 63
3. OFFSHORE 5C or 5B 84
4. UNDERARM 3B 80
5. CHESTNUT 10E 65

TOTAL: 364 POINTS

PART FOUR

Making the Ideal Play

It's one thing to be able to find the highest-scoring play. It's another to find the best play. The following chapters will give you an in-depth look and a great deal of practice at how to do so.

After finishing the following pages, I hope you'll agree with me that each game position is a unique puzzle that has the potential to excite, dazzle, and command your curiosity and devotion to this wonderful game.

CHAPTER 13

A Practical Guide for Choosing the Ideal Play

Before reading further, take a minute or two to look at the following position and ask yourself what would you play if it was your turn.

A	B	C	D	E	F	G	H	I	J	K	L	M	N	O	
TWS			DLS				TWS				DLS			TWS	1
	DWS				TLS				TLS				DWS		2
		DWS				DLS		DLS				DWS			3
DLS			DWS				DLS				DWS			DLS	4
				DWS						DWS					5
	TLS				TLS				TLS				TLS		6
		DLS				DLS B_3		DLS				DLS			7
TWS			DLS V_4	A_1	L_1	O_1	R_1				DLS			TWS	8
		DLS				DLS G_2		DLS				DLS			9
	TLS				TLS				TLS				TLS		10
				DWS						DWS					11
DLS			DWS				DLS				DWS			DLS	12
		DWS				DLS		DLS				DWS			13
	DWS				TLS				TLS				DWS		14
TWS			DLS				TWS				DLS			TWS	15

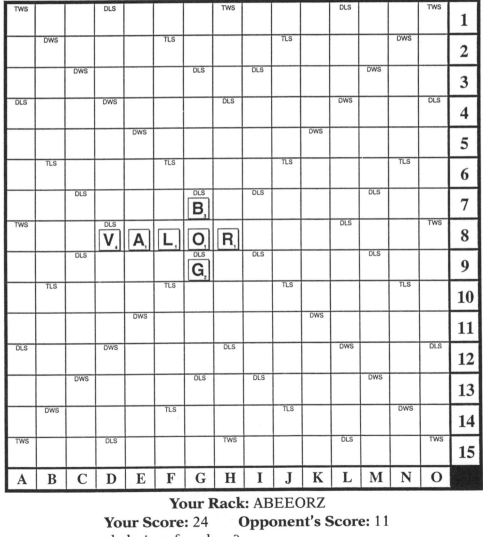

Your Rack: ABEEORZ

Your Score: 24 **Opponent's Score:** 11

What are some good choices for plays?

Now that you have some choices, the question and answer I'd like to discuss this chapter is: How did you arrive at your choices? See the end of this chapter for further analysis of this position. But don't look yet, you may change your mind after reading further.

There are literally hundreds of choices for words you can make in most situations during a typical SCRABBLE® crossword game. The player's task is to find a "good" play in a reasonably short time. How do we do that?

In this chapter I will present a method that is effective in helping you develop reasonable choices quickly. How well it serves you will depend on your ability to practice each element. Since you're probably going to be playing the game (otherwise, why are you reading this?), why not try it out when you have the chance? You may be surprised at how your thoughts may seem to develop more clarity and focus as you practice.

Please keep in mind that, in theory, the ideal play is the play that gives you the best chance to win the game.

DEVELOP THE HABIT OF ASKING YOURSELF QUESTIONS:

The very first thing to do when looking for the ideal play is to ask yourself a series of questions silently in your mind. Take a certain amount of time to answer each question and then go on to the next question. Many players get into the habit of simply looking at their rack and trying to find words, or looking at the board and trying to find places to play, without a definite purpose behind their search. While this method may sometimes delight you with a surprising high-scoring play on occasion, much like finding a $20 bill on the sidewalk, you won't necessarily develop the skills to make these "finds" a more frequent experience.

Question 1: Do I have a bingo?

In most circumstances, playing a bingo is going to give you the best chance to win. It follows that developing the ability to find more bingos will enhance your winning chances. We've already shown you in Chapter 12 how to look for bingos. If you practice with the diagrams therein and whenever you play, you will watch your skills grow.

What follows is a short list that will help you focus on the common word beginnings and endings. When you have at least one high-point tile: **Use your high-point tile to help lead you to find the common beginnings and endings of words. Use the letters L, N, R, S, and T to combine with the high-point tiles to form common combinations of letters.** The high-point tiles (worth three points or more) generally have a distinct pattern in the way they appear in seven- and eight-letter words. If you practice thinking of several words that start or end with each of these combinations of letters, you're more likely to remember these combinations during a game.

B: AB-, BE-, BI-, BL-, BR-; -MB, -BLE
C: CH-, CL-, COM-, CON-, CR-, SC-; -CH, -CK, -CLE, -ENCE, -CT, -IC
F: FL-, FR-, FOR; -FIE(D,R,S) -FY, -FLE, -FF, -LF, -RF, -FT, -FUL, -FORM
H: CH-, HEAD-, HAND-, PH-, SH-, TH-, WH-; -GH(T), -PH, -(I)SH
J: J-
K: KN-, SK-; -CK, -LK, -NK, -RK, -SK, -KLE
M: EM-, MIS-, SM-; -LM, -MB, -MP, -RM, -(I)SM, -(I)UM
P: PH-, PL-, PR(E,O,), SP-; -MP, -RP, -LP, -PT
Q: AQU-, QU-, SQU-; -QUE
V: OVER-; -LVE, -RVE, -IVE
W: SW-, TW-, WH-, WR-; -WD, -WISE, -WL, -WN, -WOOD, -WORM, -WORK
X: AX-, EX, OX-; -(B)OX; -XT
Y: -ARY, -BOY, -DAY, -ITY, -(I)LY, -LOGY
Z: -IZE, -ZLE, -ZEL, -TZ

Also keep in mind the following hints: When you have a D or G, always look for -ED and -ING as well as -AGE and DG combos. Use the R most often with RE- or -ER. The N is often used as ING, IN, EN, AN, and very frequently as UN-. The L combines well with almost all other consonants (the N being an exception), while the T is often seen with OUT, -NT, -TIC, TH-. Please refer to the beginnings and endings used in Chapter 12 for more ideas on which letters combine well together.

Here is a list of 10 letters. ABCEFILNTV. Let's say you want to find all the seven- and eight-letter words spellable with just these letters. Using the above list, which beginnings and endings would you check out first? See the end of the chapter for the answers.

Question 2: Which double- and triple-word-score bonus squares are available and onto which double- and triple-letter-score squares can I play my high-point tiles?

Take a look at each row and column, one by one, to see which bonus squares are available. Once you find one, look for your highest-scoring play using it. Then look for another play that covers it but gives you a superior leave, if that's possible. Then go on to the next bonus square. To ensure that you're being thorough, make sure you know the two-letter words. For instance, look back at Diagram 13-1 on page 193. In order to know that the F6 and F10 TLSs are available, you need to know that AB and AG are acceptable words. These sorts of openings happen frequently each game. Unless you know the twos, you'll be missing some of your best opportunities for large scores.

Question 3: Can you "hook" any words? Look at every word already on the board and ask yourself if any single letter can be added to the front or back to form another word.

If ARM is on the board, you might hook an H in front, forming HARM, and then play perpendicular to form another word. Hooking can effectively double your scores on any given play. While the S is by far the best hook letter, don't forget that many other letters can be hooked as well. For instance, many common words end in Y, such as HAND (Y), MAN (Y), DEAR (Y), HEART (Y). Many words ending in E are verbs and take a D or R: BAKE, PALE or DANCE.

Question 4: What will my "leave" be after I've made my play?

At this point you have found several potential plays. Now determine what letters you'll have left after each of these plays. That's called the "leave." Your ideal leave will consist of no high-point tiles and an equal number of consonants and vowels, or just one more consonant than vowel. The best one-point consonants to keep, from best to worst, are SRNTL, while the best vowels are E, followed by A, I, O, and U. Note that there are exceptions. If you can't use the X well, but can get rid of five other tiles, keeping the X is not a bad idea. It's often worth it.

Question 5A: Will my play change the board to give many more scoring opportunities, many fewer opportunities, or will it keep the board with about as many "hot spots" as right now? A "hot spot" is an area on the board that with the right letters can earn many points.

Question 5B: How far ahead or behind am I?

Let's look at some examples of why these two questions can be so important and are linked together.

1. More than 60 tiles are on the board. Now, imagine you're ahead by 30 points and you have a choice between a 35-point play, BRAVE and a 25-point play, VERB. Let's say that the leaves in each case are about equal. Let's also say that BRAVE creates two new bingo lines for your opponent. Looking at VERB, you notice that it doesn't create any new open lines, although it doesn't take away the one good bingo line open already. Normally, with equal leaves, you'd jump to take the extra 10 points for BRAVE, but since you're going to be up 55 points with VERB, while making it very much more difficult for your oppo-

nent to play a bingo (compared to BRAVE), I'd recommend playing it safe with VERB.

2. Imagine you're now behind by 70. You're trying to decide between a 35-point play FLAYED, keeping S, or FORTY for 28, keeping ADELS. Neither play opens or blocks bingos, and there are already two bingo lines open for S-hooks. Here you have a significantly better chance for a bingo with ADELS, so forgo the extra points and play FORTY for 28. That's because you'll probably need a bingo to win this game. If you didn't need the bingo so badly—that is, if the score was much closer or you were ahead—you might have wanted to play FLAYED.

These two situations show that noticing both the number of hot spots and the score together can give you data you can use to optimize your winning chances.

Question 6: What tiles are left to be played?

If you want to enhance your winning chances, it's important to keep track of what tiles haven't been played yet. For instance, if neither blank has been played, the scores are about even and the game half over, you're going to want to sacrifice a few points in order to play five or six tiles per turn. The blanks can be vitally important in deciding the winner of a close game. To avoid duplication, if there are 3 N's left to play and only one T, consider saving a T (usually a weaker letter) instead of the N.

Question 7: Has your opponent given you any information, either through his recent play(s) or other "tells" that might influence your thinking?

"Tells" are behaviors that indicate a player's state of mind. Expert poker players use their ability to see others' "tells" to let them know how and when to bluff. Since each player is different, you'll have to learn what they are by trial and error.

But it won't be so hard to use them. For instance, if you've learned that a player always shakes his head a certain way when he has very bad tiles, you can use that knowledge to let you know whether it's right to create more openings or shut them down. A word of warning: Many players who are aware of their own tells will occasionally fool you purposefully, so don't rely on this method too much.

To use your opponent's play to guide you, consider the following two examples:

1. Suppose your opponent, an expert player, has just played off five tiles, CORDS, for 15 points. It's highly likely that s/he has another S on his rack.

Why? Because an S is usually too valuable to waste for just 15 points. If you feel confident s/he has another S, try to use that knowledge to give you better chances to win. For instance, after CORDS is played, if the score is nearly even, and if the board is wide open with many bingo spots, and only one other S is left to be drawn, make sure you do one or more of the following three things: (1) play as many tiles off as possible to try to draw the last S. (2) Keep bingo-prone tiles. You may need to play a bingo to win if your opponent has one in the next few turns. (3) Start blocking the bingo lines—but not at the expense of scoring really well. You need to overcome your opponent's good fortune by scoring well, but you need to begin to block his/her most likely bingo lines simultaneously. Keep in mind that your opponent may not bingo and s/he may still win. Also remember that you aren't in control of what your opponent may do, so continuing to score well is your number one priority.

2. Your expert opponent's last two plays were both for 10 points using two vowels each time. There are several bingo spots open. Based on these last two plays, you can expect that s/he may bingo very soon. If you don't yet have any chances for bingos because of poor tiles, try creating an opening for one of the remaining high-point tiles, an X, for instance. Even if you don't have the X now, your opponent will be very unlikely to have it (Fishing usually entails getting rid of high-point tiles—so your opponent will only have the X if it was one of the two tiles s/he just drew.), and you may draw it first. A 52-point X-play (simultaneously using a TLS horizontally and vertically) can take the sting out of an opponent's upcoming bingo. Such a play can take advantage of the fact that your opponent will play in another part of the board with his/her bingo and you'll have your opening untouched.

These are but two of the ways you can use information your opponent's plays give you to increase your winning chances.

Question 8: What's your own internal state and how well are you processing information? Can you bring yourself to a state of intense curiosity and creativity?

Disregarding for the moment any SCRABBLE® word-finding, strategic, or vocabulary skills, it's been my experience that there are six key factors to winning SCRABBLE® Brand Crossword games:

1. Tune out distractions.
2. Forget and forgive yourself for any past mistakes or losses.
3. Be neutral to how "good" or "bad" your tiles are.
4. Bring your emotional state to an intense curiosity about what the best play is.

5. On occasion use your creativity to bend the rules of traditional theory.
6. Manifest intense desire to find a legitimate and fair way to win the game.

To whatever degree you can fulfill these factors, that will to some degree determine how well you succeed. There are no absolute rules for achieving these six factors, so I suggest you experiment with your own personal creative style. For example: During crucial tournament games, I often take an inventory of my emotions to make sure I'm following my own rules. When I'm losing a game (but not lost yet), it's often the case that my state of mind is still somewhat depressed because of a rack a few turns prior for which I couldn't find any satisfactory play. Whatever play I made seemed less than the best. Thereafter, I had a nagging feeling that I had missed a better play. This insecure feeling would interfere in future decisions, so that every future play would be somewhat tainted with the thought that it wasn't the best. With this loss of confidence, I know I won't make my best plays. I've seen this happen to others as well.

So, by using previously practiced resources to adjust my state as soon as possible, I can return to a positive, creative and energetic mode. Thereafter, I invariably play my best and often win games I otherwise would have lost.

Now that you've learned the eight categories of questions to ask yourself each turn—BINGOS, BONUS SQUARES, HOOKS, LEAVE, BOARD POSITION and SCORE, TILES REMAINING, OPPONENT'S PLAY, and EMOTIONS, you're ready to streamline these questions to quicken your pace and find the Ideal Play.

Keep in mind that while this check list may seem cumbersome, most of the time many of the items will be taken care of quickly.

Let's see how this can work for you with the following racks:

1. Your rack is AEMORRV. You don't immediately see a bingo, but you notice the -ER or RE- combination. But before you check out these combinations, you notice the V, and in keeping with the philosophy of using the high-point tiles to guide you, you remember that the V can be used with the beginning OVER-. After a few tries, you see OVERARM, and can open the game with the V on the DLS for 82 points. The remaining six items on the checklist are irrelevant. **Time used:** 30 seconds.
2. You have ABBDLNT. You realize, correctly, that you can't play a bingo. Looking for bonus squares, you see two DWSs and a TLS to play across, but only one with a vowel to use, an E. Knowing you have BLE or ED makes your word search easy. There are no usable hooks. You can play DABBLE for 16, leaving no extra hooks, or TABBED for 18 (which does leave the S-hook for STABBED) or NABBED, also for 18, and rid yourself of all but the NT or LN

or LT. DABBLE is your choice over TABBED because the NT is a much more potent combination, and two points is a minor sacrifice. However, upon further reflection, the LT combination is also a good one and so you decide to take the extra two points after all by playing NABBED. **Time used:** 2 minutes.

3. The board is wide open and you have ACDEGGH. You don't see a bingo, but you see plenty of bonus squares open. How do you narrow down your search to find the highest-scoring play in the quickest amount of time? Look first for TWSs. Failing their availability, look for TLS-DWS combinations while imagining your H or then C being placed on the TLS square. Keep looking at other bonus squares until you find a TWS or DLS for your H or C while also covering a DWS. It's by using two bonus squares that you'll reap the most points. Finally you see an E on M7 that you can use to start a word played vertically. With your letters in alphabetical order, EGG is staring at you, but it takes a while for you to realize that you still have an E to use, and EGGHEAD reaches the DWS with the G on the DLS for 32 points. Not bad, since it uses six tiles for a great score and even blocks the board. **Time used:** 6 minutes.

The key to using the concept of the Ideal Play is that whenever you ask yourself one of the questions about finding your best play, you always start by imagining that the Ideal Play exists, and that all you need to do is find it. At each question, if, after a thorough search, you don't find the Ideal Play, instead of disappointment, simply move on to the next question, full of curiosity, and imagine that the best and most Ideal Play is possible, and look for it.

Finding the Ideal Play Via Computer

Hasbro Interactive has a new SCRABBLE® CD-ROM computer game (screen name "Maven") that's sold at most electronic shops. This program enables you to play against the computer at many different skill levels, from novice to expert. It also allows you to play anyone in the world via modem. But one of its unique features is that it has a built-in simulation program that allows you to test simultaneously up to ten different plays for any given position. As the computer doesn't care who's ahead, it only calculates how many points any given play is worth. This point value is only a relative term. That means it will only have meaning when compared to the other plays simulated. This means that after 5,000 trials, if WEAR is worth 35.00 points and WORD is worth 32.45 points, then by playing WEAR you'll be earning an extra 2.55 points more, in the long run, than you would if you play WORD.

Here is how the simulation (or "sim" hereafter) works. Using the above WEAR and WORD example: The computer will play WEAR and then draw seven random tiles for the opponent and make its best play. This is followed by the computer drawing replacement tiles for WEAR and making another play for you. Now the computer will evaluate your subsequent rack leave by assigning it a value based upon the value of each letter in the leave. All these scores are computed and then the same thing is done with the first play being WORD. That being finished, one sim is complete, and the program will print a point value for each play, WEAR and WORD. This whole sequence may take one second or less.

As you watch the screen the values change rapidly at first, and often different plays may be valued higher or lower. After several hundred to 3,000 sims, the values will usually become stable. When this happens, the resulting numbers are fairly accurate. In the above case, with a difference of 2.55, assuming the position occurs in the first 60 percent of the game, I'd be nearly always confident that WEAR is the better play. With sim differences greater than 1 point, the values of the plays are probably +80 percent accurate. With differences greater than 3 points, in my opinion, the accuracy rises to +98 percent. With differences less than 1 point, there can still be some debate, and other factors may enter the argument.

An additional feature of Maven is that when there are no tiles to be drawn, and both sides' tiles are known, the endgame player plays nearly perfectly, and so you can have perfect knowledge for any endgame as to who should win with best play.

Since the invention of the SCRABBLE simulation program, many expert players have been rethinking their own strategy rules on the basis of the results from this program. As a testament to the program, I can personally say that it works, and works exceedingly well. My own strategic guidelines have changed enormously after using this program. And my tournament results have shown the changes to be an improvement. I judge that since my results have been so good, and that most everyone else has continued to improvc their word knowledge while mine has stayed the same or even weakened somewhat, it is most likely the changing strategy component that has made the primary difference in my results.

Please note: While the simulation program is a crossword game analyst's godsend, it is not infallible. In fact, there are many situations when you absolutely shouldn't believe the results. Therein lies the beauty and continuing fascination with the game. Maven (as the program is sometimes called) is only programmed to analyze for points, not winning chances. There are many situations when you don't care whether you win by 100 points or 3, you just want to win. The conflict usually happens in two different types of situations:

1. In the latter half of the game. At this point, both the board configuration and the remaining tiles to be played are so important to the outcome of the game that often the computer's results will be skewed incorrectly. Near the end of the game, when you are ahead by 55 points, you don't need to make a 35-point play if it opens a bingo line when you can make a 10-point play instead and shut down all potential bingo lines. By making the 10-point play you can ensure the win 99 percent of the time. The other play may earn you more points in the long run, but it may only win 80 percent of the time.

   This inaccuracy in sim results is debatable on a position-to-position basis, since, in many positions, there is no unusual board-configuration feature that seems to detract from the Maven simulation. So it's not a trivial exercise to understand when Maven is wrong. Please keep in mind that while the simulation data is important, even the best players are not always certain how.
2. Since Maven draws seven random tiles for the opponent, if you have any indication that your opponent may have certain tiles, any simulation will be off the mark. For instance, if you think your opponent has an S, then a simulation result shouldn't be relied upon for best results. Furthermore, since most everyone is trying to save their best tiles each play, most opponents will have better than a random rack on any turn they've just made a one-, two-, or three-tile fishing play. In such cases the simulation will also be more inaccurate.

Because of these conflicts in reaching accurate simulation results, it has become somewhat of an art form to interpret the data. That makes it endlessly fascinating, so far!

There's one more question I'd like to answer regarding simulations: Human players are fallible, don't think like computers, and certainly don't know all the words. Won't that make sim results, which includes knowing and seeing all the words, quite inaccurate in the real world? Why bother to study simulations at all if we know that our opponents won't make the best plays most of the time?

Answer: Since the best players tend to play more like the computer than most other players, the sim results will help you to improve your play against these top players. What you'll also find is that the more accurately you play, the higher your average score will be against average players, and the more games you'll win. Against most players it will help you to be aware of their weaknesses and use that info to play counter to the sim results at appropriate times. Which times are those? You must use your own experience to determine that.

Furthermore, there is at least one rule of thumb I've discovered from simulations: Let's call it Simulation Principle 1 (SP1):

When you have a choice of plays that earn about the same score (0–5

points difference), and one keeps a good leave but opens the board up, while the other keeps a poor leave but blocks the board, countless sims show that it's worth more points to you to open the board for the good leave.

This principle will apply best only in the first half of the game. Other considerations become more important in the latter half of the game. This also assumes that you know enough words and are capable of finding them. Otherwise, the novice should almost always play defensively against the expert. When do you know enough words? Only your personal experience can suggest that for you.

Answers to ABCEFILNTV: Here are the most potent beginnings and endings: AN-, BI-, BL-, EN-, FL-, IN-, V-; -ABLE, -ANT, -ATE, -CLE, -CT, -ENT, -IAL, -IC, -INE, -ITE, -TIVE, -TLE. There are actually nine acceptable words, though many are obscure: BIVALENT, CABINET, CITABLE, FINABLE, FLAVINE, INFLATE, INFLECT, VENATIC, VENTAIL. How many did you find?

Analysis of the ABEEORZ Rack:

There are no bingos available. Next, note that there are no hooks you can add. Thirdly, look at rows 7, 8, and 9, followed by columns D–H. If you found ZAREEBA E7 36 points, or BEZOAR E4 34 points, congratulations, you're probably among the .01 percent of the population that could. Perhaps you noticed ZOEA E5 26 (ABER). That's a terrific play because the leave is so good. But if you decided upon LAZE F8 36 points, then you're even better! That's because LAZE simulates as a significantly higher-scoring play in the long run than either ZAREEBA or BEZOAR (99 percent accuracy). The main reason for that is because the BEOR leave is much more likely to produce a much better play next turn than the O or AE leave after either of the other two plays. Why? Because with BEOR you already have a good start at a great rack. It doesn't much matter what your last three tiles are—even if they're horrible, you'll still have a decent play. Whereas, after drawing to an O or an AE, in a thousand trials, you will have a horrible rack a definite percentage of thc timc, and your scores at those times will reflect it.

The secondary reason to play LAZE is that it's simply the highest-scoring play of any other alternatives not mentioned here. It's too many more points than ZOEA. The BEOR leave is slightly less attractive than the ABER leave after ZOEA, but not 10 points' worth. A third reason in favor of LAZE is that if you draw a T, you may play ABBOT 7E 30 points. How did you, or could you, find LAZE quickly during a game? Answer: by simply looking at column F, knowing that only an A would play on F9, deciding that there might be a word with the Z on F10, and looking for it with the remaining letters on your rack.

CHAPTER 14

Actual Game Positions: Your Move!

Here's a chance to see real game action. The final 50 diagrams in this book show game situations that occurred between two opponents. None of these situations are made up.

It's up to you to find the "best play." Very few of these plays are considered "spectacular," in the same way that a few of the setup plays of earlier diagrams would be. These are simply typical positions that occur between two good players.

So far we've focused on finding the highest-scoring play. While it's important to be able to find the highest-scoring play if you want to win, it's even more important to know when to play it or when to play a lesser-scoring play.

Take about 5 to 10 minutes with each of the following positions and use the ideas expressed in the previous chapter to find your best play. Then check out the answers and discover what the author thinks about each position and read the computer simulation results.

Author's disclaimer: While I've used the phrase "best play," I don't claim that the answers provided are the absolute best plays to make against all of your human opponents. What I mean by "best play" more closely resembles how two top-flight champions ought to play against each other. With less-than-perfect opponents other considerations might make it more advisable to make different plays occasionally.

A	B	C	D	E	F	G	H	I	J	K	L	M	N	O	
TWS			DLS				TWS				DLS			TWS	1
	DWS				TLS				TLS				DWS		2
		DWS				DLS		DLS				DWS			3
DLS			DWS				DLS				DWS			DLS	4
				DWS						DWS					5
	TLS				TLS				TLS				TLS		6
		DLS				DLS		DLS				DLS			7
TWS			DLS								DLS			TWS	8
		DLS				DLS		DLS				DLS			9
	TLS				TLS				TLS				TLS		10
				DWS						DWS					11
DLS			DWS				DLS				DWS			DLS	12
		DWS				DLS		DLS				DWS			13
	DWS				TLS				TLS				DWS		14
TWS			DLS				TWS				DLS			TWS	15

DIAGRAM 14-1

It's the first play of the game. You're first. First consider Rack 1 and decide what play you would make. Then start again with an empty board and imagine your first rack is Rack 2. What would you play?

RACK 1: ADHLNRT **Score:** 0–0
RACK 2: AFLNTUW
What's your best play?

A	B	C	D	E	F	G	H	I	J	K	L	M	N	O	
TWS			DLS				TWS				DLS			TWS	1
	DWS				TLS				TLS				DWS		2
		DWS				DLS		DLS				DWS			3
DLS			DWS				DLS				DWS			DLS	4
				DWS						DWS					5
	TLS				TLS				TLS				TLS		6
		DLS				DLS		DLS				DLS			7
TWS			DLS B$_3$	I$_1$	O$_1$	G$_2$	E$_1$	N$_1$	Y$_4$		DLS			TWS	8
		DLS				DLS		DLS				DLS			9
	TLS				TLS				TLS				TLS		10
				DWS						DWS					11
DLS			DWS				DLS				DWS			DLS	12
		DWS				DLS		DLS				DWS			13
	DWS				TLS				TLS				DWS		14
TWS			DLS				TWS				DLS			TWS	15

DIAGRAM 14-2

Your Rack: AEHIJPW **Score:** 0–82

What's your best play?

A	B	C	D	E	F	G	H	I	J	K	L	M	N	O	
TWS			DLS				TWS				DLS			TWS	1
	DWS				TLS				TLS				DWS		2
		DWS				DLS		DLS				DWS			3
DLS			DWS				DLS				DWS			DLS	4
				DWS						DWS					5
	TLS				TLS				TLS				TLS		6
		DLS				DLS		DLS				DLS			7
TWS			DLS F	O	E	H	N				DLS			TWS	8
		DLS				DLS		DLS				DLS			9
	TLS				TLS				TLS				TLS		10
				DWS						DWS					11
DLS			DWS				DLS				DWS			DLS	12
		DWS				DLS		DLS				DWS			13
	DWS				TLS				TLS				DWS		14
TWS			DLS				TWS				DLS			TWS	15

DIAGRAM 14-3

Your Rack: EEEGHIT **Score:** 0–30
What's your best play?

A	B	C	D	E	F	G	H	I	J	K	L	M	N	O	
TWS			DLS				TWS				DLS			TWS	1
	DWS				TLS				TLS				DWS		2
		DWS				DLS		DLS				DWS			3
DLS			DWS	L (1)			DLS				DWS			DLS	4
				DWS I (1)						DWS					5
	TLS			Q (10)	TLS				TLS				TLS		6
		DLS		U (1)		DLS		DLS				DLS			7
TWS			DLS D (2)	O (1)	D (2)	G (2)	E (1)	R (1)	S (1)		DLS			TWS	8
		DLS		R (1)		DLS		DLS				DLS			9
	TLS				TLS				TLS				TLS		10
				DWS						DWS					11
DLS			DWS				DLS				DWS			DLS	12
		DWS				DLS		DLS				DWS			13
	DWS				TLS				TLS				DWS		14
TWS			DLS				TWS				DLS			TWS	15

DIAGRAM 14-4

Your Rack: ACEFKOT **Score:** 74–30

What's your best play?

A	B	C	D	E	F	G	H	I	J	K	L	M	N	O	
TWS			DLS				TWS				DLS			TWS	1
	DWS				TLS				TLS				DWS		2
		DWS		P_3		DLS		DLS				DWS			3
DLS			DWS	R_1			DLS				DWS			DLS	4
				DWS E_1						DWS					5
	TLS			V_4	TLS				TLS				TLS		6
		DLS		E_1		DLS		DLS				DLS			7
TWS			DLS A_1	N_1	U_1	R_1	A_1	N_1			DLS			TWS	8
		DLS		T_1		DLS		DLS				DLS			9
	TLS				TLS				TLS				TLS		10
				DWS						DWS					11
DLS			DWS				DLS				DWS			DLS	12
		DWS				DLS		DLS				DWS			13
	DWS				TLS				TLS				DWS		14
TWS			DLS				TWS				DLS			TWS	15

DIAGRAM 14-5

Your Rack: EIIMNOS **Score:** 14–24

What's your best play?

A	B	C	D	E	F	G	H	I	J	K	L	M	N	O	
TWS			DLS				TWS				DLS			TWS	1
	DWS				TLS				TLS				DWS		2
		DWS				DLS		DLS				DWS			3
DLS			DWS				DLS				DWS			DLS	4
				DWS						DWS					5
	TLS				TLS				TLS				TLS		6
		DLS				DLS		DLS				DLS			7
TWS			DLS			K$_5$	O$_1$	P$_3$			DLS			TWS	8
	L$_1$	DLS O$_1$	R$_1$	I$_1$	C$_3$	DLS A$_1$		DLS				DLS			9
	TLS				TLS				TLS				TLS		10
				DWS						DWS					11
DLS			DWS				DLS				DWS			DLS	12
		DWS				DLS		DLS				DWS			13
	DWS				TLS				TLS				DWS		14
TWS			DLS				TWS				DLS			TWS	15

DIAGRAM 14-6

Your Rack: MNOPSTU **Score:** 18–17
What's your best play?

	A	B	C	D	E	F	G	H	I	J	K	L	M	N	O
1	TWS			DLS				TWS				DLS			TWS
2		DWS				TLS				TLS				DWS	
3			DWS				DLS		DLS				DWS		
4	DLS			DWS				DLS				DWS			DLS
5					DWS						DWS				
6		TLS				TLS				TLS				TLS	
7			DLS				DLS		DLS				DLS		
8	TWS			DLS			T$_1$	U$_1$	N$_1$	E$_1$	D$_2$	DLS			TWS
9			DLS				DLS		DLS		J$_8$		DLS		
10		TLS				TLS				TLS	I$_1$			TLS	
11					DWS						DWS N$_1$				
12	DLS			DWS				DLS				DWS			DLS
13			DWS				DLS		DLS				DWS		
14		DWS				TLS				TLS				DWS	
15	TWS			DLS				TWS				DLS			TWS

DIAGRAM 14-7

Your Rack: ENOTW?? **Score:** 8–30
What's your best play?

	A	B	C	D	E	F	G	H	I	J	K	L	M	N	O
1	TWS			DLS				TWS				DLS			TWS
2		DWS				TLS				TLS				DWS	
3			DWS				DLS		DLS				DWS		
4	DLS			DWS				DLS				DWS			DLS
5					DWS B						DWS				
6		TLS W	A	V	E	TLS Y				TLS				TLS	
7			DLS		G		DLS		DLS				DLS		
8	TWS			DLS H	O	S	T	A	G	E		DLS			TWS
9			DLS		N		DLS		DLS				DLS		
10		TLS			E	TLS H				TLS				TLS	
11					DWS	O					DWS				
12	DLS			DWS		R		DLS				DWS			DLS
13			DWS			N	DLS		DLS				DWS		
14		DWS				TLS E				TLS				DWS	
15	TWS			DLS		T		TWS				DLS			TWS

DIAGRAM 14-8

Your Rack: DDIINPU **Score:** 110–50
What's your best play?

	A	B	C	D	E	F	G	H	I	J	K	L	M	N	O
1	TWS			DLS				TWS				DLS			TWS
2		DWS				TLS				TLS				DWS	
3			DWS				DLS		DLS W	O	F	U	DWS L		
4	DLS			DWS				DLS				DWS M			DLS
5					DWS						DWS	P			
6		TLS				TLS				TLS		I		TLS	
7			DLS				DLS		DLS			R	DLS		
8	TWS			DLS			L	E	V	Y		DLS E			TWS
9			DLS				DLS		DLS	U	N	S	DLS		
10		TLS				TLS				TLS M	A			TLS	
11					DWS						DWS W				
12	DLS			DWS				DLS				DWS			DLS
13			DWS				DLS		DLS				DWS		
14		DWS				TLS				TLS				DWS	
15	TWS			DLS				TWS				DLS			TWS

DIAGRAM 14-9

Your Rack: AGJNNNU **Score:** 101–60

What's your best play?

	A	B	C	D	E	F	G	H	I	J	K	L	M	N	O
1	TWS			DLS				TWS				DLS			TWS
2		DWS				TLS				TLS				DWS	
3			DWS				DLS		DLS				DWS		
4	DLS			DWS				DLS				DWS			DLS
5					DWS						DWS				
6		TLS				TLS				TLS				TLS	
7			DLS				DLS		DLS				DLS		
8	TWS P	R	E	DLS V	A	I	L	E	D			DLS			TWS
9			DLS		U		DLS		DLS				DLS		
10		TLS			R	TLS				TLS				TLS	
11					DWS E						DWS				
12	DLS			DWS M	I			DLS				DWS			DLS
13			DWS X	I			DLS		DLS				DWS		
14		DWS	U	M		TLS				TLS				DWS	
15	TWS			DLS				TWS				DLS			TWS

DIAGRAM 14-10

Your Rack: HINNTTY **Score:** 50–95
What's your best play?

A	B	C	D	E	F	G	H	I	J	K	L	M	N	O	
TWS			DLS				TWS				DLS			TWS	1
	DWS				TLS				TLS				DWS		2
		DWS	B_3			DLS		DLS				DWS			3
DLS	S_1	A_1	DWS R_1	K_5	I_1	E_1	DLS S_1	T_1			DWS			DLS	4
			I_1	DWS						DWS					5
	TLS		T_1		TLS O_1				TLS				TLS		6
		DLS	T_1		U_1	DLS		DLS				DLS			7
TWS			DLS L_1	O_1	N_1	G_2	E_1				DLS			TWS	8
		DLS	E_1		C_3	DLS O_1	X_8	DLS				DLS			9
	TLS		R_1		TLS E_1				TLS				TLS		10
				DWS						DWS					11
DLS			DWS				DLS				DWS			DLS	12
		DWS				DLS		DLS				DWS			13
	DWS				TLS				TLS				DWS		14
TWS			DLS				TWS				DLS			TWS	15

DIAGRAM 14-11

Your Rack: AEIMNPR **Score:** 86–107

What's your best play?

TWS			DLS				TWS				DLS			TWS	1
	DWS			U	TLS				TLS				DWS		2
		DWS C	O	V	E	DLS Y		DLS				DWS			3
DLS			DWS	E			DLS				DWS			DLS	4
				DWS A	A					DWS					5
	TLS				TLS R				TLS				TLS		6
		DLS			O	DLS		DLS				DLS			7
TWS			DLS V	A	U	L	T				DLS			TWS	8
		DLS			N	DLS		DLS				DLS			9
	TLS				TLS D				TLS				TLS		10
				DWS						DWS					11
DLS			DWS				DLS				DWS			DLS	12
		DWS				DLS		DLS				DWS			13
	DWS				TLS				TLS				DWS		14
TWS			DLS				TWS				DLS			TWS	15
A	B	C	D	E	F	G	H	I	J	K	L	M	N	O	

DIAGRAM 14-12

Your Rack: ADDEEXU **Score:** 42–47
What's your best play?

	A	B	C	D	E	F	G	H	I	J	K	L	M	N	O
1	TWS			DLS				TWS				DLS			TWS
2		DWS				TLS				TLS				DWS	
3			DWS				DLS		DLS				DWS		
4	DLS			DWS				DLS				DWS			DLS
5					DWS						DWS				
6		TLS				TLS				TLS				TLS	
7			DLS			A$_1$	DLS		DLS				DLS		
8	TWS			DLS		R$_1$	O$_1$	E$_1$				DLS			TWS
9			DLS			E$_1$	DLS		DLS				DLS		
10		TLS				TLS A$_1$				TLS				TLS	
11					DWS E$_1$	L$_1$	M$_3$	I$_1$	E$_1$	S$_1$	DWS T$_1$				
12	DLS			DWS				DLS			A$_1$	DWS V$_4$	I$_1$	D$_2$	DLS
13			DWS				DLS		DLS				DWS		
14		DWS				TLS				TLS				DWS	
15	TWS			DLS				TWS				DLS			TWS

DIAGRAM 14-13

Your Rack: EGILNOV **Score:** 95–27
What's your best play?

	A	B	C	D	E	F	G	H	I	J	K	L	M	N	O
1															
2					G										
3					R										
4					I										
5					E										
6					V										
7					O										
8				J	U	D	O	S							
9				O	S										
10				U											
11		C	Z	A	R										
12			E	L											
13			I												
14		E	N	T	R	Y				M	O	L	A	R	
15						A	U	S	P	E	X		W	E	N

DIAGRAM 14-14

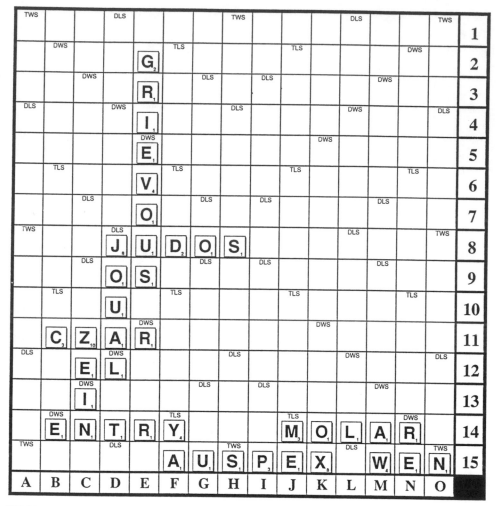

Your Rack: ABEGNTT **Score:** 127–225
What's your best play?

A	B	C	D	E	F	G	H	I	J	K	L	M	N	O	
TWS			DLS				TWS				DLS			TWS	1
	DWS				TLS				TLS				DWS		2
		DWS				DLS		DLS				DWS			3
DLS			DWS				DLS				DWS			DLS	4
				DWS						DWS					5
	TLS				TLS				TLS				TLS		6
		DLS				DLS		DLS				DLS			7
TWS W	E	N	DLS				A	B	O	O	DLS N			TWS	8
	D	DLS A	R	E	F	DLS U	L	DLS				DLS			9
	TLS				TLS		A	E	TLS C	I	A		TLS		10
				DWS						DWS					11
DLS			DWS				DLS				DWS			DLS	12
		DWS				DLS		DLS				DWS			13
	DWS				TLS				TLS				DWS		14
TWS			DLS				TWS				DLS			TWS	15

DIAGRAM 14-15

Your Rack: AEHLTTW **Score:** 23–97

What's your best play?

TWS			DLS				TWS				DLS			TWS	1
	DWS				TLS				TLS				DWS		2
		DWS				DLS		DLS				DWS			3
DLS			DWS B_3				DLS				DWS			DLS	4
			A_1	DWS						DWS					5
	TLS		R_1	E_1	TLS X_8				TLS				TLS		6
	W_4	DLS I_1	D_2	D_2	I_1	DLS E_1		DLS				DLS			7
TWS			DLS E_1			L_1	E_1	V_4	Y_4		DLS			TWS	8
		DLS				DLS		DLS				DLS			9
	TLS				TLS				TLS				TLS		10
				DWS						DWS					11
DLS			DWS				DLS				DWS			DLS	12
		DWS				DLS		DLS				DWS			13
	DWS				TLS				TLS				DWS		14
TWS			DLS				TWS				DLS			TWS	15
A	B	C	D	E	F	G	H	I	J	K	L	M	N	O	

DIAGRAM 14-16

Your Rack: DEMNNRS **Score:** 73–44
What's your best play?

	A	B	C	D	E	F	G	H	I	J	K	L	M	N	O
1	TWS			DLS				TWS				DLS			TWS
2		DWS				TLS				TLS				DWS	
3			DWS				DLS		DLS				DWS		
4	DLS			DWS N	E			DLS				DWS			DLS
5				O	DWS X						DWS				
6		TLS		D		TLS				TLS				TLS	
7			DLS	D			DLS		DLS				DLS		
8	TWS			DLS Y	A	M	U	N				DLS			TWS
9			DLS				DLS		DLS				DLS		
10		TLS				TLS				TLS				TLS	
11					DWS						DWS				
12	DLS			DWS				DLS				DWS			DLS
13			DWS				DLS		DLS				DWS		
14		DWS				TLS				TLS				DWS	
15	TWS			DLS				TWS				DLS			TWS

DIAGRAM 14-17

Your Rack: AAFOOTY **Score:** 20–66
What's your best play?

	A	B	C	D	E	F	G	H	I	J	K	L	M	N	O
1	TWS			DLS				TWS				DLS			TWS
2		DWS				TLS				TLS				DWS	
3			DWS				DLS		DLS				DWS		
4	DLS			DWS				DLS				DWS			DLS
5					DWS						DWS				
6		TLS				TLS				TLS				TLS	
7			DLS				DLS		DLS				DLS		
8	TWS			DLS			D_{2}	E_{1}	V_{4}	A_{1}		DLS			TWS
9			DLS				DLS		DLS U_{1}	H_{4}			DLS		
10		TLS				TLS			G_{2}	TLS O_{1}				TLS	
11					DWS			S_{1}	H_{4}	Y_{4}	DWS				
12	DLS			DWS				DLS T_{1}				DWS			DLS
13			DWS				DLS	A_{1}	DLS				DWS		
14		DWS				TLS J_{8}	I_{1}	G_{2}		TLS				DWS	
15	TWS			DLS				TWS E_{1}				DLS			TWS

DIAGRAM 14-18

Your Rack: DEGMMNN **Score:** 51–67
What's your best play?

	A	B	C	D	E	F	G	H	I	J	K	L	M	N	O
1	TWS			DLS				TWS				DLS			TWS
2		DWS				TLS				TLS				DWS	
3			DWS				DLS		DLS				DWS		
4	DLS			DWS				DLS				DWS			DLS
5					DWS						DWS				
6		TLS				TLS				TLS				TLS	
7			DLS				DLS		DLS				DLS		
8	TWS			DLS			J	O	G	S		DLS			TWS
9			DLS				DLS		DLS	T			DLS		
10		TLS				TLS				TLS O				TLS	
11					DWS					U	DWS				
12	DLS			DWS				DLS A	R	R	A	DWS Y	E	D	DLS
13			DWS P	A	T	E	DLS N	T	DLS	I			DWS F	A	X
14		DWS				TLS				TLS E				DWS	
15	TWS			DLS				TWS				DLS			TWS

DIAGRAM 14-19

Your Rack: AACINRZ **Score:** 112–66
What's your best play?

	A	B	C	D	E	F	G	H	I	J	K	L	M	N	O
1	TWS			DLS				TWS				DLS			TWS
2		DWS				TLS				TLS				DWS	
3			DWS				DLS		DLS				DWS		
4	DLS			DWS				DLS				DWS			DLS
5					DWS P						DWS				
6		TLS			U	TLS	W	A	M	TLS B	L	E		TLS	
7			DLS		R		DLS		DLS A	I	O	L	DLS I		
8	TWS			DLS W	A	G	G	O	N	S		DLS			TWS
9			DLS		N		DLS E	D	DLS				DLS		
10		TLS			I	TLS	Y	E	A	TLS H				TLS	
11					DWS C						DWS				
12	DLS			DWS				DLS				DWS			DLS
13			DWS				DLS		DLS				DWS		
14		DWS				TLS				TLS				DWS	
15	TWS			DLS				TWS				DLS			TWS

DIAGRAM 14-20

Your Rack: AEELMNT **Score:** 105–114

What's your best play?

A	B	C	D	E	F	G	H	I	J	K	L	M	N	O	
TWS			DLS				TWS				DLS			TWS	1
	DWS				TLS				TLS				DWS		2
		DWS				DLS		DLS				DWS			3
DLS			DWS				DLS				DWS			DLS	4
				DWS						DWS					5
	TLS				TLS W				TLS				TLS		6
		DLS		M	E	DLS L		DLS				DLS			7
TWS C			DLS B	O	R	O	N				DLS			TWS	8
I		DLS D	E	S	E	DLS X		DLS				DLS			9
O	TLS R			Q	TLS				TLS				TLS		10
N	U		A	DWS U	B	R	E	T	I	DWS A					11
DLS	T		DWS	E			DLS				DWS			DLS	12
F	I	DWS A	T	S		DLS		DLS				DWS			13
I	DWS N				TLS				TLS				DWS		14
TWS Z			DLS				TWS				DLS			TWS	15

DIAGRAM 14-21

Your Rack: DEHLOTU **Score:** 155–186
What's your best play?

A	B	C	D	E	F	G	H	I	J	K	L	M	N	O	
TWS			DLS				TWS H				DLS			TWS	1
	DWS				TLS		Y		TLS				DWS		2
		DWS				DLS V	E	DLS N	T			DWS			3
DLS			DWS		R		DLS N				DWS			DLS	4
				DWS N	A	I	A	D	S	DWS					5
	TLS				TLS J				TLS C				TLS		6
		DLS H	A	O		DLS B	E	DLS G	O	T		DLS			7
TWS		A	DLS I	R	I	E	R		F	I	DLS Z			TWS	8
		DLS				DLS		DLS	F			DLS			9
	TLS				TLS				TLS				TLS		10
				DWS						DWS					11
DLS			DWS				DLS				DWS			DLS	12
		DWS				DLS		DLS				DWS			13
	DWS				TLS				TLS				DWS		14
TWS			DLS				TWS				DLS			TWS	15

DIAGRAM 14-22

Your Rack: EINOOUU **Score:** 118–92

What's your best play?

	A	B	C	D	E	F	G	H	I	J	K	L	M	N	O
1	TWS			DLS				TWS				DLS			TWS
2		DWS				TLS				TLS				DWS	
3			DWS				DLS		DLS				DWS		
4	DLS			DWS				DLS				DWS			DLS
5					DWS						DWS E				
6		TLS				TLS				TLS	V			TLS	
7			DLS		J	I	DLS A	O	DLS		E	T	DLS		
8	TWS			DLS			E	X	P	O	S	DLS E			TWS
9			DLS				DLS		DLS R			A	DLS		
10		TLS				TLS			O	TLS		S		TLS	
11					DWS				S		DWS	I			
12	DLS			DWS				DLS	T			DWS N			DLS
13			DWS				DLS		DLS Y		A	G	DWS E	N	E
14		DWS				TLS			L	TLS				DWS	
15	TWS			DLS				TWS D	E	F	I	DLS N	I	T	E

DIAGRAM 14-23

Your Rack: ABRRSWY **Score:** 176–233
What's your best play?

	A	B	C	D	E	F	G	H	I	J	K	L	M	N	O
1	TWS			DLS				P				D			TWS
2		DWS				TLS		A	L	TLS		J	A	W	
3			DWS				DLS	W	E	L	K	I	N		
4	DLS			DWS		T		DLS	S			N			DLS
5					B	I		Y	I	R	R				
6		TLS			R	E			O	H				TLS	
7			DLS		U		DLS		N	O	T		T		
8	TWS			I	M	A	G	E	S		R	DLS	O		TWS
9			F		E		DLS		DLS	C	A	L	X		
10		TLS	E	N	S	U	I	N	G	TLS	V		E	TLS	
11	Q		A		DWS						O		M		
12	A		Z	E	B	U		DLS		R	I	V	I	N	G
13	T	H	E				DLS		DLS		S		A		
14		O	D			TLS				TLS				DWS	
15	TWS	D		DLS				TWS				DLS			TWS

DIAGRAM 14-24

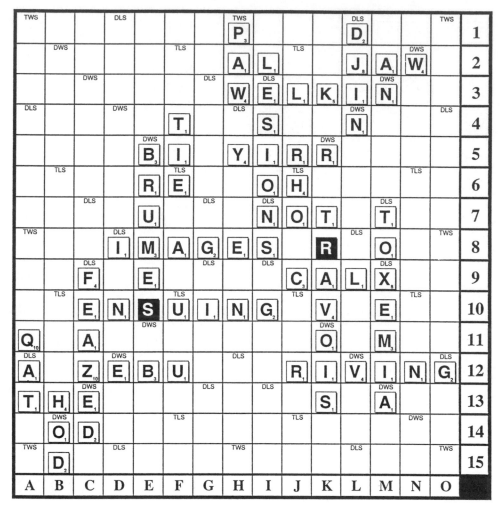

Your Rack: ADFILOS **Score:** 351–265

What's your best play?

	A	B	C	D	E	F	G	H	I	J	K	L	M	N	O
1	D	E	F	T				U			A	Z	I	N	E
2				A	N	E	U	R	I	N	S				
3		H	I	V	E			A			P	O	O	F	
4	W	A	D	S			O	R							
5	E						X	I							
6	D					J	O								
7	G					O		A							
8	Y			Q	U	E	N	C	H						
9								E							
10			C	O	C	A		T							
11			L			G	R	A	M	P	S				
12		B	I	L	G	E									
13			N												
14			K												
15															

DIAGRAM 14-25

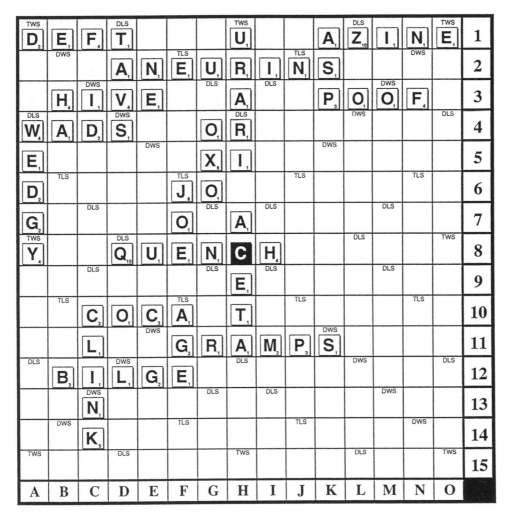

Your Rack: ALLTTUY **Score:** 206–308
What's your best play?

	A	B	C	D	E	F	G	H	I	J	K	L	M	N	O
1										B					
2	Q	U	A		G			O	V	A	T	I	O	N	
3			H	E	R	E	O	F		N					
4				H	I	N	D			A					
5					E					L					
6					V					I					
7					O					T					
8				J	U	D	O	S		Y					
9				O	S										
10				U											
11		C	Z	A	R										
12			E	L											
13			I						B	E	G	A	T		
14		E	N	T	R	Y				M	O	L	A	R	
15						A	U	S	P	E	X		W	E	N

DIAGRAM 14-26

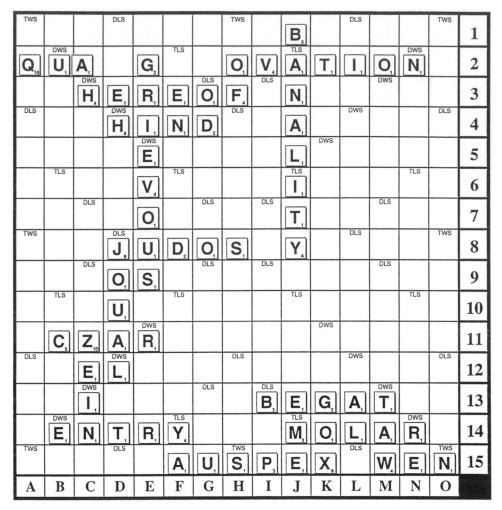

Your Rack: EEINPTT **Score:** 289–345

What's your best play?

	A	B	C	D	E	F	G	H	I	J	K	L	M	N	O
1	TWS		T	A	L	A	P	O	I	N		B	E	D	S
2		J	I	V	E	TLS		U		A	F	O	R	E	
3			DWS	A	U	G	I	T	E			W	A	I	N
4	DLS			DWS				L				DWS			DLS
5			M	A	L	E	D	I	C	T	S				
6		TLS				TLS		V		TLS	O			TLS	
7			DLS				DLS	E	DLS		F		DLS		
8	TWS			P	O	K	E	D			T	A			TWS
9			DLS				DLS		DLS			U	DLS		
10		TLS				TLS				TLS		D		TLS	
11					DWS						DWS	I			
12	DLS			DWS				DLS				O			DLS
13			DWS				DLS		DLS				DWS		
14		DWS				TLS				TLS				DWS	
15	TWS			DLS				TWS				DLS			TWS

DIAGRAM 14-27

Your Rack: AGIORTV **Score:** 276–173

What's your best play?

	A	B	C	D	E	F	G	H	I	J	K	L	M	N	O
1	TWS			DLS				TWS				DLS			TWS
2		DWS				TLS				TLS				DWS	
3			DWS				DLS		DLS				DWS		
4	DLS			DWS				DLS O	U	T	R	DWS A	T	E	DLS D
5					DWS			R			DWS				I
6		TLS				TLS	Q	A	T	TLS				TLS	A
7			DLS				DLS	T	DLS				DLS		R
8	TWS			DLS			M	O	G	G		DLS			TWS Y
9			DLS	J	I	V	DLS E	R	DLS	N			DLS		
10		TLS		E		TLS				TLS O				TLS	
11			P	E	DWS			G	U	S	DWS H	Y			
12	DLS	F	O	DWS R				DLS		T		DWS			DLS
13		A	DWS X				DLS		DLS	I			DWS		
14		DWS Z				TLS				TLS C				DWS	
15	TWS L	E	E	DLS K				TWS				DLS			TWS

DIAGRAM 14-28

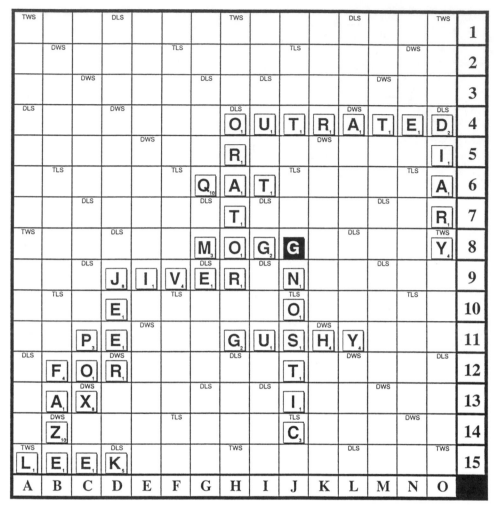

Your Rack: DEELNSS **Score:** 247–162

What's your best play?

	A	B	C	D	E	F	G	H	I	J	K	L	M	N	O
1	TWS			DLS	W	O	O	TWS F	E	D		DLS			TWS
2		DWS H	A	L	E	TLS R	S			TLS A	V	I	A	DWS N	S
3	F	I	DWS E				DLS N		DLS				DWS N		E
4	DLS			DWS			A	DLS				DWS	T		DLS P
5					DWS		B				DWS		I		A
6		TLS				TLS Q	U	O	I	TLS T			T	TLS	L
7			DLS				DLS R		DLS				DLS Y		E
8	TWS			DLS J	A	Y	G	E	E	S		DLS	P		TWS D
9			DLS D	A	G		DLS		DLS	C			DLS E		
10		TLS		B		TLS				TLS H				TLS	
11				O	DWS M			C	R	U	DWS X				
12	DLS			DWS T	O			DLS O		L		DWS			DLS
13			DWS		K		DLS	R	DLS				DWS		
14		DWS			E	TLS		I		TLS				DWS	
15	TWS			DLS				TWS A				DLS			TWS

DIAGRAM 14-29

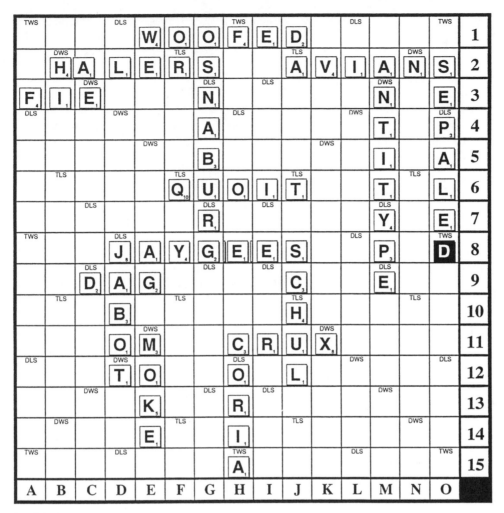

Your Rack: DDGIORT **Score:** 311–311
What's your best play?

	A	B	C	D	E	F	G	H	I	J	K	L	M	N	O
1	TWS			DLS				TWS				DLS		W	TWS
2		DWS				TLS				TLS		T		DWS A	
3			DWS				DLS		DLS			O	DWS W	L	
4	DLS			DWS				DLS				DWS Y	O	K	DLS
5					DWS						DWS		O		
6		TLS L	U	N	E	TLS T				TLS S			D	TLS	
7			DLS			I	DLS F		DLS	A			DLS E		
8	TWS			DLS			O	E		U		DLS I	N	I	TWS A
9			DLS				DLS P	R	DLS U	T	O	T	DLS		R
10		TLS				TLS				TLS E				TLS	M
11				F	DWS R	I	T	T	E	R	DWS S			J	O
12	DLS V	I	N	DWS A				DLS O		N		DWS		A	DLS R
13			DWS				DLS	Q	DLS	E			DWS	P	I
14		DWS				TLS		U		TLS				DWS E	N
15	TWS			DLS				TWS E				DLS			TWS G

DIAGRAM 14-30

Your Rack: ABELNSY **Score:** 236–283

What's your best play?

	A	B	C	D	E	F	G	H	I	J	K	L	M	N	O
1								B							I
2			C				Q	U	A	G					S
3			A			C		R							O
4			R	O	U	L	A	D	E	S		B	U	R	L
5			P		M	O	L	E		O					A
6		P	I			N		N		J					T
7	X	U			Y	E				A	E		T		E
8	I	N		K	A	R	O	O			V	O	W	E	D
9		T			I		F	E	W		A		I	T	
10		E			R					E	N		N		
11	A	D			D					F	I	T			
12	G		N	I	S	I					S	H			
13	G					T	Z	A	R		H	E			
14	I											Y			
15	E														

DIAGRAM 14-31

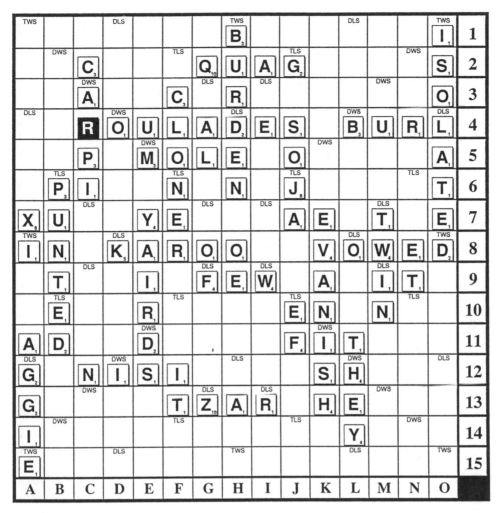

Your Rack: EMR? **Score:** 419–276
Opponent's Rack: LOV
What's your best play?

	A	B	C	D	E	F	G	H	I	J	K	L	M	N	O
1	TWS			DLS				TWS				DLS			TWS
2		DWS				TLS				TLS				DWS	
3			DWS				DLS		DLS				DWS		
4	DLS			DWS				DLS				DWS			DLS
5					DWS						DWS				
6		TLS				TLS				TLS				TLS	
7			DLS				DLS		DLS				DLS		
8	TWS			DLS B	R	O	K	E				DLS			TWS
9			DLS	L			DLS		DLS				DLS		
10		TLS		A		TLS				TLS				TLS	
11				Z	DWS E	I	N				DWS				
12	DLS			DWS E				DLS				DWS			DLS
13			DWS	R			DLS		DLS				DWS		
14		DWS				TLS				TLS				DWS	
15	TWS			DLS				TWS				DLS			TWS

DIAGRAM 14-32

Your Rack: CEELNOR **Score:** 34–54

What's your best play?

A	B	C	D	E	F	G	H	I	J	K	L	M	N	O	
TWS			DLS				TWS				DLS			TWS	1
	DWS				TLS				TLS				DWS		2
		DWS				DLS		DLS				DWS			3
DLS			DWS				DLS				DWS			DLS	4
				DWS						DWS					5
	TLS				TLS				TLS				TLS		6
		DLS H	A	O		DLS B	E	DLS G	O	T		DLS			7
TWS		A	DLS I	R	I	E	R				DLS			TWS	8
		DLS				DLS		DLS				DLS			9
	TLS				TLS				TLS				TLS		10
				DWS						DWS					11
DLS			DWS				DLS				DWS			DLS	12
		DWS				DLS		DLS				DWS			13
	DWS				TLS				TLS				DWS		14
TWS			DLS				TWS				DLS			TWS	15

DIAGRAM 14-33

Your Rack: ADFISUZ **Score:** 23–36

What's your best play?

A	B	C	D	E	F	G	H	I	J	K	L	M	N	O	
TWS			DLS				TWS				DLS			TWS	1
	DWS				TLS				TLS				DWS		2
		DWS				DLS		DLS				DWS			3
DLS			DWS				DLS				DWS			DLS	4
				DWS						DWS					5
	TLS				TLS				TLS				TLS		6
		DLS				DLS		DLS				DLS			7
TWS			DLS Z$_{10}$	I$_{1}$	T$_{1}$	I$_{1}$	S$_{1}$				DLS			TWS	8
		DLS				DLS		DLS				DLS			9
	TLS				TLS				TLS				TLS		10
				DWS						DWS					11
DLS			DWS				DLS				DWS			DLS	12
		DWS				DLS		DLS				DWS			13
	DWS				TLS				TLS				DWS		14
TWS			DLS				TWS				DLS			TWS	15

DIAGRAM 14-34

Your Rack: AEGOPTU **Score:** 0–48
What's your best play?

	A	B	C	D	E	F	G	H	I	J	K	L	M	N	O
1	TWS			DLS				TWS T				DLS			TWS G
2		DWS				TLS		O		TLS				DWS	L
3			DWS				DLS V	E	DLS T	E	R	A	DWS N		U
4	DLS			DWS		O		DLS P				DWS M	U	G	DLS G
5					DWS	U		I			DWS				
6		TLS				TLS Z		E		TLS				TLS	
7			DLS			E	DLS	C	DLS				DLS		
8	TWS			DLS H	E	L	V	E				DLS			TWS
9			DLS	O			DLS		DLS				DLS		
10		TLS		O		TLS				TLS				TLS	
11				K	DWS A						DWS				
12	DLS			DWS E	X			DLS				DWS			DLS
13			DWS	R			DLS		DLS				DWS		
14		DWS W	I	S	P	TLS Y				TLS				DWS	
15	TWS J	E	T	DLS				TWS				DLS			TWS

DIAGRAM 14-35

Your Rack: CDENRRY **Score:** 181–163

What's your best play?

A	B	C	D	E	F	G	H	I	J	K	L	M	N	O	
TWS			DLS				TWS				DLS			TWS	1
	DWS				TLS				TLS				DWS		2
		DWS				DLS		DLS				DWS			3
DLS			DWS U1				DLS				DWS			DLS	4
			N1	DWS						DWS					5
	TLS		C3		TLS				TLS				TLS		6
		DLS	L1			DLS		DLS				DLS			7
TWS			DLS A1	B3	Y4	E1	S1				DLS			TWS	8
		DLS	D2			DLS		DLS				DLS			9
	TLS				TLS				TLS				TLS		10
				DWS						DWS					11
DLS			DWS				DLS				DWS			DLS	12
		DWS				DLS		DLS				DWS			13
	DWS				TLS				TLS				DWS		14
TWS			DLS				TWS				DLS			TWS	15

DIAGRAM 14-36

Your Rack: AEFINPS **Score:** 22–18

What's your best play?

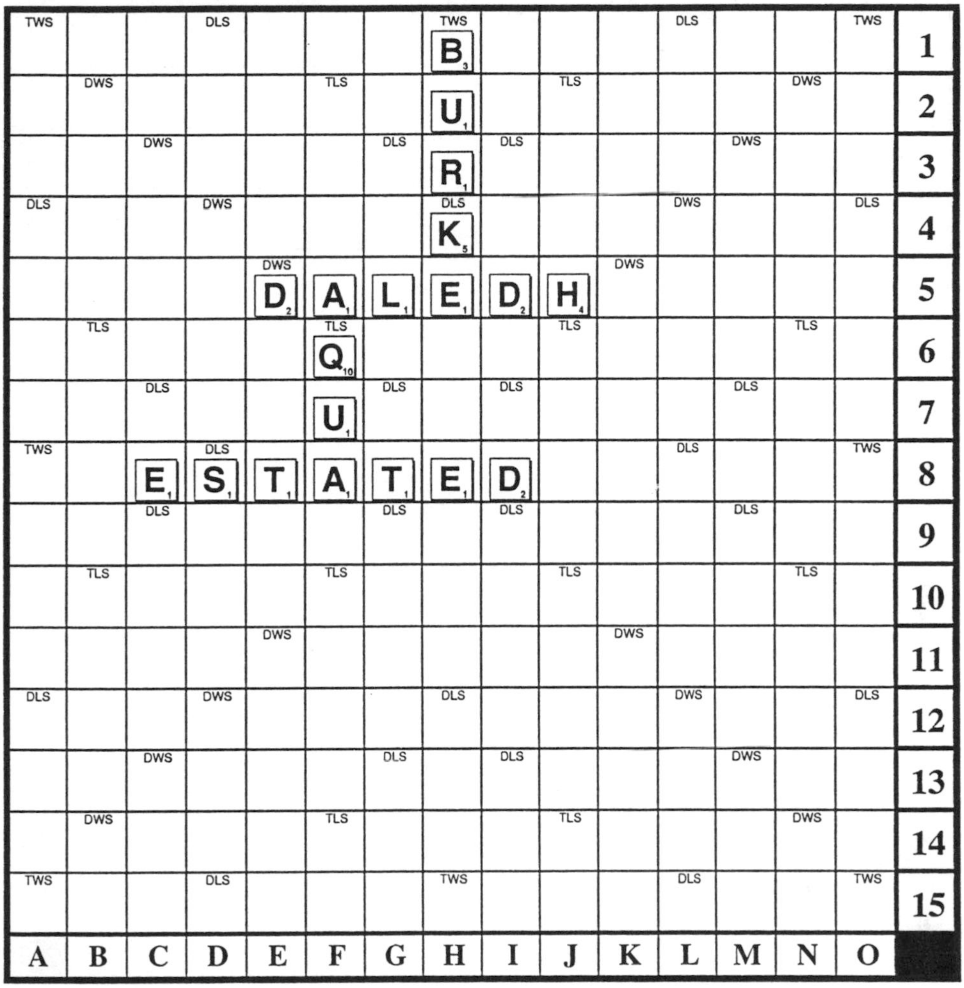

DIAGRAM 14-37

Your Rack: AGHIMNO **Score:** 90–81

What's your best play?

	A	B	C	D	E	F	G	H	I	J	K	L	M	N	O
1	TWS			DLS				TWS				DLS			TWS
2		DWS				TLS				TLS				DWS	
3			DWS				DLS		DLS				DWS		
4	DLS			DWS				DLS				DWS			DLS
5					DWS						DWS				
6		TLS				TLS			J_8	TLS				TLS	
7			DLS				DLS		DLS A_1				DLS		
8	TWS			DLS			H_4	E_1	M_3	E_1		DLS			TWS
9			DLS				DLS		DLS M_3				DLS		
10		TLS				TLS			I_1	TLS				TLS	
11					DWS W_4	I_1	D_2	E_1	N_1	E_1	DWS D_2				
12	DLS			DWS				DLS	G_2			DWS			DLS
13			DWS				DLS		DLS				DWS		
14		DWS				TLS				TLS				DWS	
15	TWS			DLS				TWS				DLS			TWS

DIAGRAM 14-38

Your Rack: AAFOTVY **Score:** 23–66
What's your best play?

A	B	C	D	E	F	G	H	I	J	K	L	M	N	O	
TWS			DLS				TWS				DLS			TWS	1
	DWS				TLS				TLS				DWS		2
		DWS				DLS		DLS				DWS			3
DLS	O_1	V_4	DWS I_1	C_3	I_1	D_2	DLS E_1				DWS			DLS	4
				DWS A_1						DWS					5
	TLS			R_1	TLS				TLS				TLS		6
		DLS		I_1		DLS		DLS				DLS			7
TWS R_1	O_1	B_3	DLS O_1	T_1			A_1	E_1		A_1	DLS G_2	E_1	N_1	TWS T_1	8
		DLS		A_1		DLS		DLS F_4	E_1	W_4		DLS			9
	TLS			S_1	TLS Q_{10}	U_1	A_1	S_1	TLS H_4				TLS		10
				DWS						DWS					11
DLS			DWS				DLS				DWS			DLS	12
		DWS				DLS		DLS				DWS			13
	DWS				TLS				TLS				DWS		14
TWS			DLS				TWS				DLS			TWS	15

DIAGRAM 14-39

Your Rack: AFHILOU **Score:** 114–143

What's your best play?

	A	B	C	D	E	F	G	H	I	J	K	L	M	N	O
1															
2												C			
3					I	N	E	R	T	I	A	L			
4												O			
5					U						A	G	A		
6				W	R	A	P				N		I		
7					A		O	F			I		R		
8					N		D	A	M	P	S		H		
9					I						O		E		
10					T						L		A	L	
11				B	E						E		D	E	
12				U	S									U	
13				I										C	
14				L		Y	U	M						I	
15	B	O	O	T	I	E			F	O	R	D	I	N	G

DIAGRAM 14-40

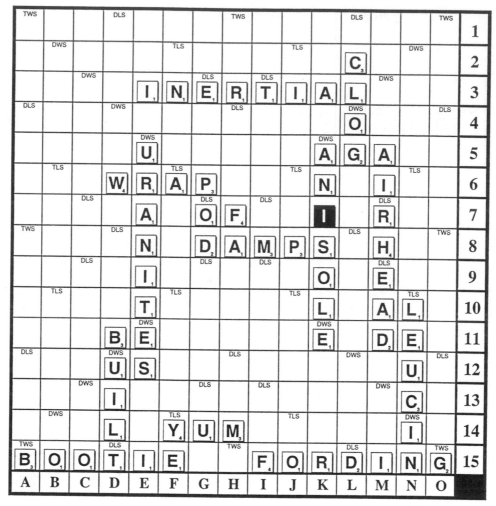

Your Rack: DEEGTVZ **Score:** 283–223

What's your best play?

	A	B	C	D	E	F	G	H	I	J	K	L	M	N	O
1	TWS			DLS				TWS				DLS			TWS
2		DWS				TLS				TLS				DWS	
3			DWS				DLS		DLS				DWS		
4	DLS	O	V	DWS I	C	I	D	DLS E				DWS			DLS
5					DWS A						DWS				
6		TLS			R	TLS				TLS				TLS	
7			DLS		I		DLS		DLS				DLS		
8	TWS			DLS	T			A	E		A	DLS G	E	N	TWS T
9			DLS		A		DLS		DLS F	E	W		DLS		
10		TLS			S	TLS Q	U	A	S	TLS H				TLS	
11					DWS						DWS				
12	DLS			DWS				DLS				DWS			DLS
13			DWS				DLS		DLS				DWS		
14		DWS				TLS				TLS				DWS	
15	TWS			DLS				TWS				DLS			TWS

DIAGRAM 14-41

Your Rack: BEORRY **Score:** 114–167

What's your best play?

	A	B	C	D	E	F	G	H	I	J	K	L	M	N	O
1												M		Y	
2		A										O		E	
3		L										U		S	
4		O	V	I	C	I	D	E				T		T	
5		O			A							H		R	
6		F			R							I		E	
7					I							N		E	
8	R	O	B	O	T			A	E		A	G	E	N	T
9					A				F	E	W				
10					S	Q	U	A	S	H					
11															
12															
13															
14															
15															

DIAGRAM 14-42

Your Rack: AEOORUU **Score:** 219–230
What's your best play?

A	B	C	D	E	F	G	H	I	J	K	L	M	N	O	
TWS			DLS				TWS				DLS			TWS	1
	DWS				TLS				TLS				DWS		2
		DWS				DLS	S	DLS				DWS			3
DLS			DWS				DLS P				DWS			DLS	4
				DWS			I		T	DWS					5
	TLS				TLS		N		TLS Z			S	TLS		6
		DLS				DLS	N	DLS	I			DLS I			7
TWS			DLS F	U	L	L	I	N	G		DLS	G		TWS	8
		DLS	A			DLS	E	DLS	A			DLS H			9
	TLS		U		TLS		S		TLS N	A		T	TLS		10
			V	DWS					E	DWS L		I			11
DLS		B	DWS E				DLS D	I	S	O	DWS W	N		DLS	12
		DWS R				DLS		DLS		W		DWS G			13
	DWS	R			TLS				TLS				DWS		14
TWS V	A	R	DLS Y				TWS				DLS			TWS	15

DIAGRAM 14-43

Your Rack: FIMOOOR **Score:** 220–216

What's your best play?

A	B	C	D	E	F	G	H	I	J	K	L	M	N	O	
							P								1
							R			B					2
							E			R	O	O	T	Y	3
							F	A	R	A	D				4
							I			N					5
					Z	A	X			N					6
										E					7
			Q				I	V	O	R	Y				8
		F	U	G	U	E	D			S					9
			O												10
			T												11
W			E												12
I			R			A	B	S	E	I	L	S			13
P	L	I	S	K	I	E									14
E															15

DIAGRAM 14-44

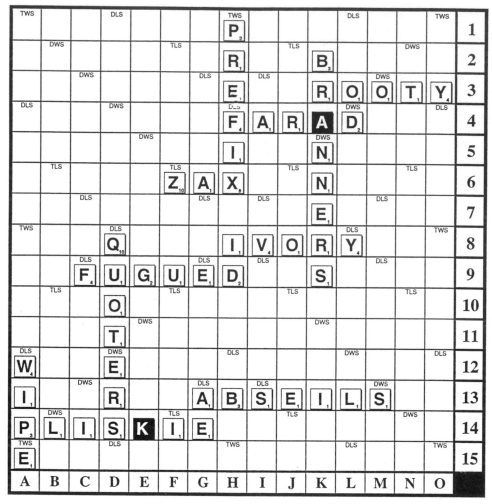

Your Rack: ANOTTUV **Score:** 254–285

What's your best play?

	A	B	C	D	E	F	G	H	I	J	K	L	M	N	O
1								G	R	O	O	M			
2												I			
3												N			
4					C					L		T			
5					A					O	N	S			
6					R					X	U				
7		U	N	O	I	L	E	D			T				
8					T			O	R	A	L				
9			Z		A				A		I				
10		Q	A	T	S				I		K		D		
11			I						A		E	T	A		
12			R	E	L	A	C	E	S			E	M		
13			E					W				U	N		
14						V	I	E	W	Y		G			
15								R				H	I	V	E

DIAGRAM 14-45

Your Rack: DDEJPS? **Score:** 368–219
What's your best play?

	A	B	C	D	E	F	G	H	I	J	K	L	M	N	O
1	TWS			DLS				TWS				DLS			TWS E
2		DWS				TLS				TLS			Q	DWS	T
3			DWS				DLS		DLS				DWS U		O
4	DLS			DWS				DLS		T		DWS	O		DLS I
5					DWS			T	R	O	DWS U	P	I	A	L
6		TLS				TLS				TLS D			N	TLS	E
7			DLS				DLS		DLS	D			DLS		
8	TWS			DLS		J	E	R	K	Y		DLS			TWS
9			DLS	B	O	O	DLS		DLS				DLS		
10		TLS				TLS W	A	I	F	TLS				TLS	
11	H	A	Z	A	DWS N	S					DWS				
12	DLS			DWS				DLS				DWS			DLS
13			DWS				DLS		DLS				DWS		
14		DWS				TLS				TLS				DWS	
15	TWS			DLS				TWS				DLS			TWS

DIAGRAM 14-46

Your Rack: ALORSUV **Score:** 135–150
What's your best play?

TWS			DLS				TWS				DLS			TWS	1
	DWS				TLS				TLS				DWS		2
		DWS				DLS		DLS				DWS			3
DLS			DWS				DLS				DWS			DLS	4
				DWS						DWS					5
	TLS				TLS				TLS				TLS		6
		DLS				DLS		DLS	G			DLS		U	7
TWS			DLS				O	X	L	I	DLS P			TWS L	8
		DLS				DLS		DLS	O			DLS		C	9
	TLS				TLS				TLS Z				TLS	E	10
				DWS					E	DWS F				R	11
DLS			DWS				DLS		S	E	DWS I			DLS A	12
		DWS				DLS		DLS		M	O	DWS		T	13
	DWS				TLS				TLS B	E	T	I	DWS D	E	14
TWS			DLS		L	O	TWS O	E	Y		DLS A		E	TWS D	15
A	B	C	D	E	F	G	H	I	J	K	L	M	N	O	

DIAGRAM 14-47

Your Rack: AAEGIMT **Score:** 126–192

What's your best play?

	A	B	C	D	E	F	G	H	I	J	K	L	M	N	O
1								H				G	E	E	Z
2								I	S		D	A			
3								D	O	S	E	R			
4									N	O	B	S			
5									A	L	T				
6									T	I					
7									I	T					
8								U	N	A	U				
9									A	R					
10										Y	E				
11											T				
12											W				M
13											E				E
14										J	E	R	I	D	S
15							C	I	A	O					A

DIAGRAM 14-48

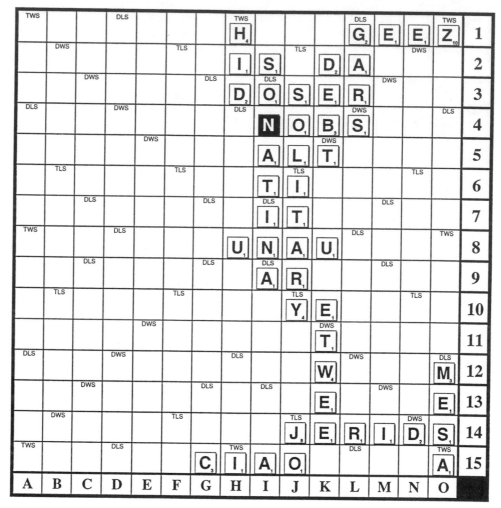

Your Rack: EGLNOUY **Score:** 210–202

What's your best play?

TWS			DLS				TWS				DLS			TWS C	1
	DWS				TLS				TLS				DWS	O	2
	F	DWS				DLS	N	DLS E	T	W	O	DWS R	K	S	3
DLS	R	E	DWS S	P	R	E	DLS A	D			DWS			DLS Y	4
	I			DWS						DWS					5
	TLS T				TLS				TLS				TLS		6
	T	DLS				DLS		DLS	J			DLS			7
TWS A	I	L	DLS E	D			O	B	E	A	DLS H			TWS	8
	N	DLS		U		DLS		DLS	U		U	DLS			9
	TLS G			V	TLS			A	TLS X		R		TLS		10
				DWS E				W		DWS	L				11
DLS			DWS	T			DLS	A			DWS Y			DLS	12
		DWS		I		DLS		DLS I				DWS			13
	DWS R	E	A	N	TLS O	I	N	T	TLS				DWS		14
TWS			DLS L	E	N	T	TWS O				DLS			TWS	15
A	B	C	D	E	F	G	H	I	J	K	L	M	N	O	

DIAGRAM 14-49

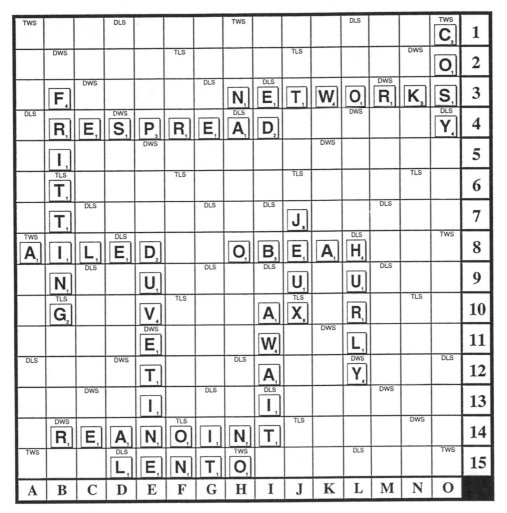

Your Rack: AABCGIN **Score:** 237–328

What's your best play?

TWS			DLS				TWS				DLS			TWS	1
	DWS				TLS				TLS				DWS		2
		DWS				DLS		DLS				DWS			3
DLS			DWS				DLS				DWS			DLS	4
				DWS						DWS					5
	TLS				TLS				TLS				TLS		6
		DLS				DLS		DLS				DLS			7
TWS			DLS			V$_{4}$	I$_{1}$	B$_{3}$	E$_{1}$		DLS			TWS	8
		DLS				DLS		DLS				DLS			9
	TLS				TLS				TLS				TLS		10
				DWS						DWS					11
DLS			DWS				DLS				DWS			DLS	12
		DWS				DLS		DLS				DWS			13
	DWS				TLS				TLS				DWS		14
TWS			DLS				TWS				DLS			TWS	15
A	B	C	D	E	F	G	H	I	J	K	L	M	N	O	

DIAGRAM 14-50

Your Rack: AEIKRUZ **Score:** 0–18
What's your best play?

ANSWERS TO CHAPTER 14

Actual Game Positions
(Letters in Parentheses Show the Leave)

Author's note on the analysis: In most cases I've imagined that the reader did NOT find the best play. Then I've constructed a plausible series of thoughts that would lead the reader to find a similar play when it occurs again.

DIAGRAM 1:

1. There are many choices for four-letter words, like HAND, HARD, LAND, THAN, HALT . . . etc., all scoring between 10 and 14 points. But all of them leave three consonants. Finding the best play means asking yourself if there are any vowelless words to be played. The best play is to save your vowel and play NTH for 12 points. This is at least 6 points better than HAND, which is probably the best of the other choices. Now, where do you play NTH? Either at 8G, 8F, or 8H. The 8G placement is 3 points better than at 8F and better still than at 8H. Why? At 8G you take away the TLSs on Columns F and J, which offer more points for your opponent.
2. The two highest-scoring plays, FLAUNT 8D 26 (W) and WALNUT 8D 26 (F), both save a high-point tile. While both are excellent plays, AWFUL 8H 24 (NT) is even better. AWFUL, far from being such, is the best way to balance your rack and score well. Saving a high-point tile, as with the other two choices, is 3–5 points weaker, as simulation shows. This, despite the L hook for LAWFUL. This is a good example of the Sim Principle 1 at work.

DIAGRAM 2:

There are many good plays, but the three best are JAPE 7F 35 (HIW), JAY J6 29 (EHIPW) and JAW 7F 32 (EHIP). JAPE is by far the best of the bunch because it closes the board down, scores the most, and leaves the tolerable WH combo.

DIAGRAM 3:

The best you can do to approach this rack is to notice the GHT combination. As soon as you notice these three letters, putting them together can lead you to spell EIGHT, and, noticing the extension, EIGHTEEN H1 98.

DIAGRAM 4:

If you found FLOCK 4E 38, you're on the right track. But, using the idea that: "if you find a good play you should look for a better one," you may extend FLOCK to FETLOCK 4B 42.

DIAGRAM 5:

Extension plays are a delight to find. If you look for one here, you'll surely find PREVENTION E3 30. When I was confronted with this position, I took a risk and played PREVENTIONISM, but, alas, it was challenged off, though I was able to play it without the ISM next turn.

DIAGRAM 6:

The key to this position is to look for a double-double. That's your most ideal play short of a bingo. With an I in position 5, look for IST, IUM and ISM endings. This may lead you to UTOPISM E5 44.

DIAGRAM 7:

There are many bingos to play. How do you choose? Looking for the ideal play, you may want to put the W on the 12H DLS as you either start at H8 and play down or go across row 12, hooking the N to make DJINN. At first you might be tempted, as I was, to try the prefix UN and see if any bingos have the W fall on the right spot. Having no luck, you may recall the other U prefix, UP. Once you think of UP, spelling TOWN on your rack may lead you to UPTOWNER H8 89, which is somewhat better than NEWTONS 12F 87.

DIAGRAM 8:

Seeing the G at 8I might motivate you to look for bingos with your ING combo, but it isn't there. Failing that, your best opening is across row 15. It will help to start by assuming your best play uses both a D and I, to get rid of your duplication. You'll also want to try to put the P on 15D, but the D is the next best, and once you try that, PUNDIT 15A 33 may come to mind.

DIAGRAM 9:

This is a difficult rack, since a reasonable but apparently impossible goal is to rid yourself of two Ns while scoring well. It's doubly hard if you know and are tempted by JUGA 2F 33 (NNN) or see JOG J2 27 (ANNNU). Don't be satisfied with these plays, since saving 3 Ns is a sure bet to having a poor next rack. Instead, keep looking. The ING at 6L might look promising, but it will prove fruitless. However, if you continue to look at that I, imagining the best (putting the J on 6N), you may remember NINJA 6K 28. While it opens the TWSs at O1 and O8, the very fact that it balances your rack and scores well makes it the overwhelming favorite. Simulation corroborates this.

DIAGRAM 10:

There are many choices here, but two plays stand out: NINTHLY 3G 22 (T) or THIRTY B5 28 (NN). Both of these plays are excellent. It's hard to choose between them because there are real pluses and minuses for each. NINTHLY opens up the board more, including a dangerous H1-H4 combination, which opponents could easily use for more than 40 points. On the other hand, THIRTY scores 6 more points but keeps the very poor NN combo.

Simulation shows that THIRTY is slightly better, but they are within a point of each other, and so I leave it for the reader's consideration.

DIAGRAM 11:

After struggling to find a bingo with these bingo-prone tiles, settling for anything less might seem anticlimactic. But a careful player checks the EX extension whenever it is available. Doing so will reap benefits: EXAMINER H8 54. I know many players who would become frustrated after not finding a bingo and simply play something like MAPS or AMPS H1 24 in the hopes of playing a bingo next turn. Don't be put off guard like that!

DIAGRAM 12:

This is very straightforward. While VEXED D8 32 is inviting, your thoroughness takes you to row 4. If you can place the X on 4H and run to 4L, you'll earn more points. EXUDED 4G 49.

DIAGRAM 13:

Two openings may spring to mind if you look carefully: bottom of columns H and/or N. On column N, putting the V on N10, your ideal choice, will lead to VIDEO N10 34 (GLN). But this is an unbalanced leave. Looking at Column H and putting the V on H12, ending it with ING, lets you play LIVING H10 42 (EO). While the EO leave is better than GLN, LIVING is worth 8 points more, which makes it the overwhelming favorite.

DIAGRAM 14:

With the board so open there are many places to find an ideal play. But before looking any further, which line of play is the most ideal? That's the line you should look at first. After you see the scoring possibilities on row 13 and check out the unusual three-letter words on our list at the front of the book, you may find BEGAT 13I 52.

DIAGRAM 15:

Finding THE 10A 32 (ALTW) is terrific since you have to remember that EDH is acceptable (see page 7). However, your first thought could have been: Maybe there is a double-double on either the E or K columns. It's not an easy find, but if you succeed you'll feel like a crossword game ATHLETE E5 40.

DIAGRAM 16:

The most promising opening for a high score is along column E. Looking carefully, noting all the unusual twos, you may find REDDENS E5 43.

DIAGRAM 17:

The key to this position is to get rid of duplication. You'd love to get rid of either the F or Y, or both, if possible. The three best choices are OAF C3 28 (AOTY), FOOTY F1 29 (AA) or TOY F4 27 (AAFO). In the latter two cases, the open board after FOOTY (row 1) and the weak leave after TOY are too risky to be desired. OAF relieves your rack of drek, scores well, and the "L" hook for "LOAF" is nothing to worry about this turn.

DIAGRAM 18:

You want to rid yourself of duplication and score decently. Your best chance to do that is on row 13. Putting an M on 13G and going across might be your first try. If so, you might discover MADMEN 13G 23. Simulation shows that MANGE 13G 19 is not far behind. I believe the reason it's so close in value to MADMEN is because the DMN leave, on this board, after opponent's next play, is far better than the GN leave after MADMEN and after opponent's next play. The GN will not produce many bingos or high-scoring plays on this board after opponent plays. However, the DMN should have good chances to score well, given you draw at least one vowel, which is quite likely.

DIAGRAM 19:

There are few words with a Z and C in them. When you see those two letters together, ZINC and CZAR might come to mind. Another careful glance at your letters could reveal the whole truth. But where do you play it? In a friendly game against a top-ranked player, I was happily surprised to find CZARINA D7 56 in this position. After another look, I was dumbfounded to find CZARINA 14A 104.

DIAGRAM 20:

If you know the word TELEMAN, you can play it at 11I 75. However, leaving the N at O11 is not optimal. Is there another bingo? My opponent looked further to find the very pretty ELEMENTAL L6 74. This is superior to TELEMAN because it doesn't leave an open TWS. However, the opponent can hook it with an S and play a word that reaches a TWS at either H15 or O15, but that's a small risk versus a big risk.

DIAGRAM 21:

Look at column H to the H15 TWS. Unfortunately, this won't lead to anything great. Another excellent "ideal" line is 12H-12L. You'd like to put the H at H12. Try it! HOTEL 2H 39 may occur to you.

DIAGRAM 22:

Nothing looks good here at first glance. The best you may find is YOU 2H 14. While this at least rids the rack of duplication, you won't have many prospects next turn on this board. In fact, with the board not particularly friendly unless you have an S, playing YOU could be deadly if opponent has a six-letter word on Row 1J-1O. It's better to exchange tiles and hope to draw one of the Ss or blanks. How many and what to exchange? Save the EN and exchange 5. This simulates better than any other exchange. There are already three Ns on the board, so duplication is unlikely, and both tiles are good for bingos or parallel plays across Row 9.

DIAGRAM 23:

As the board gets more cluttered with tiles, the possibilities for hooks goes up. If you stay alert to them, WARY M6 44 is available.

DIAGRAM 24:

The TLS-DWS combo is potent. Looking at column N can bring FINAL N10 51. Since you'll be 137 points ahead, you needn't worry about your opponent's potential bingo on Column O or Row 15. You'll still have a healthy lead.

DIAGRAM 25:

Your best chance to win this game is to score as well as possible, hope to draw the blank, and then play a bingo. OUTLAY L3 26 uses five tiles, scores the best while giving you the best chance to draw the blank. It also gives you a good place to score high with a bingo, since several high-point tiles may fit at the M7 DLS and play down to M13, scoring 80 or 90 points. If opponent blocks that spot by playing from 8L to 8O, you have the chance to play down the N or O columns.

DIAGRAM 26:

Always look for parallel plays to a TWS. In this case, that means checking out the B along Row 1. You might see BITTEN 1J 36.

DIAGRAM 27:

There are many average plays here and only one outstanding one. By looking for parallel plays on row 6, using the V as the optimal tile for 6B, VIGOR 6B 32 can show its superiority with a great score and leave.

DIAGRAM 28:

The usual first choice here is to play across the bottom row as you pluralize GNOSTIC. However, if you bother to look for a bingo, it can be found. While there is no E for LESSENED and no playable seven-letter word, by looking at the I (at E9, not 12J) you may find LINSEEDS E7 96. Note that along the E column, the I at E9 is more easily searched since any vertical play there must leave words played parallel, that is, only certain letters can be in certain positions.

DIAGRAM 29:

The most obvious place to look may also be the most difficult. If you don't at first see any good plays along column A, you might be tempted to look elsewhere quickly. There are other plays, but none matches FORDID A3 36.

DIAGRAM 30:

Here is another position awash with potential. However, using the ideal play model, you can check out the chance of putting the Y on B10 and playing to B14. After realizing that no such word could start with a Y, you might find that starting with a B leads to BYLINE B9 38 (AS). Also possible is BAILEY B10 34 and ELYSIAN B8 36. BYLINE is a clear winner since the others open hot spots and don't score as well.

DIAGRAM 31:

Although any play wins at the current score, if you bother to look for an extension play, you'll be happy you did: QUAGMIRES 2G 40.

DIAGRAM 32:

I guessed that ONCE I7 22 was the correct play here. It keeps the very nice ELR leave and doesn't open anything much for the opponent. Maven's initial thinking listed CLONER I3 24 as the best play. Simulation showed CLONE I5 21 to be better than CLONER but weaker by 1.5 points than ONCE.

DIAGRAM 33:

After checking out FIZ 8J 32 (ADSU), ZOA J6 32 (DFISU), DIAZO J3 35 (FSU), and FUTZ K5 32 (ADIS), the simulation showed that FUTZ, despite opening the O8 TWS, is a huge 5 points better than any of the others. The super ADIS leave is the main reason. Simulation Principle 1 anticipates the result.

DIAGRAM 34:

There are two excellent plays here: UPGAZE D4 36 or TOPAZ D4 32. UPGAZE gets the nod as a few points better, mostly because it's worth 4 points more during the game. The two leaves, OT vs EGU, aren't that much different in value.

DIAGRAM 35:

If you recall the list on page 8, you may see the choices: DECRY J2 23, DECRY I8 25, YEN 2J 34, CORY 10C 27, or DORY 10C 26. While each of these plays is good, best is CORY by several points. The main reasons are that it closes the board, the leave is excellent, and the D hook at I8 is still available.

DIAGRAM 36:

There are many decent choices, but only two stand out in a big way. EF 9F 23 scores very well while essentially fishing for a bingo. But DEAF 9D 30 is a big 7 extra points and the leave (INPS) is also excellent. It proves to be more than 3 points better than EF after simulation. Plays like IF 9H 11 or FINE 9G 23 are more than 10–12 points worse. Interestingly, IF, which is 12 points worse than FINE during the game, is actually better after simulation. That's because the AENPS leave is very bingo-prone.

DIAGRAM 37:

This is a fascinating position. There are a huge number of excellent plays. Some that we simulated are: HOGMANE C2 28, HOMAGE C3 28, KIANG 4H 28, AMONG 6I 30, HOGAN B6 29, and OM 6I 26. Your best bet is to play OM. The board and the AGHIN leave are so bingo-prone that that fact eclipses all other considerations. In fact, simulation shows it's a humungous favorite at 7–8 extra points. This is the Sim Principle 1 at work. However, if you haven't yet mastered the techniques for finding bingos, play KIANG or, not knowing that, AMONG.

DIAGRAM 38:

VAT F6 24 (AFOY) and FAVA 10B 23 (OTY) surpass all others. After 2,500 trials, VAT was one point better than FAVA. That was somewhat surprising since it's almost always better to rid yourself of the extra four-pointer. Since VAT was one point better over the board, and also one point better after simulation, it seems that the rack leave and board configuration after both plays have about the same value for opponent.

DIAGRAM 39:

Looking at the DWS-TLS combo at B2 and B6, you want to place the F or H on the B6 square. Play ALOOF B2 32 (HIU).

DIAGRAM 40:

Three plays look good: ZIG J2 33 (DEETV); VERGE H1 33 (DTZ), or ZEE O8 39 (DGTV). The horrible rack leave after ZEE is much worse than the DTZ leave after VERGE, since the valuable Z is missing, so it's not surprising that ZEE simulates more than 5 points less than VERGE. However, the DEETV leave is so much better than DTZ that it earns 2 extra points from the simulation, making ZIG the favorite. Using the Simulation Principle 1, this result could be inferred.

DIAGRAM 41:

Choices are: BYRE 7G 26 (OOR); ROBOT 8H 24 (ERY); BOYO 3F 24 (ERR); YORE H1 21 (BEOR); ARROYO H10 30 (BE). The leave and score make AR-

ROYO a clear favorite. ROBOT is 3.5 points worse, BOYO is 2 extra points worse than ROBOT, while YORE is even weaker.

DIAGRAM 42:

The three best plays are: AURUM 1H 21 (OOE); MAYO 1L 27 (EORUU); BUREAU C8 18 (OO). The difference in leave is what determines the value of these plays. BUREAU is the overwhelming favorite.

DIAGRAM 43:

This is a facinating position. Five plays stand out as potential winners: DOOM H12 21 (FIOR); FOLIO F6 18 (MOR); ROOF 13F 24 (IMO); FROM 14B 33 (IOOR); FRO 14B 27 (IMOOR). Prior to simulation I would have chosen ROOF, which seemed to afford the best leave. But simulation showed that FRO outshined all others by at least two points. FROM came in second and ROOF was third. I surmise from this two possibilities: (1) that the two-consonant IMOOR leave may be superior to the IMO leave and/or (2) the opening at 14B is more potent for opponent than might be expected—implying that FRO takes away a good number of opponent's best-scoring replies. Note that with all four Ss and both blanks on the board, there is less to fear from opponent playing a bingo and less disadvantage from only playing two tiles.

DIAGRAM 44:

There aren't many good plays in this position. Three that seem best are OUTATE 3C 14 (NV), TOY O1 18 (ANTUV), and VAULT L10 16 (NOT). Though the Y at O3 may seem dangerous, Simulation Principle 1 seems once again to show the way. VAULT sims best by 1.2 points over TOY and 5.2 points better than OUTATE. I see no reason to disagree. Better to have the better leave even though you're behind a little after this play.

DIAGRAM 45:

With a 150-point lead, you may well wonder why anyone would want to think about this play, since virtually any play will win. The answer to that is that in order to maintain a fascination for the game, it can be a real challenge to find the very best play each turn, regardless of the score. Another reason is that in virtually all tournaments and clubs, when more than one player has the same number of wins, ties are broken by comparing total "spread" points. Spread is a positive or negative number that shows by how many total points you've won or lost your games. That means that it's potentially to your advantage to win by the biggest margin, or lose by the smallest margin.

With this position we can use the blank for 41 points by playing PRIDED 2J (JS). Or should we play either SPIED 2J 28 (DJ?), JUS B6 26 (DDEP?) or JAPED

5D 15 (DS?)? It's instructive to learn that SPIED wins out over all other plays. And JAPED, even with its low score, is second best. The blank is simply too useful, so that by playing it now you're actually wasting it. If you save it, you're quite likely to have a playable bingo within two turns. You'll surely win by a large number by playing PRIDED, but, in the long run, you'll win by more if you play SPIED.

DIAGRAM 46:

There are three excellent plays in this position. One is an obscure word, ULVA 8A 29 (ORS), while the other two are easier to spot: VALOR B10 32 (ASU) or VALOUR B10 34 (AS). Using Simulation Principle 1, we can predict that VALOUR will be the superior play, and it doesn't disappoint. The AS leave is terrific, while even offering 2 points more than VALOR. In fact, VALOUR is worth 7 more points than VALOR due to the unbalanced ASU rack leave after VALOR. ULVA is worth only 2 fewer points than VALOUR after the sim results, since the ORS leave is actually a fairly good leave. Since ULVA is worth 5 fewer points over the board, it is the leave and board position that make up the extra 3 points.

DIAGRAM 47:

This is not a clear-cut position. There are three excellent plays. MIG M13 32 (AAEIT), IMAGE 14B 24 (AT), or AMIGA 14B 24 (ET). It's interesting to note that IMAGE and AMIGA simulated virtually identically. Since the E is a much more valuable tile than the A, a first glance would suggest that something's wrong. A second glance suggests that the difference in the board after AMIGA and IMAGE is more than minuscule. When the I is placed on 14B, it is much harder for the opponent to utilize the 15A-D line, which will be lucrative enough times after AMIGA to make up for the difference in retaining the A instead of the E.

However, the real question is if the 8 extra points earned for MIG are enough to offset the poor leave (AAEIT). Sim Principle 1 suggests that either AMIGA or IMAGE would make up several of the missing points. And that's true. However, MIG still shows up 2.5 points better than either of the other plays. I believe this is true because despite the poor leave, there are 29 seven-letter bingos you can draw to AAEIT in 23 distinct racks. All but three racks are playable across row 9, and one of these is playable as an eight-letter word to the L on F15 (PARIETAL). If you don't know or can't find most of these bingos, either of the five-letter plays is probably a tad better. Here is a complete list of those bingos: AGATIZE, AGITATE, AIRDATE (RADIATE, TIARAED), AMATIVE, AMENTIA (ANIMATE), AMIRATE, APATITE, APTERIA, ARIETTA, ARISTAE (ASTERIA, ATRESIA), ATAXIES, AVIATED, AVIATES, AWAITED, AWAITER, ENTASIA (TAENIAS), HETAIRA, IMAMATE, LABIATE, PATINAE, SATIATE, TAENIAE, VARIATE. The two racks that don't play are ARIETTA and HETAIRA.

DIAGRAM 48:

If you check the DWS-TLS combo on column N, put the Y in the ideal position on N6, and get past the obvious use of the L at N5, you may remember that the ending -LOGY is relatively common. EULOGY N1 36 may come to mind.

DIAGRAM 49:

Being behind, you might think it best to play just a few letters and keep a good leave. CAB 13A 24 (AGIN) seems excellent. However, on this board, you're not going to play an -ING bingo unless you open it up a little more. Your opponent isn't going to oblige by opening it up unless there's some profit for him/her. That's why playing your highest-scoring play, ABACI K11 29 is best. The advantage of this play is that (1) You keep the GN in case you get an I (assuming you or your opponent do create a spot for it). (2) You score the most points possible. (3) You open a TWS for either you or your opponent. With the score as it is, your opponent may not want to play to the TWS at O15 (giving you a new bingo line), yet s/he may not want to leave it for you either—especially if s/he thinks you may play the Z on 15L. So, your opponent may take a small play along row 15 to O15 and allow you to bingo down the N or O Column. What if your opponent has the Z and uses it for 80+ points on Row 15? You would most probably have lost anyway, so don't worry about it.

The sim results have ABACI beating CAB by 4.5 points., and CAWING K1 24 by 5 points.

DIAGRAM 50:

This position is a beautiful example that shows how important a good rack leave is in the early stages of a game. I simulated several plays, but the three that stood out were KUE J6 17 (AEIRZ), ZEE J6 32 (AIKRU), and RAZEE J4 34 (IKU). Using Sim Principle 1, it may be understandable why ZEE is better than RAZEE. The leave after RAZEE is much worse than after ZEE. Not only that, the board is so much more open to opponent after RAZEE that after simulation, ZEE earns a 7-point advantage over RAZEE.

Comparing KUE to ZEE, it's probably easy to see how much better the AEIRZ leave is than the AIKRU leave. But it is more than 15 points better? Yes! KUE simulates a full 4 points better than ZEE! I like KUE also because you retain the A that you may hook onto the K (KA). And opponent, if s/he decides to play on this hostile configuration, will undoubtedly give you a hot spot you'll utilize. All in all, KUE is a gem of a play!